React.js Crash Course for Beginners in 10 Hours or Less

This book may be purchased in bulk for educational, business, fundraising, or sales promotional use.

ISBN:

Published by: Ekesy In-Outdoor Company
10B, MufutauOpeifa Street, Oke-Odo,
Ile-Epo B/Stop, Alimosho,
Lagos, Nigeria

Email: dev@israeljoshua.com.ng

Tel: +234 803 815 4459, +234 813 2228 534

For information, please contact us @
dev@israeljoshua.com.ng

Call: +234 803 815 4459

Whatsapp: +234 813 2228 534

Table of Content

Dedication

I, Israel Joshua Chukwubueze, dedicate this book first to Almighty God, the source of all wisdom and understanding. Without His grace, none of this would be possible. Every line of code I've written, every lesson I've learned, and every word in this book flows from His endless mercy. To Him be all glory.

To my wonderful children, you are my greatest motivation. Every time I sit down to write or code, I think of the future I want to build for you—one where knowledge empowers you to create, solve problems, and leave your mark on the world. May this book inspire you to learn fearlessly, build boldly, and never stop growing.

To my mother, your sacrifices laid the foundation for everything I am today. You taught me resilience, faith, and the value of hard work. Even when resources were few, you made sure education was never out of reach. This book is a small part of the legacy you helped shape.

And finally, to my readers—whether you're just starting with React or refining your skills, thank you for trusting this book to guide you. Learning to code can feel overwhelming, but you've taken the first step by choosing to grow. My goal is to make React simple, practical, and accessible for you. I hope these lessons help you build amazing things, advance your career, and gain confidence as a developer.

This book is more than just a tutorial—it's a testament to the power of persistence, faith, and community. May it serve you well, and may your journey in coding bring you both success and fulfillment.

— Israel Joshua Chukwubueze

Preface

My name is Israel Joshua Chukwubueze, though many knew me earlier in my career as **Christopher Ekene Okade**. Over the past **14 years**, I've worked in web and mobile app development, building everything from small business websites to large-scale enterprise applications. Through countless projects, debugging sessions, and late-night coding marathons, one thing has remained constant—my passion for **simplifying complex ideas** and helping others learn.

That's why I wrote this book.

Why This Book Exists

When I first started learning React, I struggled to find resources that balanced **speed** with **clarity**. Some tutorials moved too fast, leaving gaps in understanding. Others were so detailed that they became overwhelming. I wanted a guide that would **cut straight to the essentials**—something that could take a beginner from zero to a working React app in the shortest time possible.

This book is my answer to that need.

Who Should Read This Book?

- **Beginners** who want a **no-fluff** introduction to React
- **JavaScript developers** transitioning to modern React
- **Bootcamp students** who need a quick but thorough reference
- **Self-taught coders** looking for a structured approach
- **Anyone** who wants to **build real apps fast**

What Makes This Book Different?

1. **Focused Learning** – Instead of lengthy explanations, each chapter delivers **key concepts in minutes**.
2. **Hands-On Approach** – You'll write code immediately, reinforcing lessons through practice.
3. **Modern React** – Covers **hooks, functional components, and best practices**—no outdated class-based examples.
4. **Real-World Skills** – Learn not just React, but **how to structure projects, debug,**

and deploy.

5. **10 Hours or Less Promise** – Designed for busy learners who need **fast, actionable knowledge**.

My Journey to Writing This Book

My career has taken me through **frontend development, UX design, backend systems, and mobile apps**. I've worked with startups, Fortune 500 companies, and everything in between. But no matter the project, one truth always stands out:

The best developers aren't just those who know the most—they're the ones who can learn quickly and adapt.

That's the mindset behind this book. I don't just want to teach you React—I want to teach you **how to learn efficiently**, so you can keep growing long after you finish reading.

How to Use This Book

- **Follow the chapters in order**—they build on each other.
- **Type out the examples**—don't just read them. Muscle memory matters.
- **Experiment**—change values, break things, then fix them. That's how real learning happens.
- **Build the final project**—applying everything you've learned is the best way to solidify knowledge.

A Personal Note

If you're feeling unsure about learning React (or coding in general), I understand. Everyone starts somewhere. What matters is that you **keep going**.

This book is my way of giving back—of taking the lessons from my 14 years in tech and packaging them into something that can help **you** succeed faster.

Let's get started.

— Israel Joshua Chukwubueze
(Formerly Christopher Ekene Okade)
Web & Mobile Developer | Instructor | Lifelong Learner

Chapter 1: Introduction to React.js

1.1 What is React.js?

Core Concepts of React.js

React.js (commonly referred to as just "React") is an open-source JavaScript library developed by Facebook (now Meta) for building user interfaces. Released in 2013, React has revolutionized the way developers approach front-end development. At its core, React provides a component-based architecture that allows developers to build encapsulated, reusable UI elements.

React isn't a full-fledged framework but rather a lightweight library focused specifically on the view layer of applications. This specialization in rendering UI is what makes React both powerful and flexible—it does one thing extremely well, leaving other aspects of application architecture to complementary libraries.

The Virtual DOM

One of React's most significant innovations is the Virtual DOM (Document Object Model). To understand its importance, let's first clarify what the DOM is: it's a programming interface that represents HTML documents as tree structures where each node represents a part of the document.

The traditional DOM manipulation can be slow, especially when dealing with complex applications that require frequent updates. React addresses this performance challenge through its Virtual DOM implementation:

1. When your data changes, React creates a new Virtual DOM representation of your UI.
2. It then compares this new representation with the previous one through a process called "diffing."
3. React calculates the minimal set of real DOM operations needed to update the UI.
4. Only these specific changes are applied to the actual DOM, minimizing performance costs.

This approach significantly improves application performance by reducing unnecessary DOM manipulations.

Declarative Programming

React employs a declarative programming paradigm. Instead of telling the computer step by step how to achieve a result (imperative programming), you simply declare what you want the final state to be, and React handles the implementation details.

For example, rather than manually manipulating DOM elements when data changes, you simply declare how your UI should look based on the current state, and React efficiently updates the DOM to match.

Component-Based Architecture

Everything in React is a component—self-contained, reusable pieces of code that return what should appear on the screen. Components can be as simple as a button or as complex as an entire page section.

Components can be classified into two types:

- **Function Components:** JavaScript functions that accept props and return React elements
- **Class Components:** ES6 classes that extend from React.Component and have additional features like local state and lifecycle methods

The component-based approach promotes:

- **Reusability:** Components can be reused across different parts of an application or even across projects
- **Maintainability:** Each component handles its own logic and rendering, making code easier to understand and maintain
- **Separation of concerns:** Components encapsulate specific functionality, promoting cleaner code organization

1.2 Why Use React?

Developer Experience and Productivity

React significantly enhances developer productivity through several key features:

Component Reusability

React's component-based architecture allows developers to create UI elements once and reuse them throughout the application. This not only saves time but also ensures consistency across the interface. For instance, a custom button component with specific styling and behavior can be reused across multiple forms and pages.

Code reusability extends beyond just visual components. Logic components, higher-order components, and custom hooks can encapsulate complex functionality for reuse. This modular approach accelerates development and reduces duplication.

Developer Tools

React offers exceptional developer tools that simplify debugging and optimization:

- **React Developer Tools:** A browser extension available for Chrome, Firefox, and Edge that allows you to inspect the React component tree, monitor component state and props, and track component renders.
- **Create React App:** A comfortable development environment that requires zero configuration, allowing developers to start building immediately.
- **Fast Refresh:** Provides near-instantaneous feedback during development by preserving component state while editing.

Strong Community and Ecosystem

React benefits from:

- **Extensive Documentation:** Comprehensive, well-maintained documentation with tutorials, guides, and API references.
- **Massive Community Support:** A large community of developers sharing knowledge through forums, blogs, and social media.
- **Rich Package Ecosystem:** Thousands of libraries and tools designed specifically to work with React.

Performance Benefits

Efficient Rendering with Virtual DOM

As mentioned earlier, React's Virtual DOM implementation offers significant performance advantages. By minimizing actual DOM manipulations, React applications can handle complex UIs with minimal performance degradation.

For large applications with frequent data updates, this optimization technique prevents the performance bottlenecks commonly associated with direct DOM manipulation.

Unidirectional Data Flow

React implements a unidirectional (or one-way) data flow, where data moves in a single direction throughout the application. This approach:

- Makes application behavior more predictable
- Simplifies debugging by providing a clear data path
- Reduces side effects and unexpected behaviors

Code Splitting and Lazy Loading

React supports advanced optimization techniques like code splitting and lazy loading:

```
// Instead of importing directly
// import ExpensiveComponent from './ExpensiveComponent';

// Use lazy loading

const ExpensiveComponent = React.lazy(() => import('./
ExpensiveComponent'));

function MyComponent() {
  return (
    <React.Suspense fallback={<div>Loading...</div>}>
      <ExpensiveComponent />
    </React.Suspense>
  );
}
```

This allows applications to load only the necessary code for the current view, reducing initial load times and improving overall performance.

Business Advantages

Faster Time-to-Market

React's component reusability, robust ecosystem, and developer productivity features translate to faster development cycles and reduced time-to-market for new features and products.

Maintainability and Scalability

Applications built with React tend to be more maintainable due to:

- Clear separation of concerns through component-based architecture
- Predictable state management
- Modular and reusable code

This maintainability becomes increasingly valuable as applications grow in size and complexity.

Cross-Platform Development

React's design principles extend beyond the web. The "learn once, write anywhere" philosophy has enabled technologies like React Native, which allows developers to use similar skills to build native mobile applications. This cross-platform capability reduces the learning curve and development costs for organizations requiring presence across multiple platforms.

1.3 React vs. Vanilla JavaScript

DOM Manipulation

Vanilla JavaScript Approach

In vanilla JavaScript, DOM manipulation typically follows an imperative approach where you manually select elements and apply changes:

```
// Vanilla JavaScript: Creating a dynamic list
function createList(items) {
  const ul = document.createElement('ul');

  items.forEach(item => {
    const li = document.createElement('li');
    li.textContent = item;
    ul.appendChild(li);
  });

  document.getElementById('container').appendChild(ul);
}

// Updating the list requires manually removing and
recreating elements
function updateList(newItems) {
  const container = document.getElementById('container');
  container.innerHTML = ''; // Remove existing content
  createList(newItems); // Recreate with new data
}
```

This approach requires careful tracking of DOM state and manual handling of elements, which can become complex and error-prone in larger applications.

React Approach

React simplifies this process with its declarative approach:

```
function ItemList({ items }) {
  return (
    <ul>
      {items.map(item => <li key={item.id}>{item.text}</
li>)}
    </ul>
  );
}

// Rendering and updating is as simple as:
ReactDOM.render(
  <ItemList items={newItems} />,
  document.getElementById('container')
);
```

React handles all the DOM updates efficiently through its Virtual DOM, determining the minimal changes needed to update the view.

State Management

Vanilla JavaScript Approach

In vanilla JavaScript, state management often involves global variables or custom solutions:

```
// Vanilla JavaScript state management
let count = 0;
const incrementButton =
document.getElementById('increment');
const counterDisplay =
document.getElementById('counter');

incrementButton.addEventListener('click', () => {
  count++;
  counterDisplay.textContent = count;
});
```

This approach works for simple cases but quickly becomes unwieldy as application complexity grows.

React Approach

React provides built-in state management through component state and hooks:

```
function Counter() {
  const [count, setCount] = React.useState(0);

  return (
    <div>
      <p>Count: {count}</p>
      <button onClick={() => setCount(count + 1)}
>Increment</button>
    </div>
  );
}
```

React's approach encapsulates state within components, making it easier to manage and reason about, especially in complex applications.

Event Handling

Vanilla JavaScript Approach

Event handling in vanilla JavaScript requires manual event listeners and callbacks:

```
// Vanilla JavaScript event handling
document.getElementById('myButton').addEventListener('cli
ck', function(event) {
  console.log('Button clicked');
  // Manually update related DOM elements
});
```

React Approach

React simplifies event handling with its synthetic event system:

```
function Button() {
  const handleClick = (event) => {
    console.log('Button clicked');
    // React will update the DOM efficiently
  };

  return <button onClick={handleClick}>Click me</button>;
}
```

React's event system normalizes browser differences and integrates seamlessly with the component lifecycle.

Code Organization and Scalability

Vanilla JavaScript Challenges

As applications grow in vanilla JavaScript:

- Code organization becomes increasingly difficult

- Separating concerns requires custom architectures
- Reusing UI elements often leads to code duplication
- Managing dependencies between components becomes complex

React Solutions

React addresses these challenges through:

- Component-based architecture that naturally separates concerns
- Clear patterns for composition and inheritance
- Well-defined component lifecycle and data flow
- Ecosystem tools for state management in larger applications

React's design encourages scalable patterns from the beginning, making it easier to maintain applications as they grow in complexity.

1.4 React vs. Other Frameworks (Angular, Vue)

React vs. Angular

Philosophy and Approach

Angular is a comprehensive framework developed and maintained by Google. It provides a complete solution with built-in tools for:

- Routing
- Form validation
- HTTP client
- Dependency injection
- Testing utilities

Angular uses TypeScript by default and follows an opinionated structure with a steeper learning curve but offers more guidance for application architecture.

React is a library focused on UI components. It's less opinionated, giving developers flexibility to choose additional libraries for routing, state management, and other functionalities. This approach offers:

- Lower entry barrier for beginners
- Greater flexibility in architectural decisions
- Lighter weight when only specific functionality is needed

Learning Curve

Angular has a steeper learning curve due to its comprehensive nature. Developers need to understand TypeScript, Angular-specific concepts like modules, decorators, services, and dependency injection.

React has a gentler learning curve, especially for developers already familiar with JavaScript. The core concepts (components, props, state) can be grasped relatively quickly, allowing developers to be productive sooner.

Performance

Both frameworks offer excellent performance when properly implemented, but they differ in their optimization strategies:

- Angular uses change detection to track and update components
- React uses Virtual DOM diffing to minimize DOM operations

For large-scale applications with complex UIs, React's Virtual DOM approach can sometimes offer performance advantages, especially when fine-tuned with techniques like memoization and pure components.

Community and Ecosystem

Both have strong communities, but React has a larger ecosystem of third-party libraries and community-driven solutions, partly due to its less opinionated nature that encourages diverse approaches to common problems.

React vs. Vue

Philosophy and Approach

Vue combines aspects of both React and Angular. Like React, it uses a Virtual DOM and component-based architecture. Like Angular, it offers more built-in features and guidance.

Vue is designed to be incrementally adoptable—it can be integrated into projects gradually, from enhancing static HTML to powering sophisticated single-page applications.

React focuses on component composition and unidirectional data flow, offering maximum flexibility for developers to structure applications according to their needs.

Template Syntax vs. JSX

Vue uses HTML-based templates with special directives:

```
<template>
  <div>
    <h1>{{ title }}</h1>
    <button v-on:click="incrementCounter">Count:
{{ counter }}</button>
  </div>
</template>

<script>
export default {
  data() {
    return {
      title: 'Vue Example',
      counter: 0
    }
  },
  methods: {
    incrementCounter() {
      this.counter++
    }
  }
}
</script>
```

React uses JSX, which allows JavaScript expressions within HTML-like syntax:

```
function VueExample() {
  const [counter, setCounter] = React.useState(0);

  return (
    <div>
      <h1>React Example</h1>
      <button onClick={() => setCounter(counter + 1)}>
        Count: {counter}
      </button>
    </div>
  );
}
```

Vue's approach might feel more familiar to traditional web developers, while React's JSX offers more direct integration with JavaScript.

State Management

Vue has Vuex as its official state management library, tightly integrated with Vue's reactivity system.

React originally used Redux as a popular state management solution, but now offers context API and hooks (like useReducer) for state management. The React ecosystem includes multiple state management options (Redux, MobX, Recoil, Zustand, etc.).

Learning Curve

Vue is often praised for having the gentlest learning curve among the three frameworks. Its template syntax is close to standard HTML, and its reactivity system works out of the box without much configuration.

React's learning curve is moderate, requiring developers to understand JavaScript concepts like functional programming and immutability for effective use.

Making the Right Choice

When choosing between React, Angular, and Vue, consider:

1. **Team Expertise:** Leveraging existing knowledge can accelerate development

2. **Project Requirements:** Complex enterprise applications might benefit from Angular's structure, while smaller projects might prefer React or Vue's flexibility
3. **Long-term Goals:** Consider the framework's community growth, corporate backing, and ecosystem health
4. **Integration Needs:** If integrating with existing systems, evaluate how easily each framework can be incorporated

React excels particularly in scenarios requiring:

- High performance user interfaces with frequent updates
- Gradual adoption into existing projects
- Maximum flexibility in architectural decisions
- Cross-platform development (web and mobile through React Native)

1.5 Setting Up Your Development Environment

System Requirements

Before setting up React, ensure your system meets these basic requirements:

- **Node.js (version 14.0.0 or higher):** React's build tools and development server depend on Node.js
- **npm (version 6.0.0 or higher) or Yarn:** Package managers for installing and managing dependencies
- **Code editor:** VS Code, WebStorm, Sublime Text, or any editor with good JavaScript support
- **Modern web browser:** Chrome, Firefox, Edge, or Safari with developer tools

Installing Node.js and npm

Node.js is essential for modern front-end development. It powers the development server, build processes, and dependency management for React applications.

Windows and macOS Installation

1. Visit the official Node.js website (https://nodejs.org/)
2. Download the LTS (Long Term Support) version
3. Run the installer and follow the installation wizard
4. Verify installation by opening a terminal/command prompt and running:

```
node -vnpm -v
```

Linux Installation

Using Ubuntu/Debian as an example:

```
# Update package lists
sudo apt update

# Install Node.js and npm
sudo apt install nodejs npm

# Verify installation
node -v
npm -v
```

For other Linux distributions, use the appropriate package manager (yum, pacman, etc.).

Code Editor Setup

While any text editor can work for React development, using an editor with good JavaScript and JSX support will significantly improve productivity.

Visual Studio Code (Recommended)

VS Code offers excellent support for React development with these recommended extensions:

1. **ESLint:** For code quality and style checking
2. **Prettier:** For automatic code formatting
3. **JavaScript and TypeScript Intellisense:** For enhanced code completion
4. **React Snippets:** For common React code patterns
5. **ES7+ React/Redux/React-Native snippets:** For quick component creation

After installing VS Code:

1. Open VS Code
2. Press `Ctrl+Shift+X` (or `Cmd+Shift+X` on macOS) to open the Extensions view
3. Search for and install the above extensions

Configuration for Optimal Development

Create these configuration files in your project root for consistent coding standards:

.eslintrc.json for code linting:

```
{
  "extends": [
    "eslint:recommended",
    "plugin:react/recommended"
  ],
  "plugins": [
    "react"
  ],
  "parserOptions": {
    "ecmaVersion": 2021,
    "sourceType": "module",
    "ecmaFeatures": {
      "jsx": true
    }
  },
  "rules": {
    "react/prop-types": "warn",
    "no-unused-vars": "warn"
  },
  "settings": {
    "react": {
      "version": "detect"
    }
  }
}
```

.prettierrc for code formatting:

```json
{
  "singleQuote": true,
  "semi": true,
  "tabWidth": 2,
  "trailingComma": "es5",
  "bracketSpacing": true,
  "jsxBracketSameLine": false
}
```

Creating Your First React Application

React offers multiple ways to create new applications. We'll cover the two most common approaches:

Method 1: Using Create React App (Recommended for Beginners)

Create React App (CRA) is an officially supported way to create single-page React applications. It provides a modern build setup with no configuration required.

```bash
# Install Create React App globally (optional)
npm install -g create-react-app

# Create a new React application
npx create-react-app my-react-app

# Navigate to the project directory
cd my-react-app

# Start the development server
npm start
```

This will create a new React application and open it in your default browser at `http://localhost:3000`.

Method 2: Using Vite (Faster Alternative)

Vite is a newer build tool that offers faster startup and hot module replacement:

```
# Create a new React project using Vite
npm create vite@latest my-react-app -- --template react

# Navigate to the project directory
cd my-react-app

# Install dependencies
npm install

# Start the development server
npm run dev
```

This will start a development server at `http://localhost:5173` (or another port if 5173 is in use).

Understanding the Project Structure

Let's examine the structure of a Create React App project:

```
my-react-app/
├── node_modules/          # Third-party libraries and
dependencies
├── public/                # Static files that don't require
processing
│   ├── favicon.ico        # Website favicon
│   ├── index.html         # HTML template
│   └── manifest.json      # Progressive Web App manifest
├── src/                   # Source code (where you'll spend
most of your time)
│   ├── App.css            # Styles for App component
│   ├── App.js             # Main App component
│   ├── App.test.js        # Tests for App component
│   ├── index.css          # Global styles
│   ├── index.js           # Application entry point
│   ├── logo.svg           # React logo
│   └── reportWebVitals.js # Performance measurement
├── .gitignore             # Git ignore file
├── package.json           # Project dependencies and
scripts
└── README.md              # Project documentation
```

Key Files Explained

public/index.html: This is the template HTML file that serves as the entry point for your application. React will inject your components into the `<div id="root"></div>` element in this file.

src/index.js: The JavaScript entry point that renders your main App component into the DOM:

```
import React from 'react';
import ReactDOM from 'react-dom/client';
import './index.css';
import App from './App';
import reportWebVitals from './reportWebVitals';

const root =
ReactDOM.createRoot(document.getElementById('root'));
root.render(
  <React.StrictMode>
    <App />
  </React.StrictMode>
);

// Performance measurement
reportWebVitals();
```

src/App.js: The main component that represents your application:

```
import React from 'react';
import logo from './logo.svg';
import './App.css';

function App() {
  return (
    <div className="App">
      <header className="App-header">
        <img src={logo} className="App-logo" alt="logo" /
>
        <p>
          Edit <code>src/App.js</code> and save to
reload.
        </p>
        <a
          className="App-link"
          href="https://reactjs.org"
          target="_blank"
          rel="noopener noreferrer"
        >
          Learn React
        </a>
      </header>
    </div>
  );
}

export default App;
```

Creating Your First Component

Let's create a simple component to understand the basics:

1. Create a new file `src/components/Welcome.js`
2. Add the following code:

```
import React from 'react';

// Function component
function Welcome(props) {
  return (
    <div className="welcome-container">
      <h1>Hello, {props.name}!</h1>
      <p>Welcome to React development</p>
    </div>
  );
}
```

```
export default Welcome;
```

3 Now modify `src/App.js` to use this component:

```
import React from 'react';
import './App.css';
import Welcome from './components/Welcome';

function App() {
  return (
    <div className="App">
      <Welcome name="Developer" />
      <p>Let's build amazing React applications together!
</p>
    </div>
  );
}

export default App;
```

4 Save both files and observe the changes in your browser.

Running and Testing Your Application

Create React App and Vite both provide several useful npm scripts for development:

Development Server

```
# For Create React App
npm start

# For Vite
npm run dev
```

This starts a development server with hot reloading, meaning your application will automatically update when you make changes to the code.

Running Tests

```
# Run all tests
npm test

# Run tests with coverage report
npm test -- --coverage
```

Building for Production

```
# For Create React App
npm run build

# For Vite
npm run build
```

This creates an optimized production build in the `build` folder (or `dist` for Vite) that's ready for deployment.

Ejecting (Create React App only)

```
npm run eject
```

Note: Ejecting is a one-way operation that exposes all the configuration files and dependencies used internally by Create React App, giving you full control over them. Only use this if you have specific configuration needs that can't be addressed otherwise.

Troubleshooting Common Setup Issues

Node Version Mismatch

Issue: Error messages about incompatible Node.js version **Solution:** Use Node Version Manager (nvm) to install and use the correct Node.js version:

Install nvm (follow instructions at https://github.com/nvm-sh/nvm)

```
```

Install and use the recommended Node.js version

```
nvm install 16
nvm use 16
```

Port Already in Use

Issue: "Something is already running on port 3000" **Solution:** Either terminate the process using the port or start React on a different port:

For Create React App

```
PORT=3001 npm start
```

For Windows Command Prompt

```
set PORT=3001 && npm start
```

For Windows PowerShell

```
$env:PORT=3001; npm start
```

Dependencies Installation Failures

Issue: npm errors during dependency installation **Solution:** Clear npm cache and retry:

```
npm cache clean --force
npm install
```

If problems persist, try using Yarn instead:

```
npm install -g yarn
yarn install
```

Moving Forward

With your development environment set up, you're ready to dive deeper into React development. As you progress through this book, you'll learn how to:

- Create and compose components effectively
- Manage state and props
- Handle events and user interactions
- Implement forms and validation
- Navigate between different views
- Connect to external APIs
- Optimize your application for performance

The foundation you've established in this chapter will serve as the groundwork for all these advanced topics. Regular practice and experimentation with the concepts introduced here will solidify your understanding of React's core principles.

Start by modifying the example components provided, changing styles, adding new features, or refactoring the code to better understand how React responds to changes. The React Developer Tools browser extension will be invaluable for inspecting components, their props, and state as you develop.

Chapter 2: Creating Your First React App

2.1 Installing Node.js and npm

Understanding Node.js and Its Role in React Development

Node.js is a JavaScript runtime environment that executes JavaScript code outside a web browser. For React development, Node.js serves multiple critical purposes:

1. **Package Management**: Node.js includes npm (Node Package Manager), which manages the libraries and dependencies your React application needs.
2. **Build Tools**: React applications use build tools that run on Node.js to compile, optimize, and bundle your code.
3. **Development Server**: When building React applications, you'll use a development server that runs on Node.js to preview your application locally.

Without Node.js, modern React development would be significantly more challenging, requiring manual management of dependencies and complex build processes.

Checking for Existing Installations

Before installing Node.js, check if it's already installed on your system:

```
# Check Node.js version
node -v

# Check npm version
npm -v
```

If these commands return version numbers, Node.js and npm are already installed. For React development in 2025, you should use Node.js version 16.0.0 or higher and npm version 7.0.0 or higher for optimal compatibility and performance.

Installation Methods

Method 1: Direct Download (Recommended for Beginners)

1. Visit the official Node.js website at https://nodejs.org/
2. Download the LTS (Long-Term Support) version, which offers the best stability
3. Run the installer and follow the on-screen instructions
4. The installer will automatically install both Node.js and npm

This method provides the simplest installation experience but offers less flexibility for managing multiple Node.js versions.

Method 2: Using a Version Manager (Recommended for Professionals)

Version managers allow you to easily switch between different Node.js versions, which is valuable when working on multiple projects with different requirements.

For macOS and Linux: nvm (Node Version Manager)

```
# Install nvm
curl -o- https://raw.githubusercontent.com/nvm-sh/nvm/
v0.39.1/install.sh | bash

# Restart your terminal or source your profile
source ~/.bashrc

# or source ~/.zshrc for Zsh users
source ~/.zshrc

# Install the latest LTS version of Node.js
nvm install --lts

# Set it as the default
nvm alias default 'lts/*'
```

For Windows: nvm-windows

1. Download the nvm-windows installer from https://github.com/coreybutler/nvm-windows/releases
2. Run the installer and follow the instructions
3. Open a new command prompt and run:

```
# Install the latest LTS version
nvm install lts

# Use the installed version
nvm use lts
```

Verifying Your Installation

After installation, verify that both Node.js and npm are correctly installed:

```
# Verify Node.js installation
```

```
node -v
```

```
# Verify npm installation
npm -v
```

```
# Test Node.js execution
node -e "console.log('Node.js is working correctly')"
```

Updating npm to the Latest Version

npm is updated more frequently than Node.js. To ensure you have the latest npm version:

```
# Update npm to the latest version
npm install -g npm@latest
```

Common Installation Issues and Solutions

Permission Errors on macOS/Linux

If you encounter "EACCES" permission errors when installing global packages:

```
# Fix npm permissions
mkdir ~/.npm-global
npm config set prefix '~/.npm-global'
```

Then add the following to your `~/.bashrc` or `~/.zshrc`:

```
export PATH=~/.npm-global/bin:$PATH
```

Path Issues on Windows

If you receive "'node' is not recognized as an internal or external command" errors:

1. Open System Properties > Advanced > Environment Variables
2. Find the PATH variable in System variables and click Edit
3. Add the directory where Node.js is installed (typically `C:\Program Files\nodejs\`)
4. Restart your command prompt

2.2 Using Create React App (CRA)

Understanding Create React App

Create React App (CRA) is an officially supported command-line tool that sets up a new React.js project with a single command. It eliminates the need for complex configuration files by providing a pre-configured development environment.

Key benefits of using CRA include:

1. **Zero Configuration**: Start developing immediately without configuring Webpack, Babel, ESLint, etc.
2. **Built-in Features**: Includes hot reloading, CSS processing, testing infrastructure, and production optimization
3. **Optimized Production Build**: Creates minified bundles with hashes and sourcemaps
4. **Modern JavaScript Support**: Write using the latest JavaScript features without worrying about browser compatibility
5. **Ecosystem Compatibility**: Designed to work with the broader React ecosystem

While alternatives like Vite and Next.js exist, CRA remains the most straightforward entry point for beginners learning React.

Installing Create React App

There are two approaches to using Create React App:

Method 1: Using npx (Recommended)

npx is a package runner tool that comes with npm 5.2+ and executes packages without installing them globally:

```
npx create-react-app my-first-app
```

This command downloads the latest version of Create React App, creates a new project called "my-first-app," and then removes CRA from your system after completion.

Method 2: Global Installation

Alternatively, you can install Create React App globally:

```
# Install globally
npm install -g create-react-app
```

```
# Create a new project
create-react-app my-first-app
```

The global installation method is less preferred as it doesn't automatically use the latest version for each new project.

Creating Your First Project

Let's create a new React application and examine what happens during the process:

```
npx create-react-app my-first-react-app
```

During execution, this command:

1. Creates a new directory called "my-first-react-app"
2. Installs React, React DOM, and React Scripts (the development dependency that includes Webpack, Babel, ESLint, etc.)
3. Generates a starter project structure with all necessary configuration files
4. Initializes a Git repository
5. Creates an initial commit with all files

The process typically takes 1-5 minutes depending on your internet connection and computer speed.

Using Templates with Create React App

Create React App supports templates that provide different starting configurations:

```
# Create a project with TypeScript
npx create-react-app my-typescript-app --template
typescript

# Create a project with Redux
npx create-react-app my-redux-app --template redux

# Create a project with TypeScript and Redux
npx create-react-app my-ts-redux-app --template redux-
typescript
```

These templates configure additional tools and provide starter code specific to their purpose.

Advanced CRA Configuration

While CRA is designed to work without configuration, you can customize its behavior:

Using Environment Variables

Create a `.env` file in your project root to define environment variables:

```
# .env file
REACT_APP_API_URL=https://api.example.com
REACT_APP_VERSION=$npm_package_version
```

Access these variables in your code:

```
// Access environment variables
const apiUrl = process.env.REACT_APP_API_URL;
console.log(`Connecting to API at ${apiUrl}`);
```

Note that only variables prefixed with `REACT_APP_` are accessible in your code.

Ejecting from Create React App

If you need deep customization beyond what CRA offers:

```
npm run eject
```

Warning: Ejecting is a one-way operation. Once you eject, you can't go back to the managed configuration.

After ejecting, you'll have:

- All configuration files (webpack.config.js, babel.config.js, etc.) exposed
- All build dependencies moved to your package.json
- Complete control over the build process

Instead of ejecting, consider using CRACO (Create React App Configuration Override) for customizations while keeping the benefits of CRA:

```
# Install CRACO
npm install @craco/craco

# Create a craco.config.js file with your customizations
```

2.3 Understanding the Project Structure

Top-Level Directory Structure

After creating a project with Create React App, you'll have the following structure:

```
my-first-react-app/
├── node_modules/
├── public/
├── src/
├── .gitignore
├── package.json
├── package-lock.json
└── README.md
```

Let's examine the purpose of each element:

node_modules/

This directory contains all the dependencies of your project, including React itself and all the libraries used by Create React App. You should never modify files in this directory directly and always include it in your `.gitignore` file to prevent it from being committed to version control.

Key points about `node_modules/`:

- It's automatically managed by npm or yarn
- It can contain thousands of files and subdirectories
- Its size can exceed 200MB, which is why we don't commit it to repositories
- It's reconstructed from `package.json` when running `npm install`

public/

The `public/` directory contains static assets that don't require processing by webpack:

```
public/
├── favicon.ico
├── index.html
├── logo192.png
├── logo512.png
├── manifest.json
└── robots.txt
```

Key files in the `public/` directory:

index.html: The HTML template for your application. This is the only HTML file in a React application since React is used to generate the content dynamically. It contains a `<div id="root"></div>` element where your React application will be mounted.

```
<!DOCTYPE html>
<html lang="en">
  <head>
    <meta charset="utf-8" />
    <link rel="icon" href="%PUBLIC_URL%/favicon.ico" />
    <meta name="viewport" content="width=device-width,
initial-scale=1" />
    <meta name="theme-color" content="#000000" />
    <meta
      name="description"
      content="Web site created using create-react-app"
    />
    <link rel="apple-touch-icon" href="%PUBLIC_URL%/
logo192.png" />
    <link rel="manifest" href="%PUBLIC_URL%/
manifest.json" />
    <title>React App</title>
  </head>
  <body>
    <noscript>You need to enable JavaScript to run this
app.</noscript>
    <div id="root"></div>
    <!-- This is where your React app will be mounted -->
  </body>
</html>
```

Note the `%PUBLIC_URL%` placeholder, which is replaced with the URL of the `public` folder during build.

manifest.json: Configuration file for Progressive Web Apps (PWA), defining how your application appears when installed on a device:

```json
{
  "short_name": "React App",
  "name": "Create React App Sample",
  "icons": [
    {
      "src": "favicon.ico",
      "sizes": "64x64 32x32 24x24 16x16",
      "type": "image/x-icon"
    },
    {
      "src": "logo192.png",
      "type": "image/png",
      "sizes": "192x192"
    },
    {
      "src": "logo512.png",
      "type": "image/png",
      "sizes": "512x512"
    }
  ],
  "start_url": ".",
  "display": "standalone",
  "theme_color": "#000000",
  "background_color": "#ffffff"
}
```

robots.txt: Instructions for web crawlers and search engines on how to interact with your site:

```
# https://www.robotstxt.org/robotstxt.html
User-agent: *
Disallow:
```

src/

The `src/` directory contains all your React source code, including components, styles, tests, and assets that need processing:

```
src/
├── App.css
├── App.js
├── App.test.js
├── index.css
├── index.js
├── logo.svg
├── reportWebVitals.js
└── setupTests.js
```

Key files in the `src/` directory:

index.js: The entry point of your React application, responsible for rendering the main App component to the DOM:

```
import React from 'react';
import ReactDOM from 'react-dom/client';
import './index.css';
import App from './App';
import reportWebVitals from './reportWebVitals';

const root =
ReactDOM.createRoot(document.getElementById('root'));
root.render(
  <React.StrictMode>
    <App />
  </React.StrictMode>
);

// Measure performance
reportWebVitals();
```

App.js: The main component of your application:

```
import logo from './logo.svg';
import './App.css';

function App() {
  return (
    <div className="App">
      <header className="App-header">
        <img src={logo} className="App-logo" alt="logo" /
>
        <p>
          Edit <code>src/App.js</code> and save to
reload.
        </p>
        <a
          className="App-link"
          href="https://reactjs.org"
          target="_blank"
          rel="noopener noreferrer"
        >
          Learn React
        </a>
      </header>
    </div>
  );
}

export default App;
```

reportWebVitals.js: Measures and reports on application performance:

```
const reportWebVitals = (onPerfEntry) => {
  if (onPerfEntry && onPerfEntry instanceof Function) {
    import('web-vitals').then(({ getCLS, getFID, getFCP,
getLCP, getTTFB }) => {
      getCLS(onPerfEntry);
      getFID(onPerfEntry);
      getFCP(onPerfEntry);
      getLCP(onPerfEntry);
      getTTFB(onPerfEntry);
    });
  }
};

export default reportWebVitals;
```

setupTests.js: Configuration for testing with Jest:

```
// jest-dom adds custom jest matchers for asserting on
DOM nodes
import '@testing-library/jest-dom';
```

Configuration Files

.gitignore: Specifies files and directories that Git should ignore:

```
# dependencies
/node_modules
/.pnp
.pnp.js

# testing
/coverage

# production
/build

# misc
.DS_Store
.env.local
.env.development.local
.env.test.local
.env.production.local

npm-debug.log*
yarn-debug.log*
yarn-error.log*
```

package.json: Defines your project's dependencies and scripts:

```json
{
  "name": "my-first-react-app",
  "version": "0.1.0",
  "private": true,
  "dependencies": {
    "@testing-library/jest-dom": "^5.16.5",
    "@testing-library/react": "^13.4.0",
    "@testing-library/user-event": "^13.5.0",
    "react": "^18.2.0",
    "react-dom": "^18.2.0",
    "react-scripts": "5.0.1",
    "web-vitals": "^2.1.4"
  },
  "scripts": {
    "start": "react-scripts start",
    "build": "react-scripts build",
    "test": "react-scripts test",
    "eject": "react-scripts eject"
  },
  "eslintConfig": {
    "extends": [
      "react-app",
      "react-app/jest"
    ]
  },
  "browserslist": {
    "production": [
      ">0.2%",
      "not dead",
      "not op_mini all"
    ],
    "development": [
      "last 1 chrome version",
      "last 1 firefox version",
      "last 1 safari version"
    ]
  }
}
```

Customizing the Project Structure

While CRA provides a default structure, you can customize it for better organization as your project grows:

Creating a Components Directory

Best practice is to organize components into dedicated directories:

```
src/
├── components/
│   ├── Button/
│   │   ├── Button.js
│   │   ├── Button.css
│   │   └── Button.test.js
│   ├── Navbar/
│   │   ├── Navbar.js
│   │   ├── Navbar.css
│   │   └── Navbar.test.js
│   └── ...
├── ...
```

Asset Organization

Group related assets by type:

```
src/
├── assets/
│   ├── images/
│   ├── fonts/
│   └── styles/
├── ...
```

Feature-Based Organization

For larger applications, consider organizing by feature:

```
src/
├── features/
│   ├── auth/
│   │   ├── components/
│   │   ├── services/
│   │   └── ...
│   ├── dashboard/
│   │   ├── components/
│   │   ├── services/
│   │   └── ...
│   └── ...
├── ...
```

2.4 Running the Development Server

Starting the Development Server

Create React App includes a development server with features like hot reloading, error reporting, and more. To start it:

```
# Navigate to your project directory
cd my-first-react-app

# Start the development server
npm start
```

After running this command:

1. The development server compiles your application
2. A new browser window opens at http://localhost:3000/
3. The server begins watching your files for changes

Understanding the Development Server

The development server provided by CRA offers several powerful features:

Hot Reloading

Hot Module Replacement (HMR) updates your application in real-time as you edit files, without losing the current state of the application. When you save changes to a file:

1. Webpack recompiles only the changed module
2. The browser receives and applies the update without a full refresh
3. Your application's state is preserved

This dramatically speeds up the development cycle by providing immediate feedback.

Error Overlay

If you make a syntax error or runtime error in your code, the development server will display a full-screen error overlay in your browser:

```
// This will cause an error
function BrokenComponent() {
  return (
    <div>
      {undefined.map(item => <p>{item}</p>)}
    </div>
  );
}
```

The error overlay shows:

- The exact error message
- The file and line number where the error occurred
- A stack trace to help locate the source of the error

Source Maps

The development server generates source maps that map the compiled code back to your original source code, making debugging much easier. When using browser developer tools:

1. Error messages reference your original code, not the compiled version
2. Breakpoints can be set in your original source files
3. You can step through your original code during debugging

HTTPS in Development

For applications that require HTTPS (e.g., for authentication or geolocation features), you can run the development server with HTTPS:

```
# Windows (cmd.exe)
set HTTPS=true&&npm start

# Windows (PowerShell)
($env:HTTPS = "true") -and (npm start)

# Linux/macOS
HTTPS=true npm start
```

This generates a self-signed certificate for development purposes.

Customizing the Development Server

You can customize various aspects of the development server:

Changing the Default Port

```
# Windows (cmd.exe)
set PORT=3001&&npm start

# Windows (PowerShell)
($env:PORT = "3001") -and (npm start)

# Linux/macOS
PORT=3001 npm start
```

Preventing the Browser from Opening

```
# Windows (cmd.exe)
set BROWSER=none&&npm start

# Windows (PowerShell)
($env:BROWSER = "none") -and (npm start)

# Linux/macOS
BROWSER=none npm start
```

Using a Different Browser

```
# Windows (cmd.exe)
set BROWSER=firefox&&npm start

# Windows (PowerShell)
($env:BROWSER = "firefox") -and (npm start)

# Linux/macOS
BROWSER=firefox npm start
```

Proxying API Requests

When your React application needs to communicate with an API server during development, you can configure the development server to proxy API requests:

Add a `proxy` field to your `package.json`:

```
{
  "name": "my-first-react-app",
  "version": "0.1.0",
  "proxy": "http://localhost:5000",
  /* other configuration... */
}
```

With this configuration:

- Requests to `/api/users` will be directed to `http://localhost:5000/api/users`
- Static assets (like CSS and images) will still be served from the development server
- The browser will see all requests coming from the same origin, avoiding CORS issues

For more complex proxying requirements, create a `src/setupProxy.js` file:

```
const { createProxyMiddleware } = require('http-proxy-
middleware');

module.exports = function(app) {
  app.use(
    '/api',
    createProxyMiddleware({
      target: 'http://localhost:5000',
      changeOrigin: true,
    })
  );

  app.use(
    '/auth',
    createProxyMiddleware({
      target: 'http://localhost:8080',
      changeOrigin: true,
    })
  );
};
```

This setup allows different API endpoints to be proxied to different servers.

Troubleshooting Common Server Issues

"Port already in use" Error

`Something is already running on port 3000.`
Solutions:

1. Find and close the process using port 3000
2. Use a different port as described above
3. Automatically find an available port:

```
# Windows (cmd.exe)
set PORT=0&&npm start

# Linux/macOS
PORT=0 npm start
```

Slow Compilation Times

If your development server becomes slow:

1. Limit the number of watched files:

```
# Windows (cmd.exe)
set FAST_REFRESH=false&&npm start
```

```
# Linux/macOS
FAST_REFRESH=false npm start
```

2. Consider splitting your application into smaller chunks
3. Use React.lazy() for code splitting:

```
const HeavyComponent = React.lazy(() => import('./
HeavyComponent'));

function App() {
  return (
    <React.Suspense fallback={<div>Loading...</div>}>
      <HeavyComponent />
    </React.Suspense>
  );
}
```

WebSocket Connection Failures

If you see "WebSocket connection failed" messages:

1. Check your firewall settings
2. Ensure your development environment allows WebSocket connections
3. Try disabling the websocket connection:

```
# Windows (cmd.exe)
set WDS_SOCKET_HOST=127.0.0.1&&npm start
```

```
# Linux/macOS
WDS_SOCKET_HOST=127.0.0.1 npm start
```

2.5 Making Your First Edit

Understanding React Components

Before making changes, let's understand the basic structure of a React component. In React, components are the building blocks of your UI.

A functional component in React is a JavaScript function that returns JSX (JavaScript XML), a syntax extension that looks similar to HTML but allows you to use JavaScript expressions:

```
function MyComponent() {
  return (
    <div className="container">
      <h1>Hello from My Component</h1>
      <p>This is a simple React component.</p>
    </div>
  );
}

export default MyComponent;
```

Key points about this component:

- It's defined as a JavaScript function
- It returns JSX, which describes what should be rendered
- `className` is used instead of `class` (since `class` is a reserved word in JavaScript)
- The component is exported so it can be imported elsewhere

Editing the App Component

Let's modify the default App component that was created by Create React App:

1. Open `src/App.js` in your code editor
2. Find the existing code:

```
import logo from './logo.svg';
import './App.css';

function App() {
  return (
    <div className="App">
      <header className="App-header">
        <img src={logo} className="App-logo" alt="logo" /
>
        <p>
          Edit <code>src/App.js</code> and save to
reload.
        </p>
        <a
          className="App-link"
          href="https://reactjs.org"
          target="_blank"
          rel="noopener noreferrer"
        >
          Learn React
        </a>
      </header>
    </div>
  );
}

export default App;
```

3 Replace it with your own content:

```
import './App.css';

function App() {
  return (
    <div className="App">
      <header className="App-header">
        <h1>My First React Application</h1>
        <p>This is a simple React app created with Create
React App.</p>
        <button
          onClick={() => alert('Button clicked!')}
          className="App-button"
        >
          Click Me
        </button>
      </header>
    </div>
  );
}

export default App;
```

4. Save the file and observe the changes in your browser

The development server automatically detects the changes and updates the browser. You should see your new heading, paragraph, and button.

Adding Styles

Let's also modify the styles to match our new content:

1. Open `src/App.css` in your code editor
2. Find the existing styles and modify them:

```
.App {
  text-align: center;
}

.App-header {
  background-color: #282c34;
  min-height: 100vh;
  display: flex;
  flex-direction: column;
  align-items: center;
  justify-content: center;
  font-size: calc(10px + 2vmin);
  color: white;
}

.App-button {
  background-color: #61dafb;
  color: #282c34;
  font-size: 1rem;
  padding: 10px 20px;
  border: none;
  border-radius: 4px;
  cursor: pointer;
  margin-top: 20px;
  transition: background-color 0.3s;
}

.App-button:hover {
  background-color: #21a1c9;
}
```

3. Save the file and observe the updated styles in the browser

Creating a New Component

Now, let's create a new component to understand how components work together:

4. Create a new file `src/components/Welcome.js`:

```
function Welcome(props) {
  return (
    <div className="welcome-container">
      <h2>Hello, {props.name}!</h2>
      <p>Welcome to React development. The time is {new
Date().toLocaleTimeString()}.</p>
    </div>
  );
}

export default Welcome;
```

2 Create a new file `src/components/Welcome.css`:

```
.welcome-container {
  background-color: #3e4451;
  padding: 20px;
  border-radius: 8px;
  margin-top: 20px;
  width: 80%;
  max-width: 500px;
}

.welcome-container h2 {
  color: #61dafb;
  margin-top: 0;
}
```

3 Update `src/App.js` to import and use this component:

```
import './App.css';
import Welcome from './components/Welcome';
import './components/Welcome.css';

function App() {
  return (
    <div className="App">
      <header className="App-header">
        <h1>My First React Application</h1>
        <p>This is a simple React app created with Create
React App.</p>
        <button
          onClick={() => alert('Button clicked!')}
          className="App-button"
        >
          Click Me
        </button>

        <Welcome name="React Developer" />
      </header>
    </div>
  );
}

export default App;
```

4 Save all files and check the browser

You should now see the Welcome component rendered within the App component, demonstrating component composition.

Adding State to Components

React's power comes from its ability to manage state and re-render components when state changes. Let's modify our application to include state:

1 Update `src/App.js` to use React's useState hook:

```
import { useState } from 'react';
import './App.css';
import Welcome from './components/Welcome';
import './components/Welcome.css';

function App() {
  const [count, setCount] = useState(0);
  const [showWelcome, setShowWelcome] = useState(true);

  const incrementCount = () => {
    setCount(count + 1);
  };

  const toggleWelcome = () => {
    setShowWelcome(!showWelcome);
  };

  return (
    <div className="App">
      <header className="App-header">
        <h1>My First React Application</h1>
        <p>This is a simple React app created with Create
React App.</p>

        <div className="counter-container">
          <p>You clicked the button {count} times</p>
          <button
            onClick={incrementCount}
            className="App-button"
          >
            Increment Counter
          </button>
        </div>

        <div className="toggle-container">
          <button
            onClick={toggleWelcome}
            className="App-button toggle-button"
          >
            {showWelcome ? 'Hide' : 'Show'} Welcome
          </button>
        </div>
```

2 Update `src/App.css` to include styles for the new elements:

```
/* Add these styles to the existing CSS */
.counter-container, .toggle-container {
  margin: 20px 0;
}

.toggle-button {
  background-color: #ff6b6b;
}

.toggle-button:hover {
  background-color: #ee5253;
}
```

3 Save all files and test the application

You now have:

- A counter that increments when the button is clicked
- A toggle button that shows/hides the Welcome component
- State management using React's useState hook

Chapter 3: Understanding JSX

3.1 What is JSX?

Introduction to JSX

JSX stands for JavaScript XML. It's a syntax extension for JavaScript recommended by React for describing what the UI should look like. JSX provides developers with a familiar syntax that resembles HTML while giving access to the full power of JavaScript.

The History and Purpose of JSX

JSX was created by Facebook specifically for React to solve the problem of separating markup from logic. Traditional web development typically separates HTML, CSS, and JavaScript into different files, which can make it challenging to track related code. JSX addresses this by allowing developers to write HTML-like code directly within JavaScript files.

How JSX Works Behind the Scenes

When you write JSX, it might look like HTML, but it's actually converted to JavaScript before being processed by browsers. This conversion is done through a process called transpilation, which is typically handled by tools like Babel. During transpilation, JSX is transformed into `React.createElement()` calls.

For example, this JSX:

```
const element = <h1>Hello, world!</h1>;
```

Gets converted to:

```
const element = React.createElement(
  'h1',
  null,
  'Hello, world!'
);
```

Why JSX is Important for React Development

JSX makes React code more readable and intuitive for developers who are familiar with HTML. It enables a clear visual structure that matches the component hierarchy, making it easier to understand how the UI is composed. JSX also helps catch errors during compilation rather than at runtime.

3.2 JSX vs. HTML

Fundamental Differences

While JSX looks very similar to HTML, there are several key differences:

1. Attribute Naming

HTML attributes use kebab-case (hyphenated lowercase) naming conventions, while JSX attributes use camelCase:

HTML:

```
<div class="container" onclick="handleClick()"></div>
```

JSX:

```
<div className="container" onClick={handleClick}></div>
```

2. Reserved Keywords

Some HTML attribute names are reserved keywords in JavaScript. React uses different naming conventions for these attributes:

- `class` → `className`
- `for` → `htmlFor`
- `tabindex` → `tabIndex`

3. Self-closing Tags

In HTML, some elements don't require closing tags, but in JSX, all elements must be explicitly closed:

HTML:

```
<input type="text">
<img src="image.jpg">
```

JSX:

```
<input type="text" />
<img src="image.jpg" />
```

4. JavaScript Expressions

JSX allows JavaScript expressions to be embedded inside curly braces:

```
const name = "John";
const element = <h1>Hello, {name}!</h1>;
```

Common Pitfalls When Transitioning from HTML to JSX

Developers new to JSX often encounter the following challenges:

Style Attribute

In HTML, the style attribute accepts a string, but in JSX, it requires a JavaScript object:

HTML:

```
<div style="color: red; font-size: 16px;"></div>
```

JSX:

```
<div style={{ color: 'red', fontSize: '16px' }}></div>
```

Event Handlers

In HTML, event handlers are strings containing JavaScript code, while in JSX, they are references to functions:

HTML:

```
<button onclick="alert('Clicked!')">Click me</button>
```

JSX:

```
<button onClick={() => alert('Clicked!')}>Click me</
button>
```

Inline Comments

Comments within JSX require a specific syntax:

```
{/* This is a JSX comment */}
```

Converting HTML to JSX

When converting existing HTML to JSX, follow these steps:

1. Change HTML attributes to their JSX equivalents (`class` → `className`, etc.)
2. Close all tags properly (`<input>` → `<input />`)
3. Transform inline styles from strings to objects
4. Replace string event handlers with function references
5. Update comments to use JSX comment syntax

Here's a comprehensive example:

HTML:

```
<div class="user-profile">
  <img src="avatar.jpg" alt="User Avatar">
  <h2>Welcome, John!</h2>
  <p style="color: gray; font-style: italic;">Last login:
Today</p>
  <button onclick="handleLogout()">Logout</button>
</div>
```

JSX:

```
<div className="user-profile">
  <img src="avatar.jpg" alt="User Avatar" />
  <h2>Welcome, {username}!</h2>
  <p style={{ color: 'gray', fontStyle: 'italic' }}>Last login: {lastLogin}</p>
  <button onClick={handleLogout}>Logout</button>
</div>
```

3.3 Embedding JavaScript in JSX

Using Expressions in JSX

JSX allows you to embed any JavaScript expression inside curly braces `{}`. An expression is any valid unit of code that resolves to a value. Here are common use cases:

Variables and Properties

```
const name = "Sarah";
const user = { age: 25 };

const element = (
  <div>
    <h1>{name}'s Profile</h1>
    <p>Age: {user.age}</p>
  </div>
);
```

Function Calls

```
function formatName(user) {
  return user.firstName + ' ' + user.lastName;
}

const user = { firstName: 'John', lastName: 'Doe' };

const element = <h1>Hello, {formatName(user)}!</h1>;
```

Arithmetic Operations

```
const price = 19.99;
const quantity = 3;

const element = <p>Total: ${price * quantity}</p>;
```

Ternary Operators

```
const isLoggedIn = true;

const element = (
  <div>
    {isLoggedIn ? <WelcomeUser /> : <LoginButton />}
  </div>
);
```

Conditional Rendering Techniques

JSX doesn't have built-in conditional statements like `if-else`, but there are several approaches to conditional rendering:

Inline Ternary Operator

```
const element = (
  <div>
    {isLoggedIn ? (
      <button onClick={handleLogout}>Logout</button>
    ) : (
      <button onClick={handleLogin}>Login</button>
    )}
  </div>
);
```

Logical && Operator

This approach works well for simple "render or don't render" scenarios:

```
const element = (
  <div>
    {unreadMessages.length > 0 && (
      <p>You have {unreadMessages.length} unread
messages.</p>
    )}
  </div>
);
```

Element Variables

```
let button;
if (isLoggedIn) {
  button = <LogoutButton onClick={handleLogout} />;
} else {
  button = <LoginButton onClick={handleLogin} />;
}

const element = (
  <div>
    <h1>Welcome</h1>
    {button}
  </div>
);
```

For complex conditionals, you can use variables to store elements:

Immediately Invoked Function Expressions (IIFE)

For more complex logic, you can use an IIFE:

```
const element = (
  <div>
    {(() => {
      if (status === 'loading') return <LoadingSpinner /
>;
      if (status === 'error') return <ErrorMessage />;
      return <Content data={data} />;
    })()}
  </div>
);
```

Working with Lists and Arrays

JSX makes it easy to render lists of elements using JavaScript's array methods:

Mapping Arrays to JSX

```
const numbers = [1, 2, 3, 4, 5];

const listItems = (
  <ul>
    {numbers.map((number) => (
      <li key={number}>{number}</li>
    ))}
  </ul>
);
```

The Importance of Keys

When creating lists in JSX, always include a unique `key` prop for each item:

```
const todoItems = todos.map((todo) => (
  <li key={todo.id}>
    {todo.text}
  </li>
));
```

Keys help React identify which items have changed, been added, or removed. Without keys, React might re-render the entire list unnecessarily, causing performance issues.

Filtering Arrays Before Rendering

```
const products = [
  { id: 1, name: 'Laptop', inStock: true },
  { id: 2, name: 'Phone', inStock: false },
  { id: 3, name: 'Tablet', inStock: true }
];

const availableProducts = (
  <ul>
    {products
      .filter(product => product.inStock)
      .map(product => (
        <li key={product.id}>{product.name}</li>
      ))}
  </ul>
);
```

Common Mistakes and Their Solutions

Forgetting That JSX Expressions Must Have a Single Parent

```
// Incorrect
const element = (
  <h1>Title</h1>
  <p>Paragraph</p>
);

// Correct
const element = (
  <div>
    <h1>Title</h1>
    <p>Paragraph</p>
  </div>
);

// Also correct (using React Fragment)
const element = (
  <>
    <h1>Title</h1>
    <p>Paragraph</p>
  </>
);
```

Trying to Use Statements Instead of Expressions

```
// Incorrect
const element = (
  <div>
    {if (isLoggedIn) { return <AdminPanel />; }}
  </div>
);

// Correct
const element = (
  <div>
    {isLoggedIn && <AdminPanel />}
  </div>
);
```

Misunderstanding the Scope of JSX Expressions

```
// Incorrect - variables declared inside the JSX aren't
accessible elsewhere
const element = (
  <div>
    {const userName = user.name}
    <h1>Hello, {userName}</h1>
  </div>
);

// Correct
const userName = user.name;
const element = (
  <div>
    <h1>Hello, {userName}</h1>
  </div>
);
```

3.4 JSX Attributes and Styling

Standard Attributes in JSX

JSX supports all standard HTML attributes, but with camelCase naming:

```
<div
  id="main"
  className="container"
  tabIndex={1}
  aria-label="Main content"
  data-testid="test-element"
>
  Content
</div>
```

Custom Data Attributes

You can add custom data attributes using the `data-` prefix:

```
<button data-value="submit" data-user-id={userId}>
  Submit
</button>
```

Boolean Attributes

For boolean attributes in JSX, `true` can be implied by just including the attribute name:

```
// These are equivalent
<input type="checkbox" checked={true} />
<input type="checkbox" checked />

// To set it to false, omit the attribute
<input type="checkbox" />
```

Inline Styling with Objects

In JSX, inline styles are specified as objects using camelCase properties:

```
const styles = {
  color: 'blue',
  backgroundColor: 'white',
  fontSize: '16px',
  padding: '10px 15px',
  borderRadius: '4px'
};

const element = <div style={styles}>Styled content</div>;

// You can also define styles inline
const inlineElement = (
  <div style={{
    color: 'blue',
    backgroundColor: 'white',
    fontSize: '16px'
  }}>
    Inline styled content
  </div>
);
```

Dynamic Styling

You can create dynamic styles based on component state or props:

```
function DynamicButton({ isActive }) {
  const buttonStyles = {
    backgroundColor: isActive ? 'green' : 'gray',
    color: 'white',
    padding: '8px 16px',
    cursor: isActive ? 'pointer' : 'not-allowed',
    opacity: isActive ? 1 : 0.5
  };

  return (
    <button style={buttonStyles}>
      {isActive ? 'Active' : 'Disabled'}
    </button>
  );
}
```

Using CSS Classes

While you can use inline styles, it's often better to use CSS classes for styling:

```
// In your CSS file
// .button { ... }
// .primary { ... }
// .large { ... }

function Button({ type, size, children }) {
  const classes = `button ${type} ${size}`;
  return <button className={classes}>{children}</button>;
}

// Usage
<Button type="primary" size="large">Click Me</Button>
```

Conditional Classes

You can conditionally apply classes based on props or state:

```
function Alert({ type, message }) {
  let className = 'alert';

  if (type === 'error') {
    className += ' alert-error';
  } else if (type === 'success') {
    className += ' alert-success';
  }

  return <div className={className}>{message}</div>;
}
```

For more complex class conditionals, libraries like `classnames` are useful:

```
import classNames from 'classnames';

function Button({ isPrimary, isDisabled, isLarge,
className }) {
  const buttonClasses = classNames('button', {
    'button-primary': isPrimary,
    'button-disabled': isDisabled,
    'button-large': isLarge
  }, className);

  return <button className={buttonClasses}>Click Me</
button>;
}
```

Event Handlers as Attributes

JSX allows you to attach event handlers as attributes:

```
function Button() {
  const handleClick = (e) => {
    e.preventDefault();
    console.log('Button clicked');
  };

  return (
    <button onClick={handleClick}>
      Click me
    </button>
  );
}
```

Common event handlers include:

- `onClick`
- `onChange`
- `onSubmit`
- `onMouseOver`
- `onKeyDown`

Attribute Spread Syntax

You can use the spread operator to pass multiple attributes at once:

```
function Card(props) {
  const { title, className, ...otherProps } = props;

  return (
    <div className={`card ${className}`} {...otherProps}>
      <h2>{title}</h2>
    </div>
  );
}

// Usage
<Card
  title="Welcome"
  className="featured"
  id="welcome-card"
  data-testid="card-component"
/>
```

3.5 JSX Best Practices

Organizational Structure

Structure your JSX for readability and maintainability:

Component Nesting

Keep nesting to a reasonable level (3-4 levels max) to maintain readability:

```
// Good practice
function App() {
  return (
    <div className="app">
      <Header />
      <main>
        <Sidebar />
        <Content>
          <ArticleList articles={articles} />
        </Content>
      </main>
      <Footer />
    </div>
  );
}
```

Breaking Down Large Components

If a component has too much JSX, break it into smaller components:

```
// Instead of this
function UserDashboard() {
  return (
    <div className="dashboard">
      <div className="header">...</div>
      <div className="sidebar">...</div>
      <div className="main-content">
        <div className="stats">...</div>
        <div className="recent-activity">...</div>
        <div className="notifications">...</div>
      </div>
      <div className="footer">...</div>
    </div>
  );
}

// Do this
function UserDashboard() {
  return (
    <div className="dashboard">
      <DashboardHeader />
      <Sidebar />
      <MainContent>
        <Stats />
        <RecentActivity />
        <Notifications />
      </MainContent>
      <Footer />
    </div>
  );
}
```

Code Formatting

Consistent formatting improves readability:

Multi-line JSX

When JSX spans multiple lines, wrap it in parentheses and indent properly:

```
// Good practice
const element = (
  <div>
    <h1>Title</h1>
    <p>Paragraph</p>
  </div>
);
```

Attribute Formatting

For components with multiple attributes, place each attribute on a new line:

```
// Good practice
<input
  type="text"
  value={value}
  onChange={handleChange}
  placeholder="Enter your name"
  required
/>
```

Using Fragments

When you don't want to add extra divs to the DOM, use React Fragments:

```
// Using the explicit syntax
<React.Fragment>
  <h1>Title</h1>
  <p>Paragraph</p>
</React.Fragment>

// Using the shorthand syntax
<>
  <h1>Title</h1>
  <p>Paragraph</p>
</>
```

Fragments are especially useful for:

- Lists where you need to return multiple items
- Components that return multiple elements
- Avoiding unnecessary DOM nodes

Component Props

Follow these guidelines when working with props in JSX:

Prop Naming Conventions

Use clear, descriptive names for props that follow camelCase convention:

```
// Good
<UserProfile
  userName="johndoe"
  userRole="admin"
  lastLoginDate="2023-03-15"
/>

// Not recommended
<UserProfile
  name="johndoe"
  role="admin"
  last="2023-03-15"
/>
```

Destructuring Props

Destructure props for cleaner code:

```
// Instead of this
function UserInfo(props) {
  return (
    <div>
      <h2>{props.name}</h2>
      <p>Role: {props.role}</p>
      <p>Email: {props.email}</p>
    </div>
  );
}

// Do this
function UserInfo({ name, role, email }) {
  return (
    <div>
      <h2>{name}</h2>
      <p>Role: {role}</p>
      <p>Email: {email}</p>
    </div>
  );
}
```

Default Props

Provide default values for optional props:

```
function Button({ type = 'default', size = 'medium',
children }) {
  return (
    <button className={`btn-${type} btn-${size}`}>
      {children}
    </button>
  );
}
```

Handling Events

Follow these best practices for event handling:

Binding Event Handlers

Define event handlers properly to maintain access to `this` and prevent unnecessary re-renders:

```
// Class component approach
class Button extends React.Component {
  // Method 1: Binding in constructor (recommended)
  constructor(props) {
    super(props);
    this.handleClick = this.handleClick.bind(this);
  }

  handleClick() {
    console.log('Button clicked');
  }

  // Method 2: Class property with arrow function
  handleHover = () => {
    console.log('Button hovered');
  }

  render() {
    return (
      <button
        onClick={this.handleClick}
        onMouseOver={this.handleHover}
      >
        Click Me
      </button>
    );
  }
}

// Function component approach (preferred)
function Button() {
  const handleClick = () => {
    console.log('Button clicked');
  };

  return <button onClick={handleClick}>Click Me</button>;
}
```

Passing Arguments to Event Handlers

When you need to pass additional data to event handlers:

```
function ItemList({ items, onItemClick }) {
  return (
    <ul>
      {items.map(item => (
        <li
          key={item.id}
          onClick={() => onItemClick(item.id)}
        >
          {item.name}
        </li>
      ))}
    </ul>
  );
}
```

Performance Considerations

Some best practices to optimize performance:

Avoiding Inline Function Definitions

Inline functions can cause unnecessary re-renders:

```
// Not recommended
function TodoList({ todos }) {
  return (
    <ul>
      {todos.map(todo => (
        <li key={todo.id} onClick={() =>
handleTodoClick(todo.id)}>
          {todo.text}
        </li>
      ))}
    </ul>
  );
}

// Better approach
function TodoList({ todos }) {
  // Define the handler outside the render method
  const handleTodoClick = useCallback((id) => {
    // Handle the click
  }, []);

  return (
    <ul>
      {todos.map(todo => (
        <TodoItem
          key={todo.id}
          todo={todo}
          onClick={handleTodoClick}
        />
      ))}
    </ul>
  );
}
```

Memoizing Components

Use React's `memo` to prevent unnecessary re-renders:

```
const TodoItem = React.memo(function TodoItem({ todo,
onClick }) {
  return (
    <li onClick={() => onClick(todo.id)}>
      {todo.text}
    </li>
  );
});
```

Testing Considerations

Design your JSX with testing in mind:

Data Attributes for Testing

Add data attributes to make your components easier to test:

```
function SubmitButton({ isDisabled }) {
  return (
    <button
      disabled={isDisabled}
      data-testid="submit-button"
    >
      Submit
    </button>
  );
}
```

Accessibility Attributes

Include accessibility attributes to make your app usable for everyone:

```
function SearchInput() {
  return (
    <div>
      <label htmlFor="search-input">Search:</label>
      <input
        id="search-input"
        type="search"
        aria-label="Search for products"
        aria-required="true"
      />
    </div>
  );
}
```

Summary of Best Practices

1. **Keep components small and focused** - Break large components into smaller, reusable pieces
2. **Use fragments to avoid unnecessary DOM elements**
3. **Format JSX for readability** - Use parentheses for multi-line JSX, proper indentation, and line breaks for attributes
4. **Choose appropriate naming conventions** - Use camelCase for props and event handlers
5. **Apply destructuring for cleaner code**
6. **Provide default values for optional props**
7. **Define event handlers correctly** - Avoid inline function definitions where possible
8. **Use keys when rendering lists**
9. **Include data attributes for testing**
10. **Add accessibility attributes**
11. **Prefer CSS classes over inline styles** for most styling needs
12. **Utilize React's performance optimization features** like `memo`, `useCallback`, and `useMemo`

Chapter 4: React Components

4.1 What Are Components?

The Building Blocks of React Applications

Components are the foundation of React applications. They are independent, reusable pieces of code that return HTML via JSX. Components allow developers to build complex UIs by breaking them down into smaller, manageable pieces that can be developed and tested in isolation.

Think of components as custom HTML elements with their own functionality, appearance, and behavior. Just as you would use standard HTML elements like `<div>`, `<header>`, or `<button>`, React allows you to create your own elements like `<Navbar>`, `<ProductCard>`, or `<CommentSection>`.

Component-Based Architecture

React adopts a component-based architecture, which offers several advantages:

Modularity

Components encapsulate their functionality, allowing developers to build complex UIs from simple building blocks. This modular approach makes the code more manageable and easier to understand.

Reusability

Well-designed components can be reused throughout an application or even across different projects. This reduces code duplication and speeds up development.

Separation of Concerns

Each component handles a specific part of the UI, making it easier to reason about the application's behavior and appearance. This separation also improves maintainability.

Testability

Individual components can be tested in isolation, which simplifies the testing process and leads to more reliable applications.

Component Structure

All React components have:

1. **Props** (optional): Input data passed from parent components
2. **State** (optional): Internal data managed by the component itself
3. **Lifecycle methods** (class components) or **Hooks** (functional components): Methods that run at different stages of a component's existence
4. **Render logic**: Code that determines what the component displays

Here's a simple example of a component's structure:

```
import React from 'react';

// A basic functional component
function Greeting(props) {
  return <h1>Hello, {props.name}!</h1>;
}

export default Greeting;
```

Types of Components

React offers two primary ways to define components:

1. **Functional Components**: JavaScript functions that accept props and return JSX
2. **Class Components**: ES6 classes that extend from React.Component and implement a render method

In modern React applications, functional components are preferred due to their simplicity and the introduction of Hooks, which allow functional components to use state and other React features that were previously only available in class components.

Component Composition

React applications are built by composing components together. Smaller components are combined to create larger ones, forming a component tree. This composition allows for the development of complex interfaces while maintaining a clean and organized codebase.

For example, a social media application might have a component hierarchy like this:

```
App
├── Header
│   ├── Logo
│   ├── SearchBar
│   └── UserMenu
├── Sidebar
│   ├── Navigation
│   └── UserProfile
└── MainContent
    ├── NewPost
    └── Feed
        └── Post (multiple instances)
            ├── PostHeader
            ├── PostContent
            └── PostFooter
                ├── LikeButton
                └── CommentSection
```

This hierarchical structure makes it easy to understand how the application is organized and how data flows between components.

4.2 Functional vs. Class Components

Functional Components

Functional components are JavaScript functions that accept props and return JSX. They are the simplest way to define a component in React.

Basic Structure

```
function Welcome(props) {
  return <h1>Hello, {props.name}</h1>;
}

// Arrow function syntax (equivalent)
const Welcome = (props) => {
  return <h1>Hello, {props.name}</h1>;
};

// Shorter syntax for simple components
const Welcome = props => <h1>Hello, {props.name}</h1>;
```

Advantages of Functional Components

1. **Simplicity**: Functional components are easier to read and write
2. **Less boilerplate**: They require less code than class components
3. **Easier testing**: They're pure functions that are easier to test
4. **Performance**: They can have slightly better performance in some cases
5. **Hooks support**: With React Hooks, functional components can now handle state and side effects

Limitations of Functional Components (Pre-Hooks)

Before the introduction of Hooks in React 16.8, functional components had several limitations:

- No state management
- No lifecycle methods
- Limited to presentation logic

However, with Hooks, functional components can now do everything that class components can do, and they are the recommended approach for new React code.

Class Components

Class components are ES6 classes that extend React.Component and implement a render method.

Basic Structure

```
import React, { Component } from 'react';

class Welcome extends Component {
  render() {
    return <h1>Hello, {this.props.name}</h1>;
  }
}
```

Advantages of Class Components

1. **Full lifecycle control**: Class components provide access to all React lifecycle methods
2. **Built-in state management**: They have built-in state handling via `this.state` and `this.setState()`
3. **Familiar for OOP developers**: They follow object-oriented programming patterns
4. **Error boundaries**: Only class components can be error boundaries (components that catch JavaScript errors)

Limitations of Class Components

1. **Verbose**: They require more boilerplate code
2. **`this` binding issues**: Handling `this` in event handlers can be tricky
3. **Harder to optimize**: More complex components can be harder to optimize
4. **Harder to understand**: Class components can be more difficult to understand, especially for developers new to React

Comparison Example

Let's compare a simple counter implemented with both functional and class components:

Class Component Version

```
import React, { Component } from 'react';

class Counter extends Component {
  constructor(props) {
    super(props);
    this.state = {
      count: 0
    };
    // Binding necessary to make `this` work in callbacks
    this.increment = this.increment.bind(this);
    this.decrement = this.decrement.bind(this);
  }

  increment() {
    this.setState({ count: this.state.count + 1 });
  }

  decrement() {
    this.setState({ count: this.state.count - 1 });
  }

  render() {
    return (
      <div>
        <h2>Counter: {this.state.count}</h2>
        <button onClick={this.increment}>Increment</
button>
        <button onClick={this.decrement}>Decrement</
button>
      </div>
    );
  }
}

export default Counter;
```

Functional Component Version (with Hooks)

```
import React, { useState } from 'react';

function Counter() {
  const [count, setCount] = useState(0);

  const increment = () => {
    setCount(count + 1);
  };

  const decrement = () => {
    setCount(count - 1);
  };

  return (
    <div>
      <h2>Counter: {count}</h2>
      <button onClick={increment}>Increment</button>
      <button onClick={decrement}>Decrement</button>
    </div>
  );
}

export default Counter;
```

When to Use Each Type

In modern React development:

- **Use functional components by default**: They're simpler, more concise, and with Hooks, they can do everything class components can do
- **Use class components when**:
  - Working with legacy code that uses class components
  - Implementing error boundaries
  - When team preference or project standards dictate their use

4.3 Creating a Simple Component

Component File Organization

Before creating components, it's important to understand how they're typically organized in a React project:

File Structure

A common convention is to place each component in its own file, named after the component:

```
src/
├── components/
│   ├── Button.js
│   ├── Navbar.js
│   ├── UserProfile.js
│   └── ...
├── App.js
└── index.js
```

For larger components, you might create a folder for the component and its related files:

```
src/
├── components/
│   ├── Button/
│   │   ├── Button.js
│   │   ├── Button.css
│   │   └── Button.test.js
│   └── ...
│
```

Creating a Functional Component

Let's create a simple Button component to demonstrate the process:

Step 1: Create the Component File

```
// src/components/Button.js
import React from 'react';

function Button(props) {
  return (
    <button
      className={`button ${props.variant || 'default'}`}
      onClick={props.onClick}
      disabled={props.disabled}
    >
      {props.children}
    </button>
  );
}

export default Button;
```

Step 2: Add PropTypes (Optional but Recommended)

PropTypes provide runtime type checking for React props:

```
// src/components/Button.js
import React from 'react';
import PropTypes from 'prop-types';

function Button(props) {
  return (
    <button
      className={`button ${props.variant || 'default'}`}
      onClick={props.onClick}
      disabled={props.disabled}
    >
      {props.children}
    </button>
  );
}

Button.propTypes = {
  variant: PropTypes.oneOf(['default', 'primary',
'secondary', 'danger']),
  onClick: PropTypes.func,
  disabled: PropTypes.bool,
  children: PropTypes.node.isRequired
};

Button.defaultProps = {
  variant: 'default',
  disabled: false,
  onClick: () => {}
};

export default Button;
```

Step 3: Using the Component

```
// src/App.js
import React from 'react';
import Button from './components/Button';

function App() {
  const handleClick = () => {
    alert('Button clicked!');
  };

  return (
    <div className="app">
      <h1>My React App</h1>
      <Button onClick={handleClick}>Click Me</Button>
      <Button variant="primary">Primary Button</Button>
      <Button variant="secondary" disabled>Disabled
Button</Button>
    </div>
  );
}

export default App;
```

Creating a Class Component

For comparison, let's create the same Button component as a class:

```
// src/components/ButtonClass.js
import React, { Component } from 'react';
import PropTypes from 'prop-types';

class Button extends Component {
  render() {
    return (
      <button
        className={`button ${this.props.variant ||
'default'}`}
        onClick={this.props.onClick}
        disabled={this.props.disabled}
      >
        {this.props.children}
      </button>
    );
  }
}

Button.propTypes = {
  variant: PropTypes.oneOf(['default', 'primary',
'secondary', 'danger']),
  onClick: PropTypes.func,
  disabled: PropTypes.bool,
  children: PropTypes.node.isRequired
};

Button.defaultProps = {
  variant: 'default',
  disabled: false,
  onClick: () => {}
};

export default Button;
```

Creating a Stateful Component

Let's create a more complex component with state - a toggle switch:

Functional Component with Hooks

```
// src/components/ToggleSwitch.js
import React, { useState } from 'react';
import PropTypes from 'prop-types';
import './ToggleSwitch.css'; // Assume we have some CSS

function ToggleSwitch(props) {
  const [isOn, setIsOn] = useState(props.defaultOn ||
false);

  const handleToggle = () => {
    const newState = !isOn;
    setIsOn(newState);

    // Call the onChange handler if provided
    if (props.onChange) {
      props.onChange(newState);
    }
  };

  return (
    <div className="toggle-switch">
      {props.label && <span className="toggle-
label">{props.label}</span>}
      <div
        className={`toggle-track ${isOn ? 'on' : 'off'}`}
        onClick={handleToggle}
      >
        <div className="toggle-thumb" />
      </div>
    </div>
  );
}

ToggleSwitch.propTypes = {
  defaultOn: PropTypes.bool,
  onChange: PropTypes.func,
  label: PropTypes.string
};

export default ToggleSwitch;
```

Class Component Version

```
// src/components/ToggleSwitchClass.js
import React, { Component } from 'react';
import PropTypes from 'prop-types';
import './ToggleSwitch.css';

class ToggleSwitch extends Component {
  constructor(props) {
    super(props);
    this.state = {
      isOn: props.defaultOn || false
    };

    this.handleToggle = this.handleToggle.bind(this);
  }

  handleToggle() {
    this.setState(prevState => {
      const newState = !prevState.isOn;

      // Call the onChange handler if provided
      if (this.props.onChange) {
        this.props.onChange(newState);
      }

      return { isOn: newState };
    });
  }

  render() {
    return (
      <div className="toggle-switch">
        {this.props.label && <span className="toggle-
label">{this.props.label}</span>}
        <div
          className={`toggle-track ${this.state.isOn ?
'on' : 'off'}`}
          onClick={this.handleToggle}
        >
          <div className="toggle-thumb" />
        </div>
```

4.4 Nesting Components

Component Composition

Component composition is a fundamental concept in React that allows you to build complex UIs by combining simpler components. Let's look at how to create nested component structures.

Parent-Child Relationships

Components can be nested inside other components, creating a parent-child relationship:

```
// src/components/Card.js
import React from 'react';
import PropTypes from 'prop-types';
import './Card.css';

function Card(props) {
  return (
    <div className={`card ${props.className || ''}`}>
      {props.title && <h2 className="card-
title">{props.title}</h2>}
      <div className="card-content">
        {props.children}
      </div>
      {props.footer && <div className="card-
footer">{props.footer}</div>}
    </div>
  );
}

Card.propTypes = {
  title: PropTypes.string,
  footer: PropTypes.node,
  className: PropTypes.string,
  children: PropTypes.node.isRequired
};

export default Card;
```

Using Children Props

The `children` prop is a special prop in React that allows you to pass components as data to other components:

```
// src/App.js
import React from 'react';
import Card from './components/Card';
import Button from './components/Button';

function App() {
  return (
    <div className="app">
      <Card
        title="Welcome to React"
        footer={<Button variant="primary">Learn More</
Button>}
      >
        <p>This is an example of component nesting in
React.</p>
        <p>The Card component is the parent, and these
paragraphs are its children.</p>
      </Card>
    </div>
  );
}

export default App;
```

Creating Compound Components

Compound components are a pattern where components are designed to work together, typically with one main component and several child components:

```
// src/components/Tabs/Tabs.js
import React, { useState } from 'react';
import PropTypes from 'prop-types';
import './Tabs.css';

function Tabs(props) {
  const [activeTab, setActiveTab] = useState(0);

  // Filter out only TabPanel components from children
  const tabPanels =
React.Children.toArray(props.children).filter(
    child => child.type && child.type.displayName ===
'TabPanel'
  );

  const handleTabClick = (index) => {
    setActiveTab(index);
  };

  return (
    <div className="tabs-container">
      <div className="tabs-header">
        {tabPanels.map((panel, index) => (
          <div
            key={index}
            className={`tab ${activeTab === index ?
'active' : ''}`}
            onClick={() => handleTabClick(index)}
          >
            {panel.props.title}
          </div>
        ))}
      </div>
      <div className="tabs-content">
        {tabPanels[activeTab]}
      </div>
    </div>
  );
}
```

Using the compound component:

```
// src/App.js
import React from 'react';
import Tabs from './components/Tabs/Tabs';

function App() {
  return (
    <div className="app">
      <h1>React Tabs Example</h1>

      <Tabs>
        <Tabs.TabPanel title="Home">
          <h2>Home Content</h2>
          <p>Welcome to the home tab!</p>
        </Tabs.TabPanel>

        <Tabs.TabPanel title="Profile">
          <h2>Profile Content</h2>
          <p>This is your profile information.</p>
        </Tabs.TabPanel>

        <Tabs.TabPanel title="Settings">
          <h2>Settings Content</h2>
          <p>Manage your account settings here.</p>
        </Tabs.TabPanel>
      </Tabs>
    </div>
  );
}

export default App;
```

Component Specialization

Another pattern is component specialization, where you create more specific components from more general ones:

```
// src/components/Button.js (base component)
// ... (code from earlier)

// src/components/IconButton.js (specialized component)
import React from 'react';
import PropTypes from 'prop-types';
import Button from './Button';
import './IconButton.css';

function IconButton(props) {
  return (
    <Button
      {...props}
      className={`icon-button ${props.className || ''}`}
    >
      <span className="icon">{props.icon}</span>
      {props.children && <span
className="text">{props.children}</span>}
    </Button>
  );
}

IconButton.propTypes = {
  ...Button.propTypes,
  icon: PropTypes.node.isRequired
};

export default IconButton;
```

Using the specialized component:

```
// src/App.js
import React from 'react';
import IconButton from './components/IconButton';

function App() {
  return (
    <div className="app">
      <h1>Icon Buttons</h1>

      <IconButton
        icon={<i className="fa fa-home"></i>}
        onClick={() => console.log('Home clicked')}
      >
        Home
      </IconButton>

      <IconButton
        icon={<i className="fa fa-cog"></i>}
        variant="primary"
      >
        Settings
      </IconButton>

      <IconButton
        icon={<i className="fa fa-trash"></i>}
        variant="danger"
      />
    </div>
  );
}

export default App;
```

Data Flow in Nested Components

When nesting components, understanding data flow is crucial:

Passing Data Down (Props)

Data flows down from parent to child components via props:

```
// UserProfile.js
import React from 'react';
import UserAvatar from './UserAvatar';
import UserInfo from './UserInfo';
import UserStats from './UserStats';

function UserProfile({ user }) {
  return (
    <div className="user-profile">
      <UserAvatar src={user.avatarUrl} size="large" />
      <UserInfo name={user.name} bio={user.bio} />
      <UserStats followers={user.followers}
following={user.following} />
    </div>
  );
}
```

Passing Data Up (Callbacks)

Data flows up from child to parent components via callback functions:

```
// ParentComponent.js
import React, { useState } from 'react';
import SearchBar from './SearchBar';
import ResultsList from './ResultsList';

function ParentComponent() {
  const [searchTerm, setSearchTerm] = useState('');
  const [results, setResults] = useState([]);

  const handleSearch = (term) => {
    setSearchTerm(term);
    // Fetch results based on term...
    setResults(/* fetched results */);
  };

  return (
    <div>
      <SearchBar onSearch={handleSearch} />
      <ResultsList results={results} />
    </div>
  );
}
```

4.5 Component Reusability

Principles of Reusable Components

Creating truly reusable components requires careful design. Here are the key principles:

Single Responsibility

Each component should do one thing and do it well. Complex components should be broken down into smaller, focused components.

Configurable

Reusable components should be configurable through props. This allows them to be customized for different use cases.

Self-Contained

Components should manage their own state and behavior, minimizing dependencies on external code.

Well-Documented

Reusable components should have clear documentation, including propTypes, default props, and usage examples.

Creating Generic Components

Let's create a generic, reusable Input component:

```
import React, { useState } from 'react';
import PropTypes from 'prop-types';

/**
 * A reusable input component with built-in validation
 */
const Input = ({
  type = 'text',
  label,
  placeholder = '',
  value = '',
  onChange,
  error = '',
  disabled = false,
  required = false,
  className = '',
  validator = () => true,
  onBlur = () => {},
}) => {
  const [touched, setTouched] = useState(false);
  const [internalError, setInternalError] = useState('');

  const handleChange = (e) => {
    const newValue = e.target.value;

    // Validate the input
    const isValid = validator(newValue);
    setInternalError(isValid === true ? '' : (isValid ||
'Invalid input'));

    // Call the parent onChange handler
    if (onChange) {
      onChange(e);
    }
  };

  const handleBlur = (e) => {
    setTouched(true);
    if (onBlur) {
      onBlur(e);
```

Usage Example

Here's how you might use this reusable Input component:

```
import React, { useState } from 'react';
import Input from './components/Input';

const ContactForm = () => {
  const [formData, setFormData] = useState({
    name: '',
    email: '',
    message: '',
  });

  const [errors, setErrors] = useState({
    name: '',
    email: '',
    message: '',
  });

  const handleChange = (e) => {
    const { name, value } = e.target;
    setFormData(prev => ({
      ...prev,
      [name]: value
    }));
  };

  // Email validator function
  const validateEmail = (email) => {
    const emailRegex = /^[^\s@]+@[^\s@]+\.[^\s@]+$/;
    return emailRegex.test(email) ? true : 'Please enter
a valid email address';
  };

  // Name validator function
  const validateName = (name) => {
    return name.length >= 2 ? true : 'Name must be at
least 2 characters';
  };

  const handleSubmit = (e) => {
    e.preventDefault();
```

Benefits of This Approach

1. **Consistency**: The Input component ensures all form inputs have the same style, behavior, and validation patterns.
2. **Reduced Code Duplication**: Common input logic like validation, error handling, and accessibility features are defined once.
3. **Ease of Maintenance**: If you need to update how inputs work across your application, you only need to modify one component.
4. **Enhanced Functionality**: The component includes built-in features like:
    - Accessible error messages
    - Required field indicators
    - Custom validation
    - Support for different input types

Extending for More Complex Use Cases

The Input component can be extended for more specific use cases:

```
// NumberInput.jsx
import React from 'react';
import Input from './Input';

const NumberInput = (props) => {
  const validateNumber = (value) => {
    if (isNaN(Number(value))) {
      return 'Please enter a valid number';
    }

    if (props.min !== undefined && Number(value) <
props.min) {
      return `Value must be at least ${props.min}`;
    }

    if (props.max !== undefined && Number(value) >
props.max) {
      return `Value must be no more than ${props.max}`;
    }

    return true;
  };

  return (
    <Input
      type="number"
      validator={validateNumber}
      {...props}
    />
  );
};

export default NumberInput;
```

Component Libraries and Design Systems

For large applications, consider organizing reusable components into a component library or design system. This approach offers:

1. **Centralized Management**: Components can be versioned and distributed as a package.
2. **Comprehensive Documentation**: Tools like Storybook help document components and their usage.
3. **Visual Testing**: Visual regression testing ensures components maintain their appearance.
4. **Design Consistency**: Components follow the same design principles and patterns.

Conclusion

Reusable components are a fundamental part of efficient React development. By designing components with clear responsibilities, configurable options, and comprehensive documentation, you create a more maintainable and consistent application. The effort invested in creating reusable components pays dividends as your application grows in complexity.

Chapter 5: Props in React

5.1 Passing Data with Props

Props (short for properties) are the primary mechanism for passing data from parent components to child components in React. They create a unidirectional data flow that makes applications predictable and easier to understand.

Understanding Props

Props are read-only pieces of information that are passed to components, similar to function parameters. They allow components to be dynamic and reusable by configuring them with different data each time they're used.

When a parent component renders a child component, it can pass any data as props. These props become accessible inside the child component through its props object.

Basic Syntax for Passing Props

```
// Parent component passing props
function ParentComponent() {
  return <ChildComponent name="John" age={25}
active={true} />;
}

// Child component receiving props
function ChildComponent(props) {
  return (
    <div>
      <p>Name: {props.name}</p>
      <p>Age: {props.age}</p>
      <p>Active: {props.active ? 'Yes' : 'No'}</p>
    </div>
  );
}
```

In this example, the parent component passes three props to the child: a string (`name`), a number (`age`), and a boolean (`active`). The child component then accesses these values via the `props` object.

Passing Different Data Types as Props

Props can be any valid JavaScript value:

- **Strings**: Passed with quotes: `name="John"`
- **Numbers**: Passed with curly braces: `age={25}`
- **Booleans**: Passed with curly braces: `active={true}`
- **Arrays**: Passed with curly braces: `items={['apple', 'orange', 'banana']}`
- **Objects**: Passed with curly braces: `user={{ name: 'John', age: 25 }}`
- **Functions**: Passed with curly braces: `onClick={() => alert('Clicked!')}`

Passing Props to Multiple Levels

Props can be passed through multiple component levels, which is sometimes called "prop drilling":

```
function GrandparentComponent() {
  const userData = { name: "John", role: "Admin" };
  return <ParentComponent userData={userData} />;
}

function ParentComponent(props) {
  return <ChildComponent userData={props.userData} />;
}

function ChildComponent(props) {
  return (
    <div>
      <p>Name: {props.userData.name}</p>
      <p>Role: {props.userData.role}</p>
    </div>
  );
}
```

While prop drilling works for small applications, it can become cumbersome in larger applications with deeply nested components. For such cases, context API or state management libraries offer better solutions.

Spreading Props

When you need to pass many props to a component, you can use the spread operator (`...`) to pass all properties of an object as individual props:

```
function ParentComponent() {
  const userProps = {
    name: "John",
    age: 25,
    location: "New York"
  };

  return <UserProfile {...userProps} />;
}

// This is equivalent to:
// <UserProfile name="John" age={25} location="New
York" />
```

Immutability of Props

One crucial aspect of props is that they are immutable. Child components should never modify the props they receive. This restriction helps maintain the unidirectional data flow in React applications and makes components more predictable.

If a component needs to modify data received as props, it should:

1. Copy the props data to its own state
2. Modify the state instead
3. Optionally, call a function passed as a prop to notify the parent of the intended change

```
function EditableProfile(props) {
  const [name, setName] = React.useState(props.name);

  const handleNameChange = (e) => {
    setName(e.target.value);
    if (props.onNameChange) {
      props.onNameChange(e.target.value);
    }
  };

  return (
    <div>
      <input value={name} onChange={handleNameChange} />
    </div>
  );
}
```

5.2 Default Props

Default props provide fallback values for props that aren't specified when a component is used. They ensure components remain functional even when some expected props are missing.

Setting Default Props

There are two common ways to set default props in React:

Method 1: Using the defaultProps Static Property (Class Components)

```
class Button extends React.Component {
  render() {
    return (
      <button className={this.props.className}>
        {this.props.label}
      </button>
    );
  }
}

Button.defaultProps = {
  className: 'default-button',
  label: 'Click Me'
};
```

Method 2: Using Default Parameters (Function Components)

```
function Button({ className = 'default-button', label =
'Click Me' }) {
  return (
    <button className={className}>
      {label}
    </button>
  );
}
```

Default Props for Complex Data Types

For complex data types like objects and arrays, be careful with default values:

```
// Good: Using a function to create a fresh object for
each component instance
function UserCard({ user = { name: 'Guest', role:
'Viewer' } }) {
  // user will be { name: 'Guest', role: 'Viewer' } if
not provided
  return (
    <div>
      <h3>{user.name}</h3>
      <p>Role: {user.role}</p>
    </div>
  );
}

// Warning: For nested objects or when default objects
are complex
function DataTable({ config = {} }) {
  // Provide defaults for nested properties
  const {
    pageSize = 10,
    sortable = true,
    columns = []
  } = config;

  return (
    <table>
      {/* Component implementation */}
    </table>
  );
}
```

When to Use Default Props

Default props are valuable in several scenarios:

1. **Making Components More Flexible**: Users of your component can provide only the props they need to customize, while other props use sensible defaults.
2. **Preventing Null/Undefined Errors**: Default props prevent "cannot read

property of undefined" errors that might occur when accessing nested properties.

3. **Documentation**: Default props serve as built-in documentation, indicating what values are expected for each prop.

4. **Testing**: Default props simplify testing by reducing the number of props you need to provide in test cases.

Conditional Rendering Based on Props

Default props work well with conditional rendering to create flexible components:

```
function Alert({ type = 'info', message, showIcon =
true }) {
  const iconMap = {
    success: '✓',
    error: '✗',
    warning: '⚠',
    info: 'i'
  };

  return (
    <div className={`alert alert-${type}`}>
      {showIcon && <span className="alert-
icon">{iconMap[type]}</span>}
      <span className="alert-message">{message}</span>
    </div>
  );
}
```

This component will display different icons based on the `type` prop and can hide the icon altogether based on the `showIcon` prop.

5.3 PropTypes for Type Checking

PropTypes provide a way to validate the data types of props passed to components. While not required, they help catch bugs by ensuring components receive the correct data types.

Setting Up PropTypes

To use PropTypes, you need to install the package:

```
npm install prop-types
```

Then, import and use it in your component:

```
import PropTypes from 'prop-types';

function UserProfile({ name, age, email }) {
  return (
    <div>
      <h2>{name}</h2>
      <p>Age: {age}</p>
      <p>Email: {email}</p>
    </div>
  );
}

UserProfile.propTypes = {
  name: PropTypes.string,
  age: PropTypes.number,
  email: PropTypes.string
};
```

Available PropTypes Validators

PropTypes offers validators for all JavaScript primitives:

```
MyComponent.propTypes = {
  // Basic types
  stringProp: PropTypes.string,
  numberProp: PropTypes.number,
  booleanProp: PropTypes.bool,
  functionProp: PropTypes.func,
  objectProp: PropTypes.object,
  arrayProp: PropTypes.array,
  symbolProp: PropTypes.symbol,

  // React elements
  elementProp: PropTypes.element,

  // Multiple types
  messageOrNumber: PropTypes.oneOfType([
    PropTypes.string,
    PropTypes.number
  ]),

  // Specific values
  status: PropTypes.oneOf(['loading', 'success',
'error']),

  // Arrays of specific types
  names: PropTypes.arrayOf(PropTypes.string),

  // Objects with specific shapes
  user: PropTypes.shape({
    name: PropTypes.string.isRequired,
    age: PropTypes.number
  }),

  // Objects with any keys but specific value types
  scores: PropTypes.objectOf(PropTypes.number),

  // Any type of data
  anyProp: PropTypes.any,

  // Custom validator
  customProp: function(props, propName, componentName) {
```

Required Props

You can mark props as required by chaining `.isRequired` to any PropTypes validator:

```
Button.propTypes = {
  label: PropTypes.string.isRequired, // Must be provided
  onClick: PropTypes.func.isRequired, // Must be provided
  className: PropTypes.string         // Optional
};
```

Custom Validators

For complex validation logic, you can create custom validators:

```
function validateEmail(props, propName, componentName) {
  const emailRegex = /^[^\s@]+@[^\s@]+\.[^\s@]+$/;
  const email = props[propName];

  if (email && !emailRegex.test(email)) {
    return new Error(
      `Invalid prop '${propName}' (value: '${email}')
supplied to ${componentName}. Expected a valid email
address.`
    );
  }
}

function ContactForm(props) {
  // Component implementation
}

ContactForm.propTypes = {
  email: validateEmail
};
```

PropTypes in Development vs. Production

PropTypes validations run only in development mode and are automatically stripped from production builds to improve performance. This means they help during development but don't impact end users.

TypeScript as an Alternative

While PropTypes are useful, many developers are moving to TypeScript, which provides stronger type checking that's verified at compile time rather than runtime:

```
interface UserProfileProps {
  name: string;
  age: number;
  email: string;
}

function UserProfile({ name, age, email }:
UserProfileProps) {
  return (
    <div>
      <h2>{name}</h2>
      <p>Age: {age}</p>
      <p>Email: {email}</p>
    </div>
  );
}
```

TypeScript offers more robust type checking but requires a build step. PropTypes are simpler to adopt in existing projects and still provide valuable runtime validation.

5.4 Destructuring Props

Destructuring props is a clean, efficient way to extract and use specific props in your components. It makes your code more readable and concise.

Basic Props Destructuring

Instead of accessing props through the `props` object, you can destructure them directly in the function parameters:

```
// Without destructuring
function Greeting(props) {
  return <h1>Hello, {props.name}!</h1>;
}

// With destructuring
function Greeting({ name }) {
  return <h1>Hello, {name}!</h1>;
}
```

Destructuring Multiple Props

You can destructure multiple props at once:

```
function UserCard({ name, title, avatar, status }) {
  return (
    <div className="user-card">
      <img src={avatar} alt={name} />
      <h3>{name}</h3>
      <p>{title}</p>
      <span className={`status ${status}`}>{status}</
span>
    </div>
  );
}
```

Combining Destructuring with Default Values

You can provide default values during destructuring:

```
function Button({ label = 'Click Me', type = 'primary',
onClick }) {
  return (
    <button className={`btn-${type}`} onClick={onClick}>
      {label}
    </button>
  );
}
```

Renaming Props During Destructuring

Sometimes you might want to use a different variable name than the prop name:

```
function ProfileHeader({ userName: name, userAvatar:
avatar }) {
  // Inside the component, use 'name' and 'avatar'
variables
  return (
    <header>
      <img src={avatar} alt={name} />
      <h2>{name}</h2>
    </header>
  );
}

// Usage:
<ProfileHeader userName="JohnDoe" userAvatar="/avatars/
john.png" />
```

Nested Destructuring

For props containing objects or arrays, you can use nested destructuring:

```
function UserDetails({ user: { name, email, address:
{ city, country } } }) {
  return (
    <div>
      <h2>{name}</h2>
      <p>Email: {email}</p>
      <p>Location: {city}, {country}</p>
    </div>
  );
}

// Usage:
<UserDetails user={{
  name: "John",
  email: "john@example.com",
  address: {
    city: "New York",
    country: "USA"
  }
}} />
```

Rest Parameters with Destructuring

You can use the rest operator (`...`) to collect remaining props:

```
function TextInput({ label, ...inputProps }) {
  // inputProps will contain all props except 'label'
  return (
    <div className="form-group">
      <label>{label}</label>
      <input {...inputProps} />
    </div>
  );
}

// Usage:
<TextInput
  label="Username"
  type="text"
  placeholder="Enter username"
  value={username}
  onChange={handleChange}
  required
/>
```

This technique is especially useful when you need to forward most props to an underlying HTML element or React component.

Destructuring in Class Components

In class components, destructuring typically happens inside the render method:

```
class ProductCard extends React.Component {
  render() {
    const { title, price, image, onAddToCart } =
this.props;

    return (
      <div className="product-card">
        <img src={image} alt={title} />
        <h3>{title}</h3>
        <p>${price.toFixed(2)}</p>
        <button onClick={onAddToCart}>Add to Cart</
button>
      </div>
    );
  }
}
```

Performance Benefits

Destructuring can slightly improve performance by avoiding repeated property lookups. Instead of accessing `props.name` multiple times, you access the `name` variable directly after destructuring.

5.5 Children Props

The `children` prop is a special prop that allows components to render content placed between their opening and closing tags. It enables the creation of wrapper components and compositional patterns.

Understanding the Children Prop

When you include content between a component's opening and closing tags, React automatically passes this content to the component as a special prop called `children`:

```
function Card({ children }) {
  return (
    <div className="card">
      {children}
    </div>
  );
}

// Usage:
<Card>
  <h2>Title</h2>
  <p>This content will be passed as the children prop.</
p>
</Card>
```

In this example, everything between `<Card>` and `</Card>` becomes the `children` prop of the `Card` component.

Children Types

The `children` prop can be:

1. **React Elements**: Other components or HTML elements
2. **Strings or Numbers**: Plain text content
3. **JavaScript Expressions**: Results of function calls or calculations
4. **Arrays**: Multiple elements
5. **null, undefined, or boolean**: Which render nothing

Creating Container Components

One common use of the `children` prop is to create container components that provide styling, layout, or functionality while being agnostic about their content:

```
function Panel({ title, children }) {
  return (
    <div className="panel">
      <div className="panel-header">
        <h3>{title}</h3>
      </div>
      <div className="panel-body">
        {children}
      </div>
    </div>
  );
}

// Usage:
<Panel title="User Information">
  <p>Name: John Doe</p>
  <p>Email: john@example.com</p>
  <button>Edit Profile</button>
</Panel>
```

Manipulating Children

You can manipulate children before rendering them. React provides utilities in the `React.Children` namespace for working with the `children` prop:

```
import React from 'react';

function List({ children }) {
  // Count children
  const childCount = React.Children.count(children);

  // Add props to each child
  const enhancedChildren = React.Children.map(children,
(child, index) => {
    return React.cloneElement(child, {
      number: index + 1,
      key: index
    });
  });

  return (
    <div>
      <p>This list has {childCount} items:</p>
      <ul>{enhancedChildren}</ul>
    </div>
  );
}

function ListItem({ number, children }) {
  return <li>Item {number}: {children}</li>;
}

// Usage:
<List>
  <ListItem>First item</ListItem>
  <ListItem>Second item</ListItem>
  <ListItem>Third item</ListItem>
</List>
```

Function as Children (Render Props)

A powerful pattern in React is passing a function as the `children` prop, often called the "render prop" pattern:

```
function DataFetcher({ url, children }) {
  const [data, setData] = React.useState(null);
  const [loading, setLoading] = React.useState(true);
  const [error, setError] = React.useState(null);

  React.useEffect(() => {
    fetch(url)
      .then(response => response.json())
      .then(data => {
        setData(data);
        setLoading(false);
      })
      .catch(error => {
        setError(error);
        setLoading(false);
      });
  }, [url]);

  return children({ data, loading, error });
}

// Usage:
<DataFetcher url="https://api.example.com/data">
  {({ data, loading, error }) => {
    if (loading) return <p>Loading...</p>;
    if (error) return <p>Error: {error.message}</p>;
    return (
      <ul>
        {data.map(item => (
          <li key={item.id}>{item.name}</li>
        ))}
      </ul>
    );
  }}
</DataFetcher>
```

This pattern provides extreme flexibility because the parent component can control the rendering logic while the child component provides the data or functionality.

Conditional Rendering with Children

You can conditionally render children based on props or state:

```
function Expandable({ title, children, initialExpanded =
false }) {
  const [expanded, setExpanded] =
React.useState(initialExpanded);

  return (
    <div className="expandable">
      <div
        className="expandable-header"
        onClick={() => setExpanded(!expanded)}
      >
        <h3>{title}</h3>
        <span>{expanded ? '▼' : '►'}</span>
      </div>
      {expanded && (
        <div className="expandable-content">
          {children}
        </div>
      )}
    </div>
  );
}

// Usage:
<Expandable title="Details">
  <p>These details are only shown when expanded.</p>
  <ul>
    <li>Item 1</li>
    <li>Item 2</li>
  </ul>
</Expandable>
```

Multiple Children Slots

Sometimes, you might want to distribute children to different parts of your component.

You can do this by having the user pass an object with named properties instead of using the standard children prop:

```
function Layout({ children: { header, sidebar, content,
footer } }) {
  return (
    <div className="layout">
      <header className="layout-header">{header}</header>
      <div className="layout-main">
        <aside className="layout-sidebar">{sidebar}</
aside>
        <main className="layout-content">{content}</main>
      </div>
      <footer className="layout-footer">{footer}</footer>
    </div>
  );
}

// Usage:
<Layout children={{
  header: <h1>My Website</h1>,
  sidebar: <nav>Navigation links...</nav>,
  content: <article>Main content...</article>,
  footer: <p>Copyright © 2025</p>
}} />
```

Alternatively, you can use specific props for each slot:

```
function Layout({ header, sidebar, content, footer }) {
  return (
    <div className="layout">
      <header className="layout-header">{header}</header>
      <div className="layout-main">
        <aside className="layout-sidebar">{sidebar}</
aside>
        <main className="layout-content">{content}</main>
      </div>
      <footer className="layout-footer">{footer}</footer>
    </div>
  );
}

// Usage:
<Layout
  header={<h1>My Website</h1>}
  sidebar={<nav>Navigation links...</nav>}
  content={<article>Main content...</article>}
  footer={<p>Copyright © 2025</p>}
/>
```

Tips for Working with Props

- Keep props simple and focused on component-specific concerns, avoiding passing unnecessary data
- Use descriptive prop names that clearly indicate their purpose
- Set default props for optional values to make components more usable
- Validate props with PropTypes or TypeScript to catch errors early
- Consider composing components instead of adding more props when component complexity increases

Actionable Strategies for Effective Prop Usage

- Implement a consistent naming convention for props across your application
- Create higher-order components to inject common props into multiple

components

- Use component composition with children props for flexible layouts instead of configuring with numerous props
- Extract complex prop logic into custom hooks for better reusability
- Document your components' props with JSDoc comments or Storybook for better team collaboration
- Minimize prop drilling by using Context API for deeply nested component structures
- Split components that require many props into smaller, more focused components

Chapter 6: State in React

6.1 What is State?

State represents the dynamic data in a React component that can change over time, typically in response to user actions or network responses. Unlike props, which are passed from parent components, state is managed internally within a component.

Core Concepts of State

State in React forms the foundation for creating interactive user interfaces. When state changes, React automatically re-renders the component and its children, updating the UI to reflect the new data. This reactive nature is what gives React its name and power.

State should contain only the minimal amount of data needed for a component to function correctly. Any data that can be derived from props or other state values should be calculated during rendering rather than stored in state.

Types of State Data

React components can manage various types of state data:

- **UI State**: Controls visual aspects of components (expanded/collapsed, active tab, etc.)
- **Form State**: Stores form input values, validation errors, and submission status
- **Application State**: Represents core application data (user information, fetched data, etc.)
- **Navigation State**: Tracks current page, URL parameters, and navigation history
- **Session State**: Manages user authentication status, permissions, and preferences

State Characteristics

State in React has several important characteristics:

Immutability

State should never be modified directly. Instead, React provides functions to replace the current state with a new value:

```
// Incorrect - direct mutation
this.state.count = this.state.count + 1;

// Correct - creating new state
setState({ count: this.state.count + 1 });
// or with hooks
setCount(count + 1);
```

Private to Components

State is fully encapsulated within its component. Parent components can't directly access or modify a child component's state. This encapsulation ensures components remain independent and reusable.

To share state between components, you either:

1. Lift state up to a common ancestor
2. Use context API
3. Implement a state management solution like Redux

Asynchronous Updates

State updates in React can be asynchronous for performance reasons. React may batch multiple setState calls into a single update. This batching optimizes rendering but means you can't rely on state updates happening immediately.

Local vs. Global State

React applications typically use a combination of local and global state:

Local State:

- Managed directly within a component
- Relevant only to that component or its immediate children
- Examples: form input values, toggle states, local UI state

Global State:

- Shared across multiple components
- Often represents application-wide data
- Examples: user authentication status, theme settings, shopping cart contents

When to Use State

State should be used when:

1. Data changes over time
2. Changes should trigger UI updates
3. Data can't be calculated from props

State should not be used for:

1. Data that doesn't change
2. Data that can be derived from props or other state
3. Data that doesn't affect rendering

Common State Mistakes

Beginners often make these mistakes with state:

1. **Storing derived data**: Calculating values during rendering is more efficient than storing them in state.

2. **Using state for one-time initializations**: For values that are computed once and never change, use regular variables or React.useMemo.

3. **Creating overly complex state structures**: Deeply nested state objects are difficult to update immutably.

4. **Not normalizing state**: When storing collections of data, organizing by IDs rather than nested arrays can simplify updates.

6.2 useState Hook Explained

The `useState` hook is the primary way to add state to function components in React. It provides a simple yet powerful mechanism for components to manage their own state.

Basic Usage of useState

The `useState` hook takes an initial state value and returns an array with two elements: the current state value and a function to update it.

```
import React, { useState } from 'react';

function Counter() {
  // Destructure the array returned by useState
  const [count, setCount] = useState(0);

  return (
    <div>
      <p>You clicked {count} times</p>
      <button onClick={() => setCount(count + 1)}>
        Click me
      </button>
    </div>
  );
}
```

In this example:

- `count` is the current state value
- `setCount` is the function to update the state
- 0 is the initial state value

Multiple State Variables

Components can have multiple state variables by calling `useState` multiple times:

```
function UserForm() {
  const [name, setName] = useState('');
  const [email, setEmail] = useState('');
  const [age, setAge] = useState(null);

  return (
    <form>
      <input
        value={name}
        onChange={(e) => setName(e.target.value)}
        placeholder="Name"
      />
      <input
        value={email}
        onChange={(e) => setEmail(e.target.value)}
        placeholder="Email"
      />
      <input
        type="number"
        value={age || ''}
        onChange={(e) => setAge(e.target.value ?
Number(e.target.value) : null)}
        placeholder="Age"
      />
    </form>
  );
}
```

Using multiple state variables allows for more precise updates and clearer code organization.

Object State with useState

You can store objects in state, but remember that the state updater function doesn't automatically merge objects like `this.setState` does in class components:

```
function ProfileForm() {
  const [profile, setProfile] = useState({
    name: '',
    email: '',
    bio: ''
  });

  const handleChange = (e) => {
    const { name, value } = e.target;

    // Must spread the existing state to avoid losing
other fields
    setProfile({
      ...profile,
      [name]: value
    });
  };

  return (
    <form>
      <input
        name="name"
        value={profile.name}
        onChange={handleChange}
      />
      <input
        name="email"
        value={profile.email}
        onChange={handleChange}
      />
      <textarea
        name="bio"
        value={profile.bio}
        onChange={handleChange}
      />
    </form>
  );
}
```

Lazy Initial State

If your initial state requires expensive computation, use a function for the initial state:

```
function TodoList() {
  // This function only runs during the first render
  const [todos, setTodos] = useState(() => {
    const savedTodos = localStorage.getItem('todos');
    if (savedTodos) {
      return JSON.parse(savedTodos);
    }
    return [];
  });

  // Component logic...
}
```

The function passed to `useState` only runs during the initial render, not on re-renders.

Functional Updates

When the new state depends on the previous state, use the functional update form:

```
function Counter() {
  const [count, setCount] = useState(0);

  const increment = () => {
    // This form is safer for multiple updates
    setCount(prevCount => prevCount + 1);
  };

  const incrementThree = () => {
    // All three updates will work correctly
    increment();
    increment();
    increment();
  };

  return (
    <div>
      <p>Count: {count}</p>
      <button onClick={increment}>Increment</button>
      <button onClick={incrementThree}>Increment Three
Times</button>
    </div>
  );
}
```

This pattern ensures you're always working with the most recent state value, even when multiple updates are scheduled.

State Initialization with Props

When initializing state with props, be aware that the state is only initialized once, during the first render:

```
function UserProfile({ userId }) {
  // This only runs once, when the component first mounts
  const [user, setUser] = useState(null);

  // Use an effect to update state when props change
  useEffect(() => {
    fetchUser(userId).then(userData =>
setUser(userData));
  }, [userId]);

  if (!user) return <p>Loading...</p>;

  return (
    <div>
      <h2>{user.name}</h2>
      <p>Email: {user.email}</p>
    </div>
  );
}
```

To react to prop changes, use `useEffect` with the prop as a dependency.

6.3 Updating State Correctly

Updating state correctly is crucial for React applications to behave predictably and efficiently. State updates in React require special attention due to their asynchronous nature and immutability requirements.

Immutability Principles

State in React should never be modified directly. Instead, create a new copy of the state with the desired changes:

```
// Array state updates
const [items, setItems] = useState(['apple', 'orange',
'banana']);

// Adding an item
setItems([...items, 'grape']);

// Removing an item
setItems(items.filter(item => item !== 'orange'));

// Updating an item
setItems(items.map(item =>
  item === 'apple' ? 'red apple' : item
));

// Object state updates
const [user, setUser] = useState({
  name: 'John',
  email: 'john@example.com',
  preferences: { theme: 'light', notifications: true }
});

// Updating a top-level property
setUser({
  ...user,
  name: 'Jane'
});

// Updating a nested property
setUser({
  ...user,
  preferences: {
    ...user.preferences,
    theme: 'dark'
  }
});
```

Handling Asynchronous Updates

State updates might be batched for performance, so the state value might not change immediately after calling the update function:

```
function Counter() {
  const [count, setCount] = useState(0);

  const handleClick = () => {
    // This might not work as expected
    setCount(count + 1);
    console.log(count); // Still shows the old value

    // For operations that depend on the updated state
    // use useEffect with dependencies
    // or continue the logic in the next render
  };

  // useEffect runs after the render with updated state
  useEffect(() => {
    console.log('Updated count:', count);
    // Perform actions that depend on the new count
  }, [count]);

  return (
    <button onClick={handleClick}>
      Increment ({count})
    </button>
  );
}
```

Functional Updates Pattern

When the new state depends on the previous state, use the functional update pattern:

```
function Counter() {
  const [count, setCount] = useState(0);

  const increment = () => {
    // This is safe for multiple sequential updates
    setCount(prevCount => prevCount + 1);
  };

  const incrementByTen = () => {
    // All updates will be applied correctly
    for (let i = 0; i < 10; i++) {
      increment();
    }
  };

  return (
    <div>
      <p>Count: {count}</p>
      <button onClick={increment}>Increment</button>
      <button onClick={incrementByTen}>+10</button>
    </div>
  );
}
```

Complex State Updates

For complex state structures, consider using helper functions or reducers to make updates more maintainable:

```
function TaskList() {
  const [tasks, setTasks] = useState([]);

  const addTask = (text) => {
    const newTask = {
      id: Date.now(),
      text,
      completed: false
    };
    setTasks(prevTasks => [...prevTasks, newTask]);
  };

  const toggleTask = (taskId) => {
    setTasks(prevTasks =>
      prevTasks.map(task =>
        task.id === taskId
          ? { ...task, completed: !task.completed }
          : task
      )
    );
  };

  const deleteTask = (taskId) => {
    setTasks(prevTasks =>
      prevTasks.filter(task => task.id !== taskId)
    );
  };

  // Component JSX...
}
```

Avoiding Common Pitfalls

Updating State Based on Props

When your state needs to be synchronized with props, use `useEffect`:

```
function SearchResults({ query }) {
  const [results, setResults] = useState([]);
  const [loading, setLoading] = useState(false);

  useEffect(() => {
    // Reset results when query changes
    setResults([]);

    if (!query) return;

    setLoading(true);
    fetchResults(query)
      .then(data => {
        setResults(data);
        setLoading(false);
      })
      .catch(error => {
        console.error(error);
        setLoading(false);
      });
  }, [query]);

  // Render results...
}
```

Updating State from Timeouts or Subscriptions

When updating state from asynchronous operations, ensure your component is still mounted:

```
function DataFetcher({ url }) {
  const [data, setData] = useState(null);
  const [loading, setLoading] = useState(true);

  useEffect(() => {
    let mounted = true;

    const fetchData = async () => {
      try {
        const response = await fetch(url);
        const result = await response.json();

        // Only update state if component is still
mounted
        if (mounted) {
          setData(result);
          setLoading(false);
        }
      } catch (error) {
        if (mounted) {
          console.error(error);
          setLoading(false);
        }
      }
    };

    fetchData();

    // Cleanup function to prevent updates on unmounted
components
    return () => {
      mounted = false;
    };
  }, [url]);

  // Render data...
}
```

Using Reducers for Complex State Logic

When state logic becomes complex, consider using the `useReducer` hook:

```
import { useReducer } from 'react';

// Define actions
const ADD_TASK = 'ADD_TASK';
const TOGGLE_TASK = 'TOGGLE_TASK';
const DELETE_TASK = 'DELETE_TASK';

// Reducer function
function tasksReducer(state, action) {
  switch (action.type) {
    case ADD_TASK:
      return [...state, {
        id: Date.now(),
        text: action.payload,
        completed: false
      }];

    case TOGGLE_TASK:
      return state.map(task =>
        task.id === action.payload
          ? { ...task, completed: !task.completed }
          : task
      );

    case DELETE_TASK:
      return state.filter(task => task.id !==
action.payload);

    default:
      return state;
  }
}

function TaskManager() {
  const [tasks, dispatch] = useReducer(tasksReducer, []);
  const [input, setInput] = useState('');

  const handleSubmit = (e) => {
    e.preventDefault();
    if (!input.trim()) return;
```

Optimizing State Updates

For better performance, consider techniques like:

1. **Memoization** with `useMemo` for expensive calculations
2. **Callback memoization** with `useCallback` for event handlers
3. **Avoiding unnecessary re-renders** with `React.memo`
4. **Debouncing or throttling** for frequent updates

6.4 State vs. Props

Understanding the differences between state and props is fundamental to building React applications correctly. While both hold data that influences rendering, they serve distinct purposes and follow different update patterns.

Key Differences

Origin and Ownership

- **Props**: Passed from parent components, owned by the parent
- **State**: Created and managed within the component, owned by the component itself

Mutability

- **Props**: Read-only, should never be modified by the receiving component
- **State**: Mutable through specific update functions (setState, useState updater)

Updates

- **Props**: Update when the parent re-renders with new values
- **State**: Updates trigger re-renders when modified using state update functions

Usage

- **Props**: Pass data down the component tree, configure child components
- **State**: Track information that changes over time within a component

When to Use Props

Use props when:

1. Passing data from parent to child components
2. Configuring reusable components with different values
3. Sharing data between sibling components (via a common parent)
4. Controlling a child component's behavior from a parent

```
// Parent component
function UserList({ users }) {
  return (
    <div>
      <h2>User List</h2>
      {users.map(user => (
        <UserCard
          key={user.id}
          name={user.name}
          email={user.email}
          role={user.role}
          onDelete={() => handleDeleteUser(user.id)}
        />
      ))}
    </div>
  );
}

// Child component - configured entirely through props
function UserCard({ name, email, role, onDelete }) {
  return (
    <div className="user-card">
      <h3>{name}</h3>
      <p>{email}</p>
      <p>Role: {role}</p>
      <button onClick={onDelete}>Delete</button>
    </div>
  );
}
```

When to Use State

Use state when:

1. Tracking data that changes over time
2. Storing user input or form values
3. Controlling UI elements (expanded/collapsed, active tab)
4. Managing component-specific data

```
// Component with internal state
function Accordion({ title, children }) {
  const [isOpen, setIsOpen] = useState(false);

  return (
    <div className="accordion">
      <div
        className="accordion-header"
        onClick={() => setIsOpen(!isOpen)}
      >
        <h3>{title}</h3>
        <span>{isOpen ? '▼' : '►'}</span>
      </div>
      {isOpen && (
        <div className="accordion-content">
          {children}
        </div>
      )}
    </div>
  );
}
```

Converting Between Props and State

Sometimes you need to convert props to state, typically when:

1. You need to track changes to a prop value
2. You need to use a prop as an initial value only

```
function SearchInput({ initialQuery }) {
  // Initialize state with prop, but after that they're
independent
  const [query, setQuery] = useState(initialQuery);

  return (
    <input
      type="text"
      value={query}
      onChange={(e) => setQuery(e.target.value)}
      placeholder="Search..."
    />
  );
}
```

Be cautious when converting props to state, as it can lead to synchronization issues. If you need to react to prop changes, consider using the prop directly or using an effect to update state when props change.

Deriving State from Props

When a value can be calculated from props or other state, don't store it in state:

```
// Bad: Storing derived data in state
function ProductList({ products }) {
  const [filteredProducts, setFilteredProducts] =
useState([]);
  const [filter, setFilter] = useState('all');

  // This creates synchronization issues
  useEffect(() => {
    if (filter === 'all') {
      setFilteredProducts(products);
    } else {
      setFilteredProducts(products.filter(p => p.category
=== filter));
    }
  }, [filter, products]);

  // Component JSX...
}

// Good: Calculating derived data during render
function ProductList({ products }) {
  const [filter, setFilter] = useState('all');

  // Calculate derived data during render
  const filteredProducts = filter === 'all'
    ? products
    : products.filter(p => p.category === filter);

  // Component JSX...
}
```

Combining Props and State

Complex components often use both props and state together:

```
function PaginatedTable({ data, itemsPerPage, columns })
{
  const [currentPage, setCurrentPage] = useState(1);
  const [sortField, setSortField] = useState(null);
  const [sortDirection, setSortDirection] =
useState('asc');

  // Calculate derived values from props and state
  const totalPages = Math.ceil(data.length /
itemsPerPage);
  const startIndex = (currentPage - 1) * itemsPerPage;
  const endIndex = startIndex + itemsPerPage;

  // Sort and paginate data
  const sortedData = sortField
    ? [...data].sort((a, b) => {
        if (a[sortField] < b[sortField]) return
sortDirection === 'asc' ? -1 : 1;
        if (a[sortField] > b[sortField]) return
sortDirection === 'asc' ? 1 : -1;
        return 0;
      })
    : data;

  const paginatedData = sortedData.slice(startIndex,
endIndex);

  const handleSort = (field) => {
    if (field === sortField) {
      setSortDirection(sortDirection === 'asc' ? 'desc' :
'asc');
    } else {
      setSortField(field);
      setSortDirection('asc');
    }
  };

  // Render table with pagination controls...
}
```

6.5 State Management Best Practices

As React applications grow in complexity, adopting good state management practices becomes increasingly important. This section covers strategies for organizing, structuring, and handling state effectively.

Minimizing State

The first rule of state management is to keep state to a minimum:

1. **Don't duplicate data**: If information exists in props or can be derived from other state, don't store it separately.
2. **Store the minimal representation**: Keep state as simple as possible and compute derived values during rendering.
3. **Avoid redundant state**: Don't maintain state that's already tracked elsewhere (like in the DOM or in parent components).

```
// Bad: Redundant state
function Form() {
  const [firstName, setFirstName] = useState('');
  const [lastName, setLastName] = useState('');
  const [fullName, setFullName] = useState(''); //
Redundant!

  useEffect(() => {
    setFullName(`${firstName} ${lastName}`.trim());
  }, [firstName, lastName]);

  // Component JSX...
}

// Good: Calculate derived values during render
function Form() {
  const [firstName, setFirstName] = useState('');
  const [lastName, setLastName] = useState('');

  // Calculate during render
  const fullName = `${firstName} ${lastName}`.trim();

  // Component JSX...
}
```

State Colocation

Place state as close as possible to where it's used:

```
// Bad: State too high in the tree
function App() {
  const [isMenuOpen, setIsMenuOpen] = useState(false);

  return (
    <div>
      <Header isMenuOpen={isMenuOpen}
setIsMenuOpen={setIsMenuOpen} />
      <MainContent />
      <Footer />
    </div>
  );
}

// Good: State colocated with the component that uses it
function App() {
  return (
    <div>
      <Header />
      <MainContent />
      <Footer />
    </div>
  );
}

function Header() {
  const [isMenuOpen, setIsMenuOpen] = useState(false);

  // Header implementation with menu controls
}
```

Lifting State Up

When multiple components need to share state, lift it to their closest common ancestor:

```
function ShoppingCart() {
  const [cartItems, setCartItems] = useState([]);

  const addToCart = (product) => {
    setCartItems([...cartItems, product]);
  };

  const removeFromCart = (productId) => {
    setCartItems(cartItems.filter(item => item.id !==
productId));
  };

  return (
    <div>
      <ProductList products={products}
addToCart={addToCart} />
      <Cart items={cartItems}
removeFromCart={removeFromCart} />
    </div>
  );
}
```

Using Context for Global State

For state that needs to be accessed by many components, use Context API:

```
// Create a context
const ThemeContext = React.createContext();

// Provider component
function ThemeProvider({ children }) {
  const [theme, setTheme] = useState('light');

  const toggleTheme = () => {
    setTheme(prevTheme => prevTheme === 'light' ?
'dark' : 'light');
  };

  return (
    <ThemeContext.Provider value={{ theme, toggleTheme }}
>
      {children}
    </ThemeContext.Provider>
  );
}

// App with context
function App() {
  return (
    <ThemeProvider>
      <Header />
      <MainContent />
      <Footer />
    </ThemeProvider>
  );
}

// Consumer component
function ThemeToggle() {
  const { theme, toggleTheme } =
useContext(ThemeContext);

  return (
    <button onClick={toggleTheme}>
      Current theme: {theme}
    </button>
```

State Normalization

For complex data structures, normalize state to make updates more efficient:

```
// Bad: Nested arrays of objects
const [posts, setPosts] = useState([
  {
    id: 1,
    title: 'First Post',
    comments: [
      { id: 101, text: 'Nice post!' },
      { id: 102, text: 'Thanks for sharing' }
    ]
  },
  // More posts...
]);

// Good: Normalized state
const [posts, setPosts] = useState({
  byId: {
    '1': { id: 1, title: 'First Post', commentIds: [101,
102] }
    // More posts...
  },
  allIds: [1, 2, 3]
});

const [comments, setComments] = useState({
  byId: {
    '101': { id: 101, postId: 1, text: 'Nice post!' },
    '102': { id: 102, postId: 1, text: 'Thanks for
sharing' }
    // More comments...
  },
  allIds: [101, 102, 103]
});
```

Using Reducers for Complex State

When state logic becomes complex or involves multiple related values, use `useReducer`:

```
const initialState = {
  isLoading: false,
  error: null,
  data: null
};

function dataReducer(state, action) {
  switch (action.type) {
    case 'FETCH_START':
      return { ...state, isLoading: true, error: null };
    case 'FETCH_SUCCESS':
      return { isLoading: false, error: null, data:
action.payload };
    case 'FETCH_ERROR':
      return { isLoading: false, error: action.payload,
data: null };
    default:
      return state;
  }
}

function DataFetcher({ url }) {
  const [state, dispatch] = useReducer(dataReducer,
initialState);

  useEffect(() => {
    const fetchData = async () => {
      dispatch({ type: 'FETCH_START' });
      try {
        const response = await fetch(url);
        const data = await response.json();
        dispatch({ type: 'FETCH_SUCCESS', payload:
data });
      } catch (error) {
        dispatch({ type: 'FETCH_ERROR', payload:
error.message });
      }
    };

    fetchData();
```

Custom Hooks for Reusable State Logic

Extract common state logic into custom hooks:

```
// Custom hook for form state
function useForm(initialValues) {
  const [values, setValues] = useState(initialValues);
  const [errors, setErrors] = useState({});
  const [touched, setTouched] = useState({});

  const handleChange = (e) => {
    const { name, value } = e.target;
    setValues({ ...values, [name]: value });
  };

  const handleBlur = (e) => {
    const { name } = e.target;
    setTouched({ ...touched, [name]: true });
  };

  const resetForm = () => {
    setValues(initialValues);
    setErrors({});
    setTouched({});
  };

  return {
    values,
    errors,
    touched,
    handleChange,
    handleBlur,
    resetForm,
    setValues,
    setErrors
  };
}

// Using the custom hook
function LoginForm() {
  const {
    values,
    errors,
    touched,
```

Performance Optimization

As your application grows, optimize state updates to prevent unnecessary renders:

1. **Split state**: Divide state into smaller pieces to minimize re-renders.
2. **Use memoization**: Utilize `useMemo` and `useCallback` to avoid recalculating values or recreating functions.
3. **Implement `React.memo`**: Prevent component re-renders when props haven't changed.

```
// Split state example
function UserDashboard() {
  // Split related state
  const [userData, setUserData] = useState(null);
  const [userPreferences, setUserPreferences] =
useState(null);

  // Only components that use userData will re-render
when it changes
  // Only components that use userPreferences will re-
render when it changes
}

// Memoization example
function ExpensiveComponent({ data, onItemClick }) {
  // Memoize expensive calculations
  const processedData = useMemo(() => {
    return expensiveCalculation(data);
  }, [data]);

  // Memoize callback functions
  const handleClick = useCallback((item) => {
    onItemClick(item.id);
  }, [onItemClick]);

  return (
    // Component JSX...
  );
}

// React.memo example
const MemoizedChildComponent = React.memo(function
ChildComponent(props) {
  // This component will only re-render if its props
change
  return (
    // Component JSX...
  );
});
```

Tips for Working with State

- Keep state as simple and flat as possible for easier updates and debugging
- Use controlled components for form elements to maintain a single source of truth
- Create custom hooks for reusable state logic to maintain clean component code
- Utilize state initialization functions for expensive calculations or operations
- Choose the right level of state management based on application complexity

Chapter 7: Handling Events in React

Events are actions or occurrences that happen in the system you're building, usually initiated by users. From clicking a button to submitting a form, handling events effectively is crucial for creating interactive React applications. This chapter thoroughly examines React's event system, demonstrating how to capture and respond to user interactions.

7.1 onClick, onChange, onSubmit

Understanding React Event Handlers

In React, event handlers follow camelCase naming convention rather than the lowercase used in standard HTML. For example, the HTML `onclick` becomes `onClick` in React. Additionally, in JSX you pass a function as the event handler rather than a string.

onClick Events

The `onClick` event handler triggers when an element is clicked. It's commonly used with buttons, links, and other interactive elements.

```
function ClickButton() {
  const handleClick = () => {
    alert('Button was clicked!');
  };

  return <button onClick={handleClick}>Click Me</button>;
}
```

You can also define the handler function directly inline:

```
function ClickButton() {
  return (
    <button onClick={() => {
      alert('Button was clicked!');
    }}>
      Click Me
    </button>
  );
}
```

onChange Events

The `onChange` event fires when the value of an input element changes. This is particularly useful for controlled components where React manages the state of form elements.

```
function InputField() {
  const [text, setText] = useState('');

  const handleChange = (event) => {
    setText(event.target.value);
  };

  return (
    <div>
      <input type="text" value={text}
onChange={handleChange} />
      <p>You typed: {text}</p>
    </div>
  );
}
```

The `onChange` event works with various form elements:

Text inputs:

```
<input type="text" onChange={handleChange} />
```

Checkboxes:

```
const [isChecked, setIsChecked] = useState(false);

const handleCheckboxChange = (event) => {
  setIsChecked(event.target.checked);
};

<input type="checkbox" checked={isChecked}
onChange={handleCheckboxChange} />
```

Radio buttons:

```
const [selected, setSelected] = useState('');

const handleRadioChange = (event) => {
  setSelected(event.target.value);
};

<div>
  <input
    type="radio"
    value="option1"
    checked={selected === 'option1'}
    onChange={handleRadioChange}
  />
  <input
    type="radio"
    value="option2"
    checked={selected === 'option2'}
    onChange={handleRadioChange}
  />
</div>
```

Select dropdowns:

```
const [selectedOption, setSelectedOption] =
useState('apple');

const handleSelectChange = (event) => {
  setSelectedOption(event.target.value);
};

<select value={selectedOption}
onChange={handleSelectChange}>
  <option value="apple">Apple</option>
  <option value="banana">Banana</option>
  <option value="orange">Orange</option>
</select>
```

onSubmit Events

The `onSubmit` event triggers when a form is submitted. It's essential for handling form submissions and often used in conjunction with preventing the default browser behavior.

```
function LoginForm() {
  const [username, setUsername] = useState('');
  const [password, setPassword] = useState('');

  const handleSubmit = (event) => {
    event.preventDefault(); // Prevent page reload
    console.log('Form submitted with:', username,
password);
    // Handle login logic here
  };

  return (
    <form onSubmit={handleSubmit}>
      <div>
        <label>
          Username:
          <input
            type="text"
            value={username}
            onChange={(e) => setUsername(e.target.value)}
          />
        </label>
      </div>
      <div>
        <label>
          Password:
          <input
            type="password"
            value={password}
            onChange={(e) => setPassword(e.target.value)}
          />
        </label>
      </div>
      <button type="submit">Login</button>
    </form>
  );
}
```

Other Common Event Handlers

React supports many other event handlers for various user interactions:

Mouse Events:

- `onMouseEnter` - Fires when the pointer enters an element
- `onMouseLeave` - Fires when the pointer leaves an element
- `onMouseDown` - Fires when a mouse button is pressed
- `onMouseUp` - Fires when a mouse button is released
- `onDoubleClick` - Fires when an element is double-clicked

Keyboard Events:

- `onKeyDown` - Fires when a key is pressed
- `onKeyUp` - Fires when a key is released
- `onKeyPress` - Fires when a key is pressed (character keys only)

Focus Events:

- `onFocus` - Fires when an element receives focus
- `onBlur` - Fires when an element loses focus

Touch Events:

- `onTouchStart` - Fires when a touch point is placed on the element
- `onTouchMove` - Fires when a touch point is moved over the element
- `onTouchEnd` - Fires when a touch point is removed from the element

7.2 Synthetic Events in React

What Are Synthetic Events?

Synthetic events are React's cross-browser wrapper around the browser's native events. They combine the behavior of different browsers into one API, ensuring events work consistently across different browsers.

The main characteristics of synthetic events include:

1. **Cross-browser compatibility:** React normalizes events so they have consistent properties across different browsers.

2. **Pool of event objects:** React reuses event objects for performance optimization (prior to React 17).
3. **Event delegation:** React uses a single event listener at the document level for many events, improving performance.

Structure of Synthetic Events

A synthetic event is an object that wraps around the native browser event with the same interface. It includes the following methods and properties:

```
function EventDemo() {
  const handleClick = (event) => {
    console.log('Event type:', event.type);
    console.log('Target:', event.target);
    console.log('Current target:', event.currentTarget);
    console.log('Native event:', event.nativeEvent);
    console.log('Is default prevented:',
event.isDefaultPrevented());
    console.log('Is propagation stopped:',
event.isPropagationStopped());
  };

  return <button onClick={handleClick}>Examine Event</
button>;
}
```

Key Properties of Synthetic Events

- `type`: The event type (e.g., "click", "change")
- `target`: The element that triggered the event
- `currentTarget`: The element that the event handler is attached to
- `nativeEvent`: The underlying browser event
- `timeStamp`: When the event was created
- `defaultPrevented`: Whether `preventDefault()` was called

Key Methods of Synthetic Events

- `preventDefault()`: Prevents the default browser behavior
- `stopPropagation()`: Stops the event from bubbling up to parent elements
- `isPropagationStopped()`: Returns whether `stopPropagation()` was called
- `isDefaultPrevented()`: Returns whether `preventDefault()` was called
- `persist()`: Removes the event from the pool (not needed in React 17+)

Event Pooling (Pre-React 17)

Before React 17, synthetic events were pooled for performance. This meant that event objects were reused after the event callback was invoked. If you needed to access the event object asynchronously, you had to call `event.persist()`.

```
// Pre-React 17
function AsyncEventAccess() {
  const handleChange = (event) => {
    event.persist(); // Keep the event object around
    setTimeout(() => {
      console.log(event.target.value); // This works
because we called persist()
    }, 1000);
  };

  return <input onChange={handleChange} />;
}
```

In React 17 and later, event pooling was removed, eliminating the need for `event.persist()`.

7.3 Binding Event Handlers

The Need for Binding

In JavaScript, the value of `this` inside a function depends on how the function is called. When using class components in React, event handlers need access to the component instance (`this`). Without proper binding, `this` becomes `undefined` within the handler.

Methods for Binding Event Handlers

1. Binding in the Constructor

```
class ToggleButton extends React.Component {
  constructor(props) {
    super(props);
    this.state = { isOn: false };
    // Binding in constructor
    this.handleClick = this.handleClick.bind(this);
  }

  handleClick() {
    this.setState(prevState => ({ isOn: !
prevState.isOn }));
  }

  render() {
    return (
      <button onClick={this.handleClick}>
        {this.state.isOn ? 'ON' : 'OFF'}
      </button>
    );
  }
}
```

2. Class Fields with Arrow Functions

Arrow functions automatically bind to the surrounding context, eliminating the need for manual binding.

```
class ToggleButton extends React.Component {
  state = { isOn: false };

  // Class field with arrow function
  handleClick = () => {
    this.setState(prevState => ({ isOn: !
prevState.isOn }));
  };

  render() {
    return (
      <button onClick={this.handleClick}>
        {this.state.isOn ? 'ON' : 'OFF'}
      </button>
    );
  }
}
```

3. Inline Arrow Functions in Render

```
class ToggleButton extends React.Component {
  state = { isOn: false };

  render() {
    return (
      <button onClick={() => {
        this.setState(prevState => ({ isOn: !
prevState.isOn }));
      }}>
        {this.state.isOn ? 'ON' : 'OFF'}
      </button>
    );
  }
}
```

Binding in Functional Components

Function components don't have issues with `this` binding since they don't use the `this` keyword. They use hooks and closure to maintain state and references.

```
function ToggleButton() {
  const [isOn, setIsOn] = useState(false);

  const handleClick = () => {
    setIsOn(prevIsOn => !prevIsOn);
  };

  return (
    <button onClick={handleClick}>
      {isOn ? 'ON' : 'OFF'}
    </button>
  );
}
```

Performance Considerations with Binding

- **Constructor binding** is performant as it creates the function once.
- **Class fields** with arrow functions are also performant.
- **Inline arrow functions** create new function instances on each render, which can impact performance in components that render frequently or in lists.

7.4 Passing Arguments to Events

There are several ways to pass arguments to event handlers in React.

Method 1: Using Arrow Functions

```
function ItemList() {
  const items = ['Apple', 'Banana', 'Cherry'];

  const handleItemClick = (item, index, event) => {
    console.log(`Clicked on ${item} at index ${index}`);
    console.log('Event:', event.type);
  };

  return (
    <ul>
      {items.map((item, index) => (
        <li
          key={index}
          onClick={(e) => handleItemClick(item, index,
e)}
        >
          {item}
        </li>
      ))}
    </ul>
  );
}
```

Method 2: Using .bind()

```
function ItemList() {
  const items = ['Apple', 'Banana', 'Cherry'];

  const handleItemClick = (item, index, event) => {
    console.log(`Clicked on ${item} at index ${index}`);
    console.log('Event:', event.type);
  };

  return (
    <ul>
      {items.map((item, index) => (
        <li
          key={index}
          onClick={handleItemClick.bind(null, item,
index)}
        >
          {item}
        </li>
      ))}
    </ul>
  );
}
```

Note that when using `.bind()`, the event object is automatically passed as the last parameter.

Method 3: Using Data Attributes

```
function ItemList() {
  const items = ['Apple', 'Banana', 'Cherry'];

  const handleItemClick = (event) => {
    const { item, index } = event.currentTarget.dataset;
    console.log(`Clicked on ${item} at index ${index}`);
  };

  return (
    <ul>
      {items.map((item, index) => (
        <li
          key={index}
          data-item={item}
          data-index={index}
          onClick={handleItemClick}
        >
          {item}
        </li>
      ))}
    </ul>
  );
}
```

Method 4: Using Closures

```
function Counter() {
  const [counters, setCounters] = useState([0, 0, 0]);

  const createIncrementHandler = (index) => {
    // This creates a closure over the index
    return () => {
      const newCounters = [...counters];
      newCounters[index] += 1;
      setCounters(newCounters);
    };
  };

  return (
    <div>
      {counters.map((count, index) => (
        <div key={index}>
          <span>Counter {index}: {count}</span>
          <button onClick={createIncrementHandler(index)}
>Increment</button>
        </div>
      ))}
    </div>
  );
}
```

Performance Considerations

When passing arguments to event handlers:

- Arrow functions in render create new function instances on each render, which may affect performance in large lists.
- Using `bind()` also creates new function references on each render.
- Creating handler factories that return functions (Method 4) can be more performant when defined outside render or using `useCallback`.
- Data attributes can be a good choice for simple data passing without creating new functions.

7.5 Preventing Default Behavior

Understanding Default Browser Behavior

Browsers have default behaviors for many events:

- Clicking a link navigates to its href
- Submitting a form causes a page reload
- Clicking a checkbox toggles its checked state

In React applications, you often want to intercept these default behaviors to handle them in JavaScript instead.

Using preventDefault()

The `preventDefault()` method stops the browser from executing the default action associated with the event.

```
function LinkExample() {
  const handleClick = (event) => {
    event.preventDefault();
    console.log('Link was clicked, but navigation was
prevented');
    // Custom handling here
  };

  return (
    <a href="https://example.com" onClick={handleClick}>
      Click me
    </a>
  );
}
```

Form Submission Example

A common use case is preventing form submission from reloading the page:

```
function ContactForm() {
  const [name, setName] = useState('');
  const [email, setEmail] = useState('');
  const [message, setMessage] = useState('');

  const handleSubmit = (event) => {
    event.preventDefault();

    // Process form data
    const formData = {
      name,
      email,
      message
    };

    console.log('Form data:', formData);
    // Send data to server, etc.
  };

  return (
    <form onSubmit={handleSubmit}>
      <div>
        <label htmlFor="name">Name:</label>
        <input
          id="name"
          type="text"
          value={name}
          onChange={(e) => setName(e.target.value)}
        />
      </div>

      <div>
        <label htmlFor="email">Email:</label>
        <input
          id="email"
          type="email"
          value={email}
          onChange={(e) => setEmail(e.target.value)}
        />
      </div>

      <div>
```

Preventing Other Default Behaviors

Preventing text selection:

```
function NoSelectText() {
  const preventSelection = (event) => {
    event.preventDefault();
  };

  return (
    <div onMouseDown={preventSelection}>
      This text cannot be selected by dragging
    </div>
  );
}
```

Preventing context menu:

```
function NoContextMenu() {
  const preventContextMenu = (event) => {
    event.preventDefault();
    console.log('Context menu prevented');
  };

  return (
    <div onContextMenu={preventContextMenu}
style={{ padding: 20 }}>
      Right-click is disabled in this area
    </div>
  );
}
```

Preventing drag behavior:

```
function NoDragImage() {
  const preventDrag = (event) => {
    event.preventDefault();
  };

  return (
    <img
      src="example.jpg"
      alt="Non-draggable image"
      onDragStart={preventDrag}
    />
  );
}
```

Conditional Prevention

Sometimes you want to prevent the default behavior only under certain conditions:

```
function ConditionalForm() {
  const [agreed, setAgreed] = useState(false);
  const [email, setEmail] = useState('');

  const handleSubmit = (event) => {
    // Only allow submission if terms are agreed
    if (!agreed) {
      event.preventDefault();
      alert('You must agree to the terms');
      return;
    }

    // Validate email
    if (!email.includes('@')) {
      event.preventDefault();
      alert('Please enter a valid email');
      return;
    }

    // If all validations pass, form will submit normally
    console.log('Form submitted successfully');
  };

  return (
    <form onSubmit={handleSubmit}>
      <input
        type="email"
        value={email}
        onChange={(e) => setEmail(e.target.value)}
        placeholder="Enter your email"
      />

      <label>
        <input
          type="checkbox"
          checked={agreed}
          onChange={(e) => setAgreed(e.target.checked)}
        />
        I agree to the terms
      </label>

      <button type="submit">Submit</button>
```

Best Practices for preventDefault()

1. Always call `preventDefault()` at the beginning of your event handler to ensure it runs before any code that might throw errors.
2. Be mindful of accessibility - some default behaviors are important for keyboard navigation and screen readers.
3. Consider providing visual feedback when preventing default behaviors so users understand what's happening.
4. When preventing form submission, validate inputs and provide clear error messages.

Event Handling Tips

- Use semantic event names in your handler functions (e.g., `handleSubmit`, `handleInputChange`)
- Keep event handlers focused on a single responsibility
- Extract complex logic from event handlers into separate functions
- Test event handlers separately from the components
- Use the React DevTools to debug event-related issues

Actionable Strategies for Effective Event Handling

- Always bind methods in class components either in the constructor or using class properties
- Extract event handling logic into pure functions for easier testing and reuse
- Implement debouncing or throttling for events that fire rapidly (like resize, scroll, or input)
- Use event delegation patterns for lists with many items to improve performance
- Properly clean up event listeners when components unmount to prevent memory leaks
- Create specialized custom hooks for common event handling patterns
- Validate user input and provide clear feedback during form interactions

Chapter 8: Conditional Rendering

Conditional rendering forms the backbone of dynamic user interfaces in React applications. It allows components to display different content based on the current state or props, creating responsive and interactive experiences. This chapter examines various techniques for implementing conditional logic in your React components, providing you with the tools to build flexible UIs that adapt to changing data and user interactions.

8.1 if-else in JSX

Basic Conditional Rendering

At its core, conditional rendering in React relies on JavaScript's capabilities. Since JSX is an extension of JavaScript, you can use familiar control flow statements like `if` and `else` to determine what gets rendered.

The most straightforward approach involves using an `if` statement outside the JSX return statement:

```
function UserGreeting({ isLoggedIn, username }) {
  if (isLoggedIn) {
    return <h1>Welcome back, {username}!</h1>;
  } else {
    return <h1>Please sign in to continue</h1>;
  }
}
```

This pattern works well when the conditional branches require completely different UI structures.

Using Variables to Store JSX

For more complex conditional scenarios, you can use variables to store JSX elements:

```
function NotificationPanel({ notifications }) {
  let content;

  if (notifications.length === 0) {
    content = <p>You have no new notifications</p>;
  } else if (notifications.length <= 3) {
    content = (
      <div>
        <p>You have {notifications.length} new
notifications:</p>
        <NotificationList notifications={notifications} /
>
      </div>
    );
  } else {
    content = (
      <div>
        <p>You have many notifications
({notifications.length})</p>
        <NotificationList
          notifications={notifications.slice(0, 3)}
          preview={true}
        />
        <button>View all</button>
      </div>
    );
  }

  return (
    <div className="notification-panel">
      <h2>Notifications</h2>
      {content}
    </div>
  );
}
```

This approach helps organize more complex conditional rendering logic while keeping the return statement clean.

Component Functions with Conditions

Another pattern involves creating helper functions within your component that handle specific rendering cases:

```
function ProductDisplay({ product, inventory }) {
  function renderPricing() {
    if (product.onSale) {
      return (
        <div className="pricing">
          <span className="original-price">$
{product.price.toFixed(2)}</span>
          <span className="sale-price">$
{product.salePrice.toFixed(2)}</span>
          <span className="discount">
            {Math.round((1 - product.salePrice /
product.price) * 100)}% off
          </span>
        </div>
      );
    }

    return <div className="pricing">$
{product.price.toFixed(2)}</div>;
  }

  function renderAvailability() {
    if (inventory <= 0) {
      return <div className="out-of-stock">Out of stock</
div>;
    } else if (inventory < 5) {
      return <div className="low-stock">Only {inventory}
left!</div>;
    }

    return <div className="in-stock">In stock</div>;
  }

  return (
    <div className="product">
      <h3>{product.name}</h3>
      <div className="product-image">
        <img src={product.imageUrl} alt={product.name} />
      </div>
      {renderPricing()}
      {renderAvailability()}
      <button disabled={inventory <= 0}>
```

This pattern excels at organizing complex rendering logic into manageable chunks while maintaining readability.

8.2 Ternary Operators

Inline Conditions with Ternary Operator

When your conditional rendering logic is simpler, the ternary operator (`condition ? true : false`) offers a concise inline alternative:

```
function Button({ isLoading, onClick, children }) {
  return (
    <button
      className={isLoading ? 'button loading' : 'button'}
      disabled={isLoading}
      onClick={onClick}
    >
      {isLoading ? 'Processing...' : children}
    </button>
  );
}
```

The ternary operator allows you to handle conditional rendering directly within JSX, making it ideal for toggling between two states or values.

Nested Ternary Operators

For scenarios requiring multiple conditions, ternary operators can be nested:

```
function TrafficLight({ status }) {
  return (
    <div className="traffic-light">
      {status === 'stop' ? (
        <div className="light red">Stop</div>
      ) : status === 'caution' ? (
        <div className="light yellow">Caution</div>
      ) : status === 'go' ? (
        <div className="light green">Go</div>
      ) : (
        <div className="light off">Off</div>
      )}
    </div>
  );
}
```

However, be cautious with nested ternaries—they can quickly become difficult to read. If you find yourself using multiple nested ternaries, consider refactoring to use if-else statements or a switch statement instead.

Combining with Destructuring

Ternary operators work particularly well with destructuring assignments:

```
function UserAvatar({ user }) {
  const { name, avatarUrl, isOnline } = user;

  return (
    <div className={`avatar ${isOnline ? 'online' :
'offline'}`}>
      <img
        src={avatarUrl || '/default-avatar.png'}
        alt={`${name}'s avatar`}
      />
      <span className="status-indicator"></span>
    </div>
  );
}
```

This pattern combines multiple React patterns for clean, expressive code.

8.3 Logical && Operator

Conditional Rendering with &&

The logical AND operator (`&&`) provides a simple way to conditionally render elements when you only need to include something or nothing based on a condition:

```
function TodoItem({ todo, isEditing }) {
  return (
    <div className="todo-item">
      {isEditing && (
        <input
          type="text"
          defaultValue={todo.title}
          className="edit-input"
        />
      )}

      {!isEditing && (
        <span className={todo.completed ? 'completed' :
''}>
          {todo.title}
        </span>
      )}

      {todo.dueDate && (
        <div className="due-date">
          Due: {new
Date(todo.dueDate).toLocaleDateString()}
        </div>
      )}
    </div>
  );
}
```

The `&&` pattern works because in JavaScript, if the first operand evaluates to `false`, the expression short-circuits and returns the first operand. If the first operand is `true`, the expression returns the second operand.

Pitfalls with Falsy Values

Be careful when using `&&` with values that might be `0`, empty strings, or other falsy values:

```
function ItemCounter({ count }) {
  return (
    <div>
      {/* Problematic: will render "0" when count is 0
*/}
      {count && <div>Items: {count}</div>}

      {/* Better approach */}
      {count > 0 && <div>Items: {count}</div>}

      {/* Or using ternary for the zero case */}
      {count > 0 ? <div>Items: {count}</div> : <div>No
items</div>}
    </div>
  );
}
```

When the first operand is `0`, the entire expression evaluates to `0`, which React will render as the string "0" instead of rendering nothing. Always ensure your condition evaluates specifically to a boolean when using the `&&` operator.

Using Multiple Conditions

The `&&` operator can be chained for multiple conditions:

```
function CommentSection({ comments, isLoggedIn,
isAdmin }) {
  return (
    <div className="comments-section">
      <h3>Comments ({comments.length})</h3>

      {comments.length > 0 && (
        <div className="comment-list">
          {comments.map(comment => (
            <Comment
              key={comment.id}
              comment={comment}
              canDelete={isLoggedIn && (isAdmin ||
comment.userId === currentUser.id)}
            />
          ))}
        </div>
      )}

      {comments.length === 0 && (
        <p className="no-comments">No comments yet. Be
the first to comment!</p>
      )}

      {isLoggedIn && <CommentForm />}
      {!isLoggedIn && <p>Please log in to comment</p>}
    </div>
  );
}
```

This approach works well for simple conditional chains but becomes harder to read with complex logic.

8.4 Switch-Case in Components

Using Switch Statements for Multiple Conditions

When dealing with multiple mutually exclusive conditions, a switch statement can provide clarity:

```
function PaymentStatus({ status }) {
  let statusMessage;

  switch (status) {
    case 'processing':
      statusMessage = (
        <div className="status processing">
          <Spinner size="small" />
          <span>Processing payment...</span>
        </div>
      );
      break;
    case 'success':
      statusMessage = (
        <div className="status success">
          <CheckIcon />
          <span>Payment successful!</span>
        </div>
      );
      break;
    case 'failed':
      statusMessage = (
        <div className="status error">
          <ErrorIcon />
          <span>Payment failed. Please try again.</span>
        </div>
      );
      break;
    case 'refunded':
      statusMessage = (
        <div className="status info">
          <InfoIcon />
          <span>Payment refunded.</span>
        </div>
      );
      break;
    default:
      statusMessage = (
        <div className="status pending">
          <span>Awaiting payment</span>
        </div>
      );
```

This approach works well for components that need to render significantly different UIs based on a single variable with multiple possible values.

Object Lookup Pattern

As an alternative to switch statements, you can use object lookups for cleaner conditional rendering:

```
function StepIndicator({ currentStep }) {
  const steps = {
    account: {
      number: 1,
      title: 'Account Details',
      icon: <UserIcon />
    },
    shipping: {
      number: 2,
      title: 'Shipping Information',
      icon: <TruckIcon />
    },
    payment: {
      number: 3,
      title: 'Payment Method',
      icon: <CreditCardIcon />
    },
    confirmation: {
      number: 4,
      title: 'Order Confirmation',
      icon: <CheckmarkIcon />
    }
  };

  const stepOrder = ['account', 'shipping', 'payment',
'confirmation'];
  const currentStepIndex =
stepOrder.indexOf(currentStep);

  return (
    <div className="step-indicator">
      {stepOrder.map((step, index) => {
        const stepData = steps[step];
        const status = index < currentStepIndex ?
'completed' :
                      index === currentStepIndex ?
'active' : 'pending';

        return (
          <div key={step} className={`step ${status}`}>
            <div className="step-number">
              {status === 'completed' ? <CheckIcon /> :
```

This pattern works exceptionally well when you have complex data structures associated with each condition.

Component Mapping

For the most flexible approach, you can map states to specific components:

```
function Wizard({ step, userData, onNext, onPrevious }) {
  const steps = {
    userInfo: <UserInfoStep userData={userData}
onNext={onNext} />,
    preferences: <PreferencesStep userData={userData}
onNext={onNext} onPrevious={onPrevious} />,
    confirmation: <ConfirmationStep userData={userData}
onSubmit={onSubmit} onPrevious={onPrevious} />,
    success: <SuccessStep />
  };

  return (
    <div className="wizard">
      <h2>Account Setup</h2>
      <ProgressIndicator currentStep={step}
totalSteps={Object.keys(steps).length} />

      <div className="wizard-content">
        {steps[step] || <div>Unknown step</div>}
      </div>
    </div>
  );
}
```

This approach promotes composition and separation of concerns, making it easier to maintain complex UI flows.

8.5 Dynamic Class Names

Conditional Class Assignment

One of the most common uses of conditional rendering is toggling CSS classes based on component state:

```
function TabButton({ active, onClick, children }) {
  return (
    <button
      className={active ? 'tab active' : 'tab'}
      onClick={onClick}
    >
      {children}
    </button>
  );
}
```

This basic pattern works well for simple class toggling.

Class Building with Template Literals

For more complex class combinations, template literals provide a flexible solution:

```
function Card({ variant, size, elevated, disabled,
className }) {
  const cardClass = `
    card
    ${variant ? `card--${variant}` : ''}
    ${size ? `card--${size}` : ''}
    ${elevated ? 'card--elevated' : ''}
    ${disabled ? 'card--disabled' : ''}
    ${className || ''}
  `.trim().replace(/\s+/g, ' ');

  return (
    <div className={cardClass}>
      {/* Card content */}
    </div>
  );
}
```

Template literals allow you to build class strings dynamically, though they can become unwieldy for very complex class logic.

Using ClassNames Library

For more sophisticated class name management, the `classnames` (or `clsx`) library provides a cleaner solution:

```
import classNames from 'classnames';

function Button({
  primary,
  danger,
  size = 'medium',
  outline,
  rounded,
  disabled,
  className,
  children,
  ...props
}) {
  const buttonClasses = classNames(
    'button',
    {
      'button--primary': primary && !danger,
      'button--danger': danger,
      'button--outline': outline,
      'button--rounded': rounded,
      'button--disabled': disabled,
      [`button--${size}`]: size
    },
    className
  );

  return (
    <button
      className={buttonClasses}
      disabled={disabled}
      {...props}
    >
      {children}
    </button>
  );
}
```

Libraries like `classnames` handle the complexities of combining conditional classes, avoiding duplication, and managing edge cases.

CSS Modules and Conditional Classes

When using CSS Modules, you can apply conditional classes in a type-safe manner:

```
import styles from './Alert.module.css';
import classNames from 'classnames';

function Alert({ type = 'info', title, message,
onClose }) {
  const alertClasses = classNames(
    styles.alert,
    {
      [styles.info]: type === 'info',
      [styles.success]: type === 'success',
      [styles.warning]: type === 'warning',
      [styles.error]: type === 'error'
    }
  );

  const iconMap = {
    info: <InfoIcon className={styles.icon} />,
    success: <CheckCircleIcon className={styles.icon} />,
    warning: <WarningIcon className={styles.icon} />,
    error: <ErrorIcon className={styles.icon} />
  };

  return (
    <div className={alertClasses} role="alert">
      <div className={styles.iconContainer}>
        {iconMap[type] || iconMap.info}
      </div>
      <div className={styles.content}>
        {title && <h4 className={styles.title}>{title}</
h4>}
        <p className={styles.message}>{message}</p>
      </div>
      {onClose && (
        <button
          className={styles.closeButton}
          onClick={onClose}
          aria-label="Close alert"
        >
          <CloseIcon />
        </button>
      )}
    </div>
```

This approach combines conditional class assignment with CSS Modules, providing both flexibility and compile-time safety.

Styled Components and Dynamic Styling

With styled-components or emotion, you can handle conditional styling through props:

```
import styled from 'styled-components';

const StyledButton = styled.button`
  padding: ${props => props.size === 'small' ? '0.5rem
1rem' :
          props.size === 'large' ? '1rem 2rem' :
'0.75rem 1.5rem'};
  background-color: ${props => props.primary ? 'var(--
primary-color)' :
                      props.danger ? 'var(--danger-
color)' : 'transparent'};
  color: ${props => (props.primary || props.danger) ?
'white' : 'var(--text-color)'};
  border: ${props => (props.primary || props.danger) && !
props.outline ? 'none' :
          props.primary ? '2px solid var(--primary-
color)' :
          props.danger ? '2px solid var(--danger-
color)' : '2px solid var(--border-color)'};
  border-radius: ${props => props.rounded ? '9999px' :
'4px'};
  opacity: ${props => props.disabled ? 0.6 : 1};
  cursor: ${props => props.disabled ? 'not-allowed' :
'pointer'};

  &:hover:not(:disabled) {
    background-color: ${props => props.primary ? 'var(--
primary-dark)' :
                        props.danger ? 'var(--danger-
dark)' : 'var(--hover-bg)'};
  }
`;

function Button({ children, ...props }) {
  return <StyledButton {...props}>{children}</
StyledButton>;
}
```

This approach moves the conditional logic into the styled component definition, keeping your JSX clean while maintaining the flexibility of conditional styling.

Tips for Effective Conditional Rendering

- Keep conditional rendering logic simple and focus on readability over brevity
- Extract complex rendering logic into separate functions or components
- Prefer ternary operators for simple binary conditions
- Use logical `&&` when conditionally rendering a single element
- Consider object mapping or switch statements for multi-state rendering
- Test all possible rendering paths to ensure your UI handles all states correctly
- Use CSS transitions between different conditional states for smoother UIs

Actionable Strategies for Conditional Rendering

- Start with component state diagrams to identify all possible rendering states before coding
- Create reusable condition hooks for sharing complex conditional logic between components
- Implement error boundaries around conditionally rendered components to prevent cascading failures
- Organize conditional rendering by creating "container" and "presentational" component pairs
- Use data-testid attributes on conditionally rendered elements for reliable testing
- Apply conditional logic at the highest appropriate level in your component tree to minimize re-renders
- Document all conditional paths with comments for complex rendering scenarios to aid maintenance

Chapter 9: Lists and Keys

9.1 Rendering Lists with map()

Understanding List Rendering in React

List rendering is a fundamental concept in React applications. Nearly every application requires displaying collections of data, whether they're product listings, user comments, task items, or navigation links. In React, the primary method for rendering lists is using JavaScript's built-in `map()` function.

The `map()` function transforms each item in an array according to a provided function and returns a new array with the transformed items. When rendering lists in React, each transformed item typically becomes a React element.

Basic List Rendering

Let's start with a simple example of rendering a list of names:

```
function NamesList() {
  const names = ['Alice', 'Bob', 'Charlie', 'David'];

  return (
    <div>
      <h2>Names List</h2>
      <ul>
        {names.map(name => (
          <li>{name}</li>
        ))}
      </ul>
    </div>
  );
}
```

In this example, we have an array of names and we're using the `map()` function to transform each name string into a `<li>` element. React will render these elements as a list.

However, if you run this code, you'll notice a warning in the console about missing "keys" for list items. This warning introduces us to one of the most important concepts when working with lists in React: keys.

Rendering Objects in a List

Often, you'll be working with arrays of objects rather than simple strings. Here's how to render properties from objects:

```
function UsersList() {
  const users = [
    { id: 1, name: 'Alice', role: 'Developer' },
    { id: 2, name: 'Bob', role: 'Designer' },
    { id: 3, name: 'Charlie', role: 'Manager' },
    { id: 4, name: 'David', role: 'Tester' }
  ];

  return (
    <div>
      <h2>Users List</h2>
      <ul>
        {users.map(user => (
          <li key={user.id}>
            {user.name} - {user.role}
          </li>
        ))}
      </ul>
    </div>
  );
}
```

Notice that we've added a `key` prop to each list item. This is a critical improvement over our first example and addresses the warning we received.

Rendering Complex Components

For more complex UI, you might want to render custom components for each item in your list:

```
function UserCard({ user }) {
  return (
    <div className="user-card">
      <h3>{user.name}</h3>
      <p>Role: {user.role}</p>
      <p>Email: {user.email}</p>
    </div>
  );
}

function UsersGrid() {
  const users = [
    { id: 1, name: 'Alice', role: 'Developer', email:
'alice@example.com' },
    { id: 2, name: 'Bob', role: 'Designer', email:
'bob@example.com' },
    { id: 3, name: 'Charlie', role: 'Manager', email:
'charlie@example.com' },
    { id: 4, name: 'David', role: 'Tester', email:
'david@example.com' }
  ];

  return (
    <div>
      <h2>Users Grid</h2>
      <div className="users-grid">
        {users.map(user => (
          <UserCard key={user.id} user={user} />
        ))}
      </div>
    </div>
  );
}
```

In this example, we're mapping each user object to a `UserCard` component. Notice the `key` prop is added to the component we're returning from the `map()` function, not inside the component itself.

Common Patterns for List Rendering

Conditional Rendering Within Lists

Sometimes you need to conditionally render items or elements within a list:

```
function TaskList() {
  const tasks = [
    { id: 1, text: 'Complete project', completed:
false },
    { id: 2, text: 'Review code', completed: true },
    { id: 3, text: 'Deploy application', completed:
false },
    { id: 4, text: 'Write documentation', completed:
true }
  ];

  return (
    <div>
      <h2>Task List</h2>
      <ul>
        {tasks.map(task => (
          <li key={task.id} className={task.completed ?
'completed' : ''}>
            {task.text}
            {task.completed && <span
className="check">✓</span>}
          </li>
        ))}
      </ul>
    </div>
  );
}
```

Nested Lists

You may also need to render nested lists:

```
function CategoryList() {
  const categories = [
    {
      id: 1,
      name: 'Fruits',
      items: ['Apple', 'Banana', 'Orange']
    },
    {
      id: 2,
      name: 'Vegetables',
      items: ['Carrot', 'Broccoli', 'Spinach']
    },
    {
      id: 3,
      name: 'Dairy',
      items: ['Milk', 'Cheese', 'Yogurt']
    }
  ];

  return (
    <div>
      <h2>Categories</h2>
      <ul>
        {categories.map(category => (
          <li key={category.id}>
            <h3>{category.name}</h3>
            <ul>
              {category.items.map((item, index) => (
                <li key={`${category.id}-${index}`}
>{item}</li>
              ))}
            </ul>
          </li>
        ))}
      </ul>
    </div>
  );
}
```

In this nested list example, notice how we create composite keys for the inner list items by combining the category ID with the item index.

9.2 Importance of Keys

What Are Keys in React?

Keys are special attributes you need to include when creating lists of elements in React. Keys help React identify which items have changed, been added, or been removed, which is crucial for efficient updates and rendering.

Why Keys Matter

1. **Performance Optimization**: React uses keys to determine which list items have changed, enabling it to update only the necessary components rather than re-rendering the entire list.

2. **Maintaining Component State**: When list items have stable keys, React can preserve the state of components even when the list changes.

3. **Avoiding Rendering Bugs**: Proper keys prevent issues like incorrect element updating when the list order changes.

What Happens Without Keys

When you don't provide keys (or use inadequate keys), several problems can occur:

1. **Warning Messages**: React will display warning messages in the console.

2. **Performance Degradation**: React might re-render more components than necessary.

3. **State Loss**: Components might lose their state when the list changes.

4. **Unexpected Behavior**: Elements might update incorrectly when items are added, removed, or reordered.

Let's see an example of what can go wrong without proper keys:

```
function CounterList() {
  const [counters, setCounters] = useState([
    { value: 0 },
    { value: 0 },
    { value: 0 }
  ]);

  const handleIncrement = (index) => {
    const newCounters = [...counters];
    newCounters[index].value += 1;
    setCounters(newCounters);
  };

  const handleRemoveFirst = () => {
    setCounters(counters.slice(1));
  };

  return (
    <div>
      <button onClick={handleRemoveFirst}>Remove First
Counter</button>
      <div>
        {counters.map((counter, index) => (
          <div>
            <span>{counter.value}</span>
            <button onClick={() =>
handleIncrement(index)}>Increment</button>
          </div>
        ))}
      </div>
    </div>
  );
}
```

In this example, if you increment some counters and then click "Remove First Counter," you might see unexpected behavior because React doesn't know which counter was removed.

Let's fix it with proper keys:

```
function CounterList() {
  const [counters, setCounters] = useState([
    { id: 1, value: 0 },
    { id: 2, value: 0 },
    { id: 3, value: 0 }
  ]);

  const handleIncrement = (id) => {
    const newCounters = counters.map(counter =>
      counter.id === id ? { ...counter, value:
counter.value + 1 } : counter
    );
    setCounters(newCounters);
  };

  const handleRemoveFirst = () => {
    setCounters(counters.slice(1));
  };

  return (
    <div>
      <button onClick={handleRemoveFirst}>Remove First
Counter</button>
      <div>
        {counters.map(counter => (
          <div key={counter.id}>
            <span>{counter.value}</span>
            <button onClick={() =>
handleIncrement(counter.id)}>Increment</button>
          </div>
        ))}
      </div>
    </div>
  );
}
```

With proper keys, React can correctly preserve the state of each counter even when the list changes.

9.3 Handling Unique Keys

Choosing Effective Keys

The most important property of a key is that it must be unique among siblings in a list. Here are some guidelines for choosing effective keys:

Using Stable IDs

The best keys are stable, unique identifiers that don't change between renders. Typically, these are IDs from your data:

```
function ProductList({ products }) {
  return (
    <ul>
      {products.map(product => (
        <li key={product.id}>{product.name}</li>
      ))}
    </ul>
  );
}
```

When IDs Are Not Available

If your data doesn't have stable IDs, you might need to generate them:

```
import { v4 as uuidv4 } from 'uuid';

function generateProducts() {
  return [
    { id: uuidv4(), name: 'Product 1' },
    { id: uuidv4(), name: 'Product 2' },
    { id: uuidv4(), name: 'Product 3' }
  ];
}
```

Using Index as Keys (and when to avoid it)

In some cases, you might use the array index as a key if you have no other option:

```
function SimpleList({ items }) {
  return (
    <ul>
      {items.map((item, index) => (
        <li key={index}>{item}</li>
      ))}
    </ul>
  );
}
```

However, using indexes as keys can lead to problems if:

- The list can reorder items
- Items can be added or removed from anywhere other than the end
- List items have state

When indexes are used as keys in these situations, React may confuse which elements have changed, leading to unintended consequences and bugs.

Creating Composite Keys

Sometimes you need to create composite keys, especially for nested lists:

```
function CommentThread({ threads }) {
  return (
    <div>
      {threads.map(thread => (
        <div key={thread.id}>
          <h3>{thread.title}</h3>
          <ul>
            {thread.comments.map((comment, commentIndex)
=> (
              <li key={`${thread.id}-comment-$
{commentIndex}`}>
                {comment.text}
              </li>
            ))}
          </ul>
        </div>
      ))}
    </div>
  );
}
```

Key Generation Strategies

Using a Counter

For temporary client-side items without IDs:

```
let nextId = 0;

function createNewTodo(text) {
  return {
    id: `todo-${nextId++}`,
    text,
    completed: false
  };
}
```

Using Item Properties as Keys

For items with unique natural identifiers:

```
function CountryList({ countries }) {
  return (
    <ul>
      {countries.map(country => (
        <li key={country.code}>{country.name}</li>
      ))}
    </ul>
  );
}
```

Using String Concatenation

For creating unique identifiers from multiple properties:

```
function EmployeeSchedule({ shifts }) {
  return (
    <table>
      <tbody>
        {shifts.map(shift => (
          <tr key={`${shift.employeeId}-${shift.date}`}>
            <td>{shift.employeeName}</td>
            <td>{shift.date}</td>
            <td>{shift.hours} hours</td>
          </tr>
        ))}
      </tbody>
    </table>
  );
}
```

Common Key Mistakes

Generating Keys During Render

One common mistake is generating keys inside the render method:

```
// Bad practice
function BadListExample({ items }) {
  return (
    <ul>
      {items.map(item => (
        <li key={Math.random()}>{item}</li> // DON'T DO
THIS
      ))}
    </ul>
  );
}
```

This approach creates a new key on every render, defeating the purpose of keys.

Using Non-Unique Values

Another mistake is using values that aren't guaranteed to be unique:

```
// Potentially problematic
function UserList({ users }) {
  return (
    <ul>
      {users.map(user => (
        <li key={user.name}>{user.name}</li> // Names
might not be unique
      ))}
    </ul>
  );
}
```

9.4 Filtering Lists

Filtering is a common operation when working with lists in React. It allows you to display only items that match certain criteria.

Basic List Filtering

The most common way to filter a list is using JavaScript's `filter()` method before mapping:

```
function TaskList({ tasks }) {
  const [showCompleted, setShowCompleted] =
useState(false);

  // Filter tasks based on the showCompleted state
  const filteredTasks = tasks.filter(task =>
    showCompleted ? task.completed : !task.completed
  );

  return (
    <div>
      <button onClick={() => setShowCompleted(!
showCompleted)}>
        Show {showCompleted ? 'Active' : 'Completed'}
Tasks
      </button>

      <ul>
        {filteredTasks.map(task => (
          <li key={task.id}>{task.text}</li>
        ))}
      </ul>
    </div>
  );
}
```

Implementing a Search Filter

Here's an example of implementing a search feature:

```
function ProductSearch({ products }) {
  const [searchTerm, setSearchTerm] = useState('');

  const filteredProducts = products.filter(product =>

product.name.toLowerCase().includes(searchTerm.toLowerCas
e())
  );

  return (
    <div>
      <input
        type="text"
        placeholder="Search products..."
        value={searchTerm}
        onChange={e => setSearchTerm(e.target.value)}
      />

      <ul>
        {filteredProducts.map(product => (
          <li key={product.id}>{product.name}</li>
        ))}
      </ul>
    </div>
  );
}
```

Multiple Filter Criteria

For more complex filtering needs, you can combine multiple criteria:

```
function AdvancedProductFilter({ products }) {
  const [filters, setFilters] = useState({
    searchTerm: '',
    minPrice: '',
    maxPrice: '',
    category: 'all'
  });

  const handleFilterChange = (key, value) => {
    setFilters({
      ...filters,
      [key]: value
    });
  };

  const filteredProducts = products.filter(product => {
    // Check if product name matches search term
    const matchesSearch = filters.searchTerm === '' ||

product.name.toLowerCase().includes(filters.searchTerm.to
LowerCase());

    // Check if product price is within range
    const matchesMinPrice = filters.minPrice === '' ||
      product.price >= Number(filters.minPrice);
    const matchesMaxPrice = filters.maxPrice === '' ||
      product.price <= Number(filters.maxPrice);

    // Check if product category matches selected
category
    const matchesCategory = filters.category === 'all' ||
      product.category === filters.category;

    return matchesSearch && matchesMinPrice &&
matchesMaxPrice && matchesCategory;
  });

  return (
    <div>
      <div className="filters">
```

Filter with Pagination

For large lists, it's often useful to combine filtering with pagination:

```
function PaginatedProductList({ products }) {
  const [searchTerm, setSearchTerm] = useState('');
  const [currentPage, setCurrentPage] = useState(1);
  const productsPerPage = 5;

  // Filter products based on search term
  const filteredProducts = products.filter(product =>

product.name.toLowerCase().includes(searchTerm.toLowerCas
e())
  );

  // Calculate pagination values
  const indexOfLastProduct = currentPage *
productsPerPage;
  const indexOfFirstProduct = indexOfLastProduct -
productsPerPage;
  const currentProducts =
filteredProducts.slice(indexOfFirstProduct,
indexOfLastProduct);
  const totalPages = Math.ceil(filteredProducts.length /
productsPerPage);

  // Generate page numbers
  const pageNumbers = [];
  for (let i = 1; i <= totalPages; i++) {
    pageNumbers.push(i);
  }

  return (
    <div>
      <input
        type="text"
        placeholder="Search products..."
        value={searchTerm}
        onChange={e => {
          setSearchTerm(e.target.value);
          setCurrentPage(1); // Reset to first page on
new search
        }}
```

Optimizing Filtered Lists

For large datasets, consider optimizing your filtering logic to avoid performance issues:

```
function OptimizedProductList({ products }) {
  const [searchTerm, setSearchTerm] = useState('');

  // Memoize filtered products to prevent unnecessary
recalculations
  const filteredProducts = useMemo(() => {
    return products.filter(product =>

product.name.toLowerCase().includes(searchTerm.toLowerCas
e())
    );
  }, [products, searchTerm]);

  return (
    <div>
      <input
        type="text"
        placeholder="Search products..."
        value={searchTerm}
        onChange={e => setSearchTerm(e.target.value)}
      />

      <ul>
        {filteredProducts.map(product => (
          <li key={product.id}>{product.name}</li>
        ))}
      </ul>
    </div>
  );
}
```

9.5 Sorting Lists

Sorting is another common operation when working with lists in React. It allows you to arrange items in a specific order based on their properties.

Basic List Sorting

To sort a list, you can use JavaScript's `sort()` method before mapping:

```
function SortableProductList({ products }) {
  const [sortOrder, setSortOrder] = useState('asc');

  // Create a new sorted array to avoid mutating the
original data
  const sortedProducts = [...products].sort((a, b) => {
    if (sortOrder === 'asc') {
      return a.price - b.price;
    } else {
      return b.price - a.price;
    }
  });

  return (
    <div>
      <button onClick={() => setSortOrder(prev => prev
=== 'asc' ? 'desc' : 'asc')}>
        Sort by Price: {sortOrder === 'asc' ? 'Low to
High' : 'High to Low'}
      </button>

      <ul>
        {sortedProducts.map(product => (
          <li key={product.id}>
            {product.name} - ${product.price}
          </li>
        ))}
      </ul>
    </div>
  );
}
```

Implementing Multiple Sort Options

For more advanced sorting, you might want to allow sorting by different fields:

```
function AdvancedSortableList({ products }) {
  const [sortConfig, setSortConfig] = useState({
    key: 'name',
    direction: 'asc'
  });

  const requestSort = (key) => {
    let direction = 'asc';
    if (sortConfig.key === key && sortConfig.direction
=== 'asc') {
      direction = 'desc';
    }
    setSortConfig({ key, direction });
  };

  const sortedProducts = [...products].sort((a, b) => {
    if (a[sortConfig.key] < b[sortConfig.key]) {
      return sortConfig.direction === 'asc' ? -1 : 1;
    }
    if (a[sortConfig.key] > b[sortConfig.key]) {
      return sortConfig.direction === 'asc' ? 1 : -1;
    }
    return 0;
  });

  return (
    <div>
      <table>
        <thead>
          <tr>
            <th onClick={() => requestSort('name')}>
              Name {sortConfig.key === 'name' &&
(sortConfig.direction === 'asc' ? '↑' : '↓')}
            </th>
            <th onClick={() => requestSort('price')}>
              Price {sortConfig.key === 'price' &&
(sortConfig.direction === 'asc' ? '↑' : '↓')}
            </th>
            <th onClick={() => requestSort('category')}>
              Category {sortConfig.key === 'category' &&
```

Combining Sorting and Filtering

In real applications, you'll often need to combine sorting and filtering:

```
function ProductTable({ products }) {
  const [filters, setFilters] = useState({
    searchTerm: '',
    category: 'all'
  });

  const [sortConfig, setSortConfig] = useState({
    key: 'name',
    direction: 'asc'
  });

  const handleFilterChange = (key, value) => {
    setFilters({
      ...filters,
      [key]: value
    });
  };

  const requestSort = (key) => {
    let direction = 'asc';
    if (sortConfig.key === key && sortConfig.direction
=== 'asc') {
      direction = 'desc';
    }
    setSortConfig({ key, direction });
  };

  // First, filter the products
  const filteredProducts = products.filter(product => {
    const matchesSearch =
product.name.toLowerCase().includes(filters.searchTerm.to
LowerCase());
    const matchesCategory = filters.category === 'all' ||
product.category === filters.category;
    return matchesSearch && matchesCategory;
  });

  // Then, sort the filtered products
  const sortedProducts = [...filteredProducts].sort((a,
b) => {
```

Optimizing Sorted Lists

For improved performance with large datasets, you can memoize the sorted list:

```
function OptimizedSortedList({ products }) {
  const [sortConfig, setSortConfig] = useState({
    key: 'name',
    direction: 'asc'
  });

  // Memoize sorted products to prevent unnecessary
recalculations
  const sortedProducts = useMemo(() => {
    const sortableProducts = [...products];
    sortableProducts.sort((a, b) => {
      if (a[sortConfig.key] < b[sortConfig.key]) {
        return sortConfig.direction === 'asc' ? -1 : 1;
      }
      if (a[sortConfig.key] > b[sortConfig.key]) {
        return sortConfig.direction === 'asc' ? 1 : -1;
      }
      return 0;
    });
    return sortableProducts;
  }, [products, sortConfig]);

  return (
    <div>
      {/* Sorting controls and product display */}
    </div>
  );
}
```

Custom Sort Functions

For more complex sorting needs, you might need custom sort functions:

```
function ComplexSortExample({ users }) {
  const [sortBy, setSortBy] = useState('nameAsc');

  const getSortedUsers = () => {
    const usersCopy = [...users];

    switch (sortBy) {
      case 'nameAsc':
        return usersCopy.sort((a, b) =>
a.name.localeCompare(b.name));
      case 'nameDesc':
        return usersCopy.sort((a, b) =>
b.name.localeCompare(a.name));
      case 'recentActivity':
        return usersCopy.sort((a, b) => new
Date(b.lastActive) - new Date(a.lastActive));
      case 'mostPosts':
        return usersCopy.sort((a, b) => b.postCount -
a.postCount);
      default:
        return usersCopy;
    }
  };

  const sortedUsers = getSortedUsers();

  return (
    <div>
      <div className="sort-controls">
        <select value={sortBy} onChange={e =>
setSortBy(e.target.value)}>
          <option value="nameAsc">Name (A-Z)</option>
          <option value="nameDesc">Name (Z-A)</option>
          <option value="recentActivity">Recent
Activity</option>
          <option value="mostPosts">Most Posts</option>
        </select>
      </div>

      <ul>
```

Tips for Working with Lists and Keys

1. Always provide unique and stable keys for list items to improve performance and prevent rendering issues.
2. Consider extracting list items into their own components when they become complex or contain their own state.
3. Perform filtering and sorting operations before rendering to improve code readability and maintainability.
4. Use the `useMemo` hook to optimize expensive filtering and sorting operations for large lists.
5. Avoid using array indexes as keys unless the list is static and will never change order or have items added/removed.

Chapter 10: Forms in React

Forms are essential components of any interactive web application, allowing users to input data and submit it to the application. In React, forms present unique challenges due to the framework's state-driven architecture. This chapter examines how to create, manage, and validate forms in React applications.

10.1 Controlled Components

Understanding Controlled Components

In HTML, form elements such as `<input>`, `<textarea>`, and `<select>` typically maintain their own state and update it based on user input. In React, mutable state is typically kept in the state property of components and updated using `setState()`.

A controlled component is a form element whose value is controlled by React state. With controlled components, the form data is handled by the React component rather than the DOM. This approach gives you more control over the form's behavior and allows for immediate validation and formatting of user input.

Basic Implementation

Here's how you can create a controlled component:

```
import React, { useState } from 'react';

function SimpleInput() {
  const [value, setValue] = useState('');

  const handleChange = (event) => {
    setValue(event.target.value);
  };

  return (
    <div>
      <input type="text" value={value}
onChange={handleChange} />
      <p>You typed: {value}</p>
    </div>
  );
}
```

In this example, the `useState` hook initializes a state variable `value` with an empty string. The `handleChange` function updates this state every time the user types in the input field. The input's value is then tied to the component's state, creating a controlled component.

Controlled Forms with Multiple Inputs

For forms with multiple inputs, you can manage all inputs in a single state object:

```
import React, { useState } from 'react';

function RegistrationForm() {
  const [formData, setFormData] = useState({
    username: '',
    email: '',
    password: ''
  });

  const handleChange = (event) => {
    const { name, value } = event.target;
    setFormData({
      ...formData,
      [name]: value
    });
  };

  return (
    <form>
      <div>
        <label htmlFor="username">Username:</label>
        <input
          type="text"
          id="username"
          name="username"
          value={formData.username}
          onChange={handleChange}
        />
      </div>
      <div>
        <label htmlFor="email">Email:</label>
        <input
          type="email"
          id="email"
          name="email"
          value={formData.email}
          onChange={handleChange}
        />
      </div>
      <div>
```

This approach uses the ES6 computed property name syntax `[name]: value` to update the property in the state object that corresponds to the input name. The spread operator (`...formData`) ensures that all other form data remains intact when updating a single field.

Handling Different Input Types

Controlled components work with all types of form elements:

Text and Textarea

For text inputs and textareas, the value attribute is used:

```
const [text, setText] = useState('');

// For input
<input type="text" value={text} onChange={e =>
setText(e.target.value)} />

// For textarea
<textarea value={text} onChange={e =>
setText(e.target.value)} />
```

Checkboxes

For checkboxes, the `checked` attribute is used instead of `value`:

```
const [isChecked, setIsChecked] = useState(false);

<input
  type="checkbox"
  checked={isChecked}
  onChange={e => setIsChecked(e.target.checked)}
/>
```

Select Dropdowns

For select dropdowns, the value attribute is used to control the selected option:

```
const [selectedOption, setSelectedOption] =
useState('react');

<select value={selectedOption} onChange={e =>
setSelectedOption(e.target.value)}>
  <option value="react">React</option>
  <option value="angular">Angular</option>
  <option value="vue">Vue</option>
</select>
```

Radio Buttons

For radio buttons, you maintain a state variable for the selected value:

```
const [selectedRadio, setSelectedRadio] = useState('');

<div>
  <input
    type="radio"
    id="option1"
    name="options"
    value="option1"
    checked={selectedRadio === 'option1'}
    onChange={e => setSelectedRadio(e.target.value)}
  />
  <label htmlFor="option1">Option 1</label>
</div>
<div>
  <input
    type="radio"
    id="option2"
    name="options"
    value="option2"
    checked={selectedRadio === 'option2'}
    onChange={e => setSelectedRadio(e.target.value)}
  />
  <label htmlFor="option2">Option 2</label>
</div>
```

Advantages of Controlled Components

Controlled components offer several advantages:

1. **Single Source of Truth**: The state of your form inputs is kept in your component state, making it the single source of truth.
2. **Immediate Validation**: You can validate input as the user types, providing immediate feedback.
3. **Conditional Rendering**: You can conditionally render UI elements based on input values.
4. **Format Inputs**: You can format input values on the fly (e.g., credit card numbers, phone numbers).
5. **Disable Submit Button**: You can disable the submit button until all form validation rules are satisfied.

10.2 Handling Input Changes

The `onChange` Event Handler

The `onChange` event handler is the cornerstone of controlled components in React. It fires whenever the user changes the input value. The handler receives an event object that contains information about the event, including the current value of the input element.

Dynamic Input Handling

For applications with many form inputs, writing individual handlers for each input would be inefficient. Instead, you can create a dynamic handler that works for multiple inputs:

```
import React, { useState } from 'react';

function DynamicForm() {
  const [formData, setFormData] = useState({
    firstName: '',
    lastName: '',
    email: '',
    phone: '',
    message: ''
  });

  const handleInputChange = (event) => {
    const { name, value, type, checked } = event.target;

    // Handle different input types
    const inputValue = type === 'checkbox' ? checked :
value;

    setFormData({
      ...formData,
      [name]: inputValue
    });
  };

  return (
    <form>
      <div>
        <label htmlFor="firstName">First Name:</label>
        <input
          type="text"
          id="firstName"
          name="firstName"
          value={formData.firstName}
          onChange={handleInputChange}
        />
      </div>
      <div>
        <label htmlFor="lastName">Last Name:</label>
        <input
          type="text"
          id="lastName"
          name="lastName"
```

Input Transformation

Sometimes you need to transform input values before updating the state. Common examples include:

Numeric Inputs

To ensure that a field only accepts numbers:

```
const handleNumberChange = (event) => {
  const value = event.target.value;
  // Only update state if input is a number or empty
  if (value === '' || /^\d+$/.test(value)) {
    setNumber(value);
  }
};
```

Format Inputs While Typing

For formatting inputs like phone numbers, credit cards, or currency:

```
const handlePhoneChange = (event) => {
  const input = event.target.value.replace(/\D/g, ''); //
Remove non-digits
  let formattedPhone = '';

  if (input.length > 0) {
    formattedPhone = '(' + input.substring(0, 3);
    if (input.length > 3) {
      formattedPhone += ') ' + input.substring(3, 6);
      if (input.length > 6) {
        formattedPhone += '-' + input.substring(6, 10);
      }
    }
  }

  setPhone(formattedPhone);
};
```

Custom Input Masks

For more complex input patterns, consider using input mask libraries that work with

React, like `react-input-mask` or `react-text-mask`.

Debouncing Input Changes

For performance optimization, especially with input fields that trigger expensive operations (like API calls), you can implement debouncing:

```
import React, { useState, useEffect } from 'react';

function DebouncedInput() {
  const [inputValue, setInputValue] = useState('');
  const [debouncedValue, setDebouncedValue] =
useState('');

  useEffect(() => {
    // Set a timer to update the debounced value after
500ms
    const timer = setTimeout(() => {
      setDebouncedValue(inputValue);
    }, 500);

    // Clear the timer if inputValue changes before the
delay expires
    return () => clearTimeout(timer);
  }, [inputValue]);

  const handleChange = (event) => {
    setInputValue(event.target.value);
  };

  return (
    <div>
      <input
        type="text"
        value={inputValue}
        onChange={handleChange}
        placeholder="Type to search..."
      />
      <p>Debounced value: {debouncedValue}</p>
    </div>
  );
}
```

This approach ensures that expensive operations are only triggered after the user has stopped typing for a specified period.

10.3 Form Submission

Handling Form Submission

In React, form submission is typically handled by an `onSubmit` event handler attached to the form element. The default browser behavior is to refresh the page upon form submission, so you need to prevent this using `event.preventDefault()`.

```
import React, { useState } from 'react';

function SubmitForm() {
  const [formData, setFormData] = useState({
    username: '',
    email: ''
  });

  const handleChange = (event) => {
    const { name, value } = event.target;
    setFormData({
      ...formData,
      [name]: value
    });
  };

  const handleSubmit = (event) => {
    event.preventDefault();
    console.log('Form submitted with:', formData);
    // Process the form data (e.g., send to an API)
  };

  return (
    <form onSubmit={handleSubmit}>
      <div>
        <label htmlFor="username">Username:</label>
        <input
          type="text"
          id="username"
          name="username"
          value={formData.username}
          onChange={handleChange}
        />
      </div>
      <div>
        <label htmlFor="email">Email:</label>
        <input
          type="email"
          id="email"
          name="email"
          value={formData.email}
          onChange={handleChange}
```

Form Submission with Fetch API

To submit form data to a server, you can use the Fetch API:

```
const handleSubmit = async (event) => {
  event.preventDefault();

  try {
    const response = await fetch('https://
api.example.com/submit', {
      method: 'POST',
      headers: {
        'Content-Type': 'application/json'
      },
      body: JSON.stringify(formData)
    });

    if (!response.ok) {
      throw new Error(`HTTP error! Status: $
{response.status}`);
    }

    const responseData = await response.json();
    console.log('Success:', responseData);

    // Reset form after successful submission
    setFormData({
      username: '',
      email: ''
    });
  } catch (error) {
    console.error('Error submitting form:', error);
  }
};
```

Form Submission States

To provide feedback to users during form submission, you can track the submission state:

```
import React, { useState } from 'react';

function SubmissionStateForm() {
  const [formData, setFormData] = useState({
    name: '',
    email: ''
  });

  const [submissionState, setSubmissionState] =
useState({
    isSubmitting: false,
    isSuccess: false,
    isError: false,
    errorMessage: ''
  });

  const handleChange = (event) => {
    const { name, value } = event.target;
    setFormData({
      ...formData,
      [name]: value
    });
  };

  const handleSubmit = async (event) => {
    event.preventDefault();

    setSubmissionState({
      isSubmitting: true,
      isSuccess: false,
      isError: false,
      errorMessage: ''
    });

    try {
      // Simulate API call
      await new Promise(resolve => setTimeout(resolve,
1500));

      // Process the form data (e.g., send to an API)
      console.log('Form submitted with:', formData);
```

Custom Submit Buttons

Sometimes you may want to have custom submit buttons outside the form. You can achieve this using the `form` attribute:

```
<form id="myForm" onSubmit={handleSubmit}>
  {/* Form fields */}
</form>

<button type="submit" form="myForm">
  Submit Form
</button>
```

This approach allows you to place submit buttons anywhere in your UI while still maintaining the form submission behavior.

10.4 Form Validation

Client-Side Validation

Form validation ensures that user inputs meet the required criteria before being submitted. Client-side validation provides immediate feedback to users, improving the user experience.

Built-in HTML5 Validation

HTML5 provides several attributes for basic form validation:

```
<form onSubmit={handleSubmit}>
  <input
    type="text"
    name="username"
    required
    minLength={3}
    maxLength={20}
    pattern="[A-Za-z0-9]+"
  />
  <input
    type="email"
    name="email"
    required
  />
  <input
    type="number"
    name="age"
    min={18}
    max={120}
  />
  <button type="submit">Submit</button>
</form>
```

To use HTML5 validation with React, you need to prevent React from overriding the browser's validation. To do this, simply avoid calling `event.preventDefault()` until after validation occurs:

```
const handleSubmit = (event) => {
  if (!event.target.checkValidity()) {
    // Form is invalid, let browser handle validation
    return;
  }

  // Form is valid, prevent default and handle submission
  event.preventDefault();
  console.log('Form data:', formData);
};
```

Custom Validation Logic

For more complex validation rules, you can implement custom validation logic:

```
import React, { useState } from 'react';

function ValidationForm() {
  const [formData, setFormData] = useState({
    username: '',
    email: '',
    password: '',
    confirmPassword: ''
  });

  const [errors, setErrors] = useState({});

  const handleChange = (event) => {
    const { name, value } = event.target;
    setFormData({
      ...formData,
      [name]: value
    });

    // Clear the error for this field when it changes
    if (errors[name]) {
      setErrors({
        ...errors,
        [name]: null
      });
    }
  };

  const validateForm = () => {
    const newErrors = {};

    // Username validation
    if (!formData.username) {
      newErrors.username = 'Username is required';
    } else if (formData.username.length < 3) {
      newErrors.username = 'Username must be at least 3
characters';
    }

    // Email validation
    if (!formData.email) {
      newErrors.email = 'Email is required';
```

Real-Time Validation

For a better user experience, you can validate inputs in real-time as the user types:

```
const handleChange = (event) => {
  const { name, value } = event.target;
  setFormData({
    ...formData,
    [name]: value
  });

  // Validate this field in real-time
  validateField(name, value);
};

const validateField = (name, value) => {
  let errorMessage = '';

  switch (name) {
    case 'username':
      if (!value) {
        errorMessage = 'Username is required';
      } else if (value.length < 3) {
        errorMessage = 'Username must be at least 3
characters';
      }
      break;
    case 'email':
      if (!value) {
        errorMessage = 'Email is required';
      } else if (!/\S+@\S+\.\S+/.test(value)) {
        errorMessage = 'Email is invalid';
      }
      break;
    // Add other field validations
    default:
      break;
  }

  setErrors(prevErrors => ({
    ...prevErrors,
    [name]: errorMessage || null
  }));

  return !errorMessage;
};
```

Displaying Validation Messages

To provide clear feedback about validation errors, you should display error messages next to the corresponding input fields:

```
<div>
  <label htmlFor="username">Username:</label>
  <input
    type="text"
    id="username"
    name="username"
    value={formData.username}
    onChange={handleChange}
    aria-invalid={errors.username ? 'true' : 'false'}
    aria-describedby={errors.username ? 'username-
error' : undefined}
  />
  {errors.username && (
    <div id="username-error" className="error-message"
role="alert">
      {errors.username}
    </div>
  )}
</div>
```

Note the use of WAI-ARIA attributes to enhance accessibility:

- `aria-invalid`: Indicates that the input value is invalid
- `aria-describedby`: Links the input to the error message
- `role="alert"`: Ensures that screen readers announce the error message

Form Validation Libraries

For complex forms, consider using form validation libraries like:

- **Formik**: Provides form state management, validation, and error handling
- **React Hook Form**: Lightweight form validation with performance optimization
- **Yup**: Schema-based validation that works well with Formik

Here's an example using Formik with Yup:

```
import React from 'react';
import { Formik, Form, Field, ErrorMessage } from
'formik';
import * as Yup from 'yup';

const validationSchema = Yup.object({
  username: Yup.string()
    .min(3, 'Username must be at least 3 characters')
    .required('Username is required'),
  email: Yup.string()
    .email('Invalid email address')
    .required('Email is required'),
  password: Yup.string()
    .min(8, 'Password must be at least 8 characters')
    .matches(
      /(?=.*\d)(?=.*[a-z])(?=.*[A-Z])/,
      'Password must contain at least one number, one
lowercase and one uppercase letter'
    )
    .required('Password is required'),
  confirmPassword: Yup.string()
    .oneOf([Yup.ref('password'), null], 'Passwords must
match')
    .required('Confirm password is required')
});

function FormikValidationForm() {
  return (
    <Formik
      initialValues={{
        username: '',
        email: '',
        password: '',
        confirmPassword: ''
      }}
      validationSchema={validationSchema}
      onSubmit={(values, { setSubmitting }) => {
        setTimeout(() => {
          console.log('Form data:', values);
          setSubmitting(false);
        }, 400);
      }}
```

10.5 Uncontrolled Components (useRef)

Understanding Uncontrolled Components

Uncontrolled components are an alternative approach to handling form data in React. Unlike controlled components, uncontrolled components keep form data in the DOM rather than in React state. Instead of writing an event handler for every state update, you can use a `ref` to access form values from the DOM directly.

Using the `useRef` Hook

The `useRef` hook creates a mutable reference object that persists for the full lifetime of the component. You can use this reference to access DOM elements directly:

```
import React, { useRef } from 'react';

function UncontrolledForm() {
  const nameInputRef = useRef(null);
  const emailInputRef = useRef(null);

  const handleSubmit = (event) => {
    event.preventDefault();

    const formData = {
      name: nameInputRef.current.value,
      email: emailInputRef.current.value
    };

    console.log('Form data:', formData);
  };

  return (
    <form onSubmit={handleSubmit}>
      <div>
        <label htmlFor="name">Name:</label>
        <input
          type="text"
          id="name"
          ref={nameInputRef}
          defaultValue=""
        />
      </div>

      <div>
        <label htmlFor="email">Email:</label>
        <input
          type="email"
          id="email"
          ref={emailInputRef}
          defaultValue=""
        />
      </div>

      <button type="submit">Submit</button>
    </form>
  );
```

Note the use of `defaultValue` instead of `value`. This allows the input to be an uncontrolled component while still setting an initial value.

Default Values

You can specify default values for uncontrolled components using the `defaultValue` (for inputs and textareas) or `defaultChecked` (for checkboxes and radio buttons) attributes:

```
<input type="text" ref={inputRef} defaultValue="Default
text" />
<textarea ref={textareaRef} defaultValue="Default text
for textarea" />
<input type="checkbox" ref={checkboxRef}
defaultChecked={true} />
```

File Inputs

File inputs are always uncontrolled components because their value can only be set by a user action, not programmatically:

```
import React, { useRef } from 'react';

function FileUploadForm() {
  const fileInputRef = useRef(null);

  const handleSubmit = (event) => {
    event.preventDefault();

    const file = fileInputRef.current.files[0];
    if (file) {
      console.log('Selected file:', file.name);
      // Process the file (e.g., upload to a server)
    }
  };

  return (
    <form onSubmit={handleSubmit}>
      <div>
        <label htmlFor="file">Select a file:</label>
        <input
          type="file"
          id="file"
          ref={fileInputRef}
        />
      </div>

      <button type="submit">Upload</button>
    </form>
  );
}
```

Accessing Multiple Form Elements

For forms with multiple elements, you can use named refs:

```
import React, { useRef } from 'react';

function MultipleRefsForm() {
  const formRefs = {
    name: useRef(null),
    email: useRef(null),
    message: useRef(null)
  };

  const handleSubmit = (event) => {
    event.preventDefault();

    const formData = {
      name: formRefs.name.current.value,
      email: formRefs.email.current.value,
      message: formRefs.message.current.value
    };

    console.log('Form data:', formData);
  };

  return (
    <form onSubmit={handleSubmit}>
      <div>
        <label htmlFor="name">Name:</label>
        <input
          type="text"
          id="name"
          ref={formRefs.name}
          defaultValue=""
        />
      </div>

      <div>
        <label htmlFor="email">Email:</label>
        <input
          type="email"
          id="email"
          ref={formRefs.email}
          defaultValue=""
        />
      </div>
```

Comparing Controlled and Uncontrolled Components

When to Use Controlled Components

- Complex form logic
- Real-time validation
- Immediate input formatting
- Dynamic form behavior
- When you need to control input values programmatically

When to Use Uncontrolled Components

- Simple forms with minimal state management
- Performance-critical applications
- File uploads
- Working with third-party non-React libraries
- When you want to minimize re-renders

Hybrid Approach

You can also combine controlled and uncontrolled approaches:

```
import React, { useState, useRef } from 'react';

function HybridForm() {
  const [email, setEmail] = useState('');
  const nameInputRef = useRef(null);

  const handleSubmit = (event) => {
    event.preventDefault();

    const formData = {
      name: nameInputRef.current.value,
      email: email
    };

    console.log('Form data:', formData);
  };

  return (
    <form onSubmit={handleSubmit}>
      <div>
        <label htmlFor="name">Name:</label>
        <input
          type="text"
          id="name"
          ref={nameInputRef}
          defaultValue=""
        />
      </div>

      <div>
        <label htmlFor="email">Email:</label>
        <input
          type="email"
          id="email"
          value={email}
          onChange={(e) => setEmail(e.target.value)}
        />
      </div>

      <button type="submit">Submit</button>
    </form>
  );
```

Advanced Form Techniques

Form State Management

For complex forms, consider using more advanced state management techniques:

```
import React, { useReducer } from 'react';

// Reducer function for form state
const formReducer = (state, action) => {
  switch (action.type) {
    case 'UPDATE_FIELD':
      return {
        ...state,
        [action.field]: action.value
      };
    case 'RESET_FORM':
      return action.initialState;
    default:
      return state;
  }
};

function ComplexForm() {
  const initialState = {
    username: '',
    email: '',
    password: '',
    preferences: {
      newsletter: false,
      notifications: false
    }
  };

  const [formState, dispatch] = useReducer(formReducer,
initialState);

  const handleChange = (event) => {
    const { name, value, type, checked } = event.target;

    // Handle different input types
    const inputValue = type === 'checkbox'
      ? checked
      : value;

    dispatch({
      type: 'UPDATE_FIELD',
      field: name,
```

Form Performance Optimization

To optimize form performance:

1. Use `React.memo()` to prevent unnecessary re-renders
2. Implement debounce for input changes
3. Minimize state updates
4. Use `useCallback()` for event handlers

```
import React, { useState, useCallback, useMemo } from
'react';

const MemoizedInput = React.memo(({ label, name, value,
onChange }) => (
  <div>
    <label htmlFor={name}>{label}</label>
    <input
      type="text"
      id={name}
      name={name}
      value={value}
      onChange={onChange}
    />
  </div>
));

function PerformanceOptimizedForm() {
  const [formData, setFormData] = useState({
    firstName: '',
    lastName: '',
    email: ''
  });

  // Memoized change handler
  const handleChange = useCallback((event) => {
    const { name, value } = event.target;
    setFormData(prev => ({
      ...prev,
      [name]: value
    }));
  }, []);

  // Memoized computed value
  const fullName = useMemo(() => {
    return `${formData.firstName} ${formData.lastName}
`.trim();
  }, [formData.firstName, formData.lastName]);

  const handleSubmit = useCallback((event) => {
    event.preventDefault();
    console.log('Form submitted:', formData);
```

5 Tips for Effective React Forms

1. Always handle form state systematically, preferring controlled components for most use cases.
2. Implement real-time validation to provide immediate user feedback.
3. Use appropriate validation libraries for complex form requirements.
4. Optimize form performance by minimizing unnecessary re-renders.
5. Ensure accessibility by using proper labels, ARIA attributes, and error messaging.

7 Actionable Strategies for React Form Development

1. Create a reusable form validation utility that can be applied across different forms.
2. Implement progressive form enhancement with fallback for non-JavaScript environments.
3. Use form state management libraries for complex multi-step or dynamic forms.
4. Centralize form logic in custom hooks for better code organization.
5. Implement client-side and server-side validation for robust data integrity.
6. Design forms with accessibility and screen reader compatibility in mind.
7. Utilize TypeScript for type-safe form implementations and improved developer experience.

Chapter 11: useEffect Hook

11.1 Side Effects in React

Understanding Component Lifecycle and Side Effects

In React, side effects represent operations that can impact components beyond their primary rendering responsibility. These effects encompass a wide range of interactions, including:

- Data fetching from APIs
- Directly manipulating the DOM
- Setting up subscriptions
- Managing timers
- Synchronizing with external systems

Why Side Effects Matter

React components typically focus on rendering UI based on current state and props. However, real-world applications require interactions that extend beyond pure rendering. Side effects bridge this gap, allowing components to:

- Interact with browser APIs
- Communicate with external services
- Manage complex state synchronization
- Perform background operations

Lifecycle of Side Effects

Prior to React Hooks, side effects were managed through lifecycle methods in class components:

- `componentDidMount()`
- `componentDidUpdate()`
- `componentWillUnmount()`

The `useEffect` Hook consolidates these lifecycle methods into a single, more flexible API for functional components.

11.2 useEffect Basics

Fundamental Syntax

The `useEffect` Hook follows a straightforward structure:

```
useEffect(() => {
  // Side effect logic

  // Optional cleanup function
  return () => {
    // Cleanup logic
  };
}, [/* dependency array */]);
```

Core Parameters

1. **Effect Function**: The primary callback containing side effect logic
2. **Dependency Array**: Controls when the effect runs

Execution Patterns

1. Effect Without Dependencies

```
useEffect(() => {
  // Runs after EVERY render
  document.title = `Current Count`;
});
```

2. Effect with Empty Dependency Array

```
useEffect(() => {
  // Runs ONLY on initial render (component mount)
  fetchInitialData();
}, []);
```

3. Effect with Specific Dependencies

```
useEffect(() => {
  // Runs when specific state/props change
  updateUserProfile(username);
}, [username]);
```

11.3 Dependency Array

Dependency Control Mechanisms

Precise Dependency Management

The dependency array determines effect re-execution:

- Empty array `[ ]`: Effect runs once on mount
- No array: Effect runs on every render
- Array with variables: Effect runs when those variables change

Dependency Tracking Best Practices

Comprehensive Dependency Inclusion

```
function UserProfile({ userId, theme }) {
  useEffect(() => {
    // Include ALL variables used inside the effect
    loadUserDetails(userId, theme);
  }, [userId, theme]);
}
```

Avoiding Stale Closures

```
function ChatComponent() {
  const [message, setMessage] = useState('');
  const [socket, setSocket] = useState(null);

  useEffect(() => {
    // Correctly tracking socket dependency
    socket?.send(message);
  }, [socket, message]);
}
```

11.4 Cleanup Function

Preventing Memory Leaks

Cleanup functions are crucial for managing resources and preventing unintended behaviors.

Common Cleanup Scenarios

```
useEffect(() => {
  // Setting up a timer
  const intervalId = setInterval(() => {
    // Periodic task
  }, 1000);

  // Cleanup function
  return () => {
    clearInterval(intervalId);
  };
}, []);
```

Subscription Management

```
useEffect(() => {
  const subscription = dataSource.subscribe();

  // Cleanup subscription when component unmounts
  return () => {
    subscription.unsubscribe();
  };
}, [dataSource]);
```

11.5 Common useEffect Use Cases

1. Data Fetching

```
function UserDataFetcher({ userId }) {
  const [userData, setUserData] = useState(null);
  const [loading, setLoading] = useState(true);

  useEffect(() => {
    async function fetchData() {
      setLoading(true);
      try {
        const response = await axios.get(`/users/$
{userId}`);
        setUserData(response.data);
      } catch (error) {
        console.error('Fetch failed', error);
      } finally {
        setLoading(false);
      }
    }

    fetchData();
  }, [userId]);
}
```

2. Event Listeners

```
function WindowResizeTracker() {
  const [windowSize, setWindowSize] = useState({
    width: window.innerWidth,
    height: window.innerHeight
  });

  useEffect(() => {
    function handleResize() {
      setWindowSize({
        width: window.innerWidth,
        height: window.innerHeight
      });
    }

    window.addEventListener('resize', handleResize);

    // Cleanup listener
    return () => {
      window.removeEventListener('resize', handleResize);
    };
  }, []);
}
```

3. WebSocket Connections

```
function LiveChatComponent() {
  const [messages, setMessages] = useState([]);

  useEffect(() => {
    const socket = new WebSocket('wss://
chat.example.com');

    socket.onmessage = (event) => {
      const newMessage = JSON.parse(event.data);
      setMessages(prev => [...prev, newMessage]);
    };

    return () => {
      socket.close();
    };
  }, []);
}
```

4. Authentication State

```
function AuthValidator() {
  useEffect(() => {
    const token = localStorage.getItem('authToken');

    if (token) {
      validateTokenWithServer(token);
    }
  }, []);
}
```

5. Third-Party Library Integration

```
function ChartComponent() {
  const chartRef = useRef(null);

  useEffect(() => {
    const chart = new Chart(chartRef.current, {
      // Chart configuration
    });

    return () => {
      chart.destroy();
    };
  }, []);
}
```

5 Tips for Effective useEffect Usage

- Minimize effect complexity by extracting logic into separate functions
- Always include all dependencies used within the effect
- Prefer custom hooks for reusable effect logic
- Use TypeScript to enforce strict dependency tracking
- Remember that effects run after render, so avoid blocking rendering

7 Actionable Strategies for useEffect Mastery

- Create separate effects for different concerns
- Leverage useMemo and useCallback to optimize dependency management
- Implement robust error handling within effects
- Use AbortController for cancelable async operations
- Simulate complex lifecycle scenarios through strategic effect composition
- Prioritize performance by reducing unnecessary effect executions
- Develop a systematic approach to dependency array management

Chapter 12: useContext Hook

12.1 Understanding the Context API

The Problem of Prop Drilling

In React applications, data typically flows from parent to child components through props. As applications grow more complex, passing props through multiple layers of components becomes increasingly challenging. This process, known as prop drilling, leads to several significant issues:

- **Code Complexity**: Components receive props they don't directly use
- **Reduced Readability**: Prop passing becomes verbose and hard to track
- **Performance Overhead**: Unnecessary re-renders and prop passing

Context API: A Solution to Prop Drilling

The Context API provides a powerful mechanism to share values across multiple components without explicitly passing props through every intermediate component. It acts as a global state management system that allows data to be accessible to many components at different nesting levels.

Key Characteristics of Context

- **Centralized State Management**: Share data across component tree
- **Reduced Prop Passing**: Eliminate multiple layers of prop transmission
- **Flexible Data Distribution**: Works with various data types
- **Performance Optimization**: Minimizes unnecessary re-renders

12.2 Creating a Context

Basic Context Creation

Here's a comprehensive example of creating a context:

```
import React, { createContext, useState } from 'react';

// Create the context with a default value
const ThemeContext = createContext({
  isDarkMode: false,
  toggleTheme: () => {}
});

// Context Provider Component
function ThemeProvider({ children }) {
  const [isDarkMode, setIsDarkMode] = useState(false);

  const toggleTheme = () => {
    setIsDarkMode(prevMode => !prevMode);
  };

  return (
    <ThemeContext.Provider value={{ isDarkMode,
toggleTheme }}>
      {children}
    </ThemeContext.Provider>
  );
}
```

Context Provider Patterns

1. Simple Provider

```
function App() {
  return (
    <ThemeProvider>
      <MainApplication />
    </ThemeProvider>
  );
}
```

2. Complex Provider with Multiple Values

```
const UserContext = createContext({
  user: null,
  login: () => {},
  logout: () => {}
});

function UserProvider({ children }) {
  const [user, setUser] = useState(null);

  const login = (userData) => {
    setUser(userData);
  };

  const logout = () => {
    setUser(null);
  };

  return (
    <UserContext.Provider value={{ user, login, logout }}
>
      {children}
    </UserContext.Provider>
  );
}
```

12.3 useContext for State Management

Consuming Context

The `useContext` hook provides a straightforward method to access context values:

```
import React, { useContext } from 'react';

function ThemeToggleButton() {
  const { isDarkMode, toggleTheme } =
useContext(ThemeContext);

  return (
    <button
      onClick={toggleTheme}
      style={{
        backgroundColor: isDarkMode ? '#333' : '#fff',
        color: isDarkMode ? '#fff' : '#333'
      }}
    >
      {isDarkMode ? 'Light Mode' : 'Dark Mode'}
    </button>
  );
}
```

Multiple Context Usage

React allows combining multiple contexts:

```
function ProfilePage() {
  const themeContext = useContext(ThemeContext);
  const userContext = useContext(UserContext);

  return (
    <div className={themeContext.isDarkMode ? 'dark-
mode' : 'light-mode'}>
      {userContext.user ? (
        <UserProfile user={userContext.user} />
      ) : (
        <LoginPrompt />
      )}
    </div>
  );
}
```

12.4 Avoiding Prop Drilling

Traditional Prop Passing

```
function App() {
  const [theme, setTheme] = useState('light');
  return (
    <Layout theme={theme}>
      <Sidebar theme={theme}>
        <Navigation theme={theme}>
          <Content theme={theme} />
        </Navigation>
      </Sidebar>
    </Layout>
  );
}
```

Context-Based Solution

```
const ThemeContext = createContext('light');

function App() {
  const [theme, setTheme] = useState('light');
  return (
    <ThemeContext.Provider value={theme}>
      <Layout>
        <Sidebar>
          <Navigation>
            <Content />
          </Navigation>
        </Sidebar>
      </Layout>
    </ThemeContext.Provider>
  );
}

function Content() {
  const theme = useContext(ThemeContext);
  return <div className={theme}>...</div>;
}
```

12.5 Global State with Context

Complex State Management

While Context is powerful, it's not a complete state management solution for large applications. For more complex scenarios, consider:

```
const GlobalStateContext = createContext();

function GlobalStateProvider({ children }) {
  const [state, dispatch] = useReducer(rootReducer,
initialState);

  return (
    <GlobalStateContext.Provider value={{ state,
dispatch }}>
      {children}
    </GlobalStateContext.Provider>
  );
}

function rootReducer(state, action) {
  switch(action.type) {
    case 'UPDATE_USER':
      return { ...state, user: action.payload };
    case 'UPDATE_PREFERENCES':
      return { ...state, preferences: action.payload };
    default:
      return state;
  }
}
```

Performance Considerations

- Use `React.memo()` to prevent unnecessary re-renders
- Split contexts to minimize re-render scope
- Consider using `useCallback` for stable function references

Advanced Context Techniques

Dynamic Context Updates

```
function DynamicThemeProvider({ children }) {
  const [theme, setTheme] = useState('light');

  const themeContextValue = useMemo(() => ({
    theme,
    setTheme
  }), [theme]);

  return (
    <ThemeContext.Provider value={themeContextValue}>
      {children}
    </ThemeContext.Provider>
  );
}
```

5 Essential Tips for Effective Context Usage

- Optimize component performance with targeted context design
- Minimize context scope to prevent unnecessary re-renders
- Use separate contexts for different concerns
- Leverage `useMemo` and `useCallback` for stable references
- Combine context with other hooks for complex state management

7 Actionable Strategies for Context Implementation

- Break large contexts into smaller, focused contexts
- Implement lazy initialization for context values
- Use type checking with PropTypes or TypeScript
- Create custom hooks for complex context logic
- Implement fallback values for context consumers

- Utilize context for dependency injection
- Design context providers with clear, predictable interfaces

Chapter 13: useRef Hook in React.js

13.1 Accessing DOM Elements

Understanding DOM Element References

The `useRef` hook provides a powerful mechanism for directly interacting with DOM elements in React applications. Unlike traditional DOM manipulation, `useRef` offers a React-friendly approach to accessing and managing element references without triggering unnecessary re-renders.

Creating Basic DOM References

```
import React, { useRef, useEffect } from 'react';

function TextInputFocus() {
  const inputRef = useRef(null);

  useEffect(() => {
    // Automatically focus the input when component
mounts
    inputRef.current.focus();
  }, []);

  return (
    <div>
      <input
        ref={inputRef}
        type="text"
        placeholder="I'll be focused automatically"
      />
    </div>
  );
}
```

Advanced DOM Manipulation Techniques

Refs allow precise control over DOM elements, enabling scenarios like:

- Measuring element dimensions
- Triggering imperative animations
- Managing focus and selection
- Integrating with third-party DOM libraries

Measuring Element Dimensions

```
function ElementSizeMeasurer() {
  const divRef = useRef(null);

  const measureDimensions = () => {
    if (divRef.current) {
      const { width, height } =
divRef.current.getBoundingClientRect();
      console.log(`Element dimensions: ${width}x${height}
`);
    }
  };

  return (
    <div>
      <div
        ref={divRef}
        style={{ width: '200px', height: '100px',
background: 'lightblue' }}
      >
        Measurable Element
      </div>
      <button onClick={measureDimensions}>
        Measure Dimensions
      </button>
    </div>
  );
}
```

13.2 Storing Mutable Values

Persistent Values Across Renders

`useRef` provides a unique capability to store mutable values that persist between component renders without causing re-renders.

Tracking Render Counts

```
function RenderTracker() {
  const renderCount = useRef(0);

  useEffect(() => {
    renderCount.current += 1;
  });

  return (
    <div>
      <p>This component has rendered
{renderCount.current} times</p>
    </div>
  );
}
```

Comparison with Traditional State Management

While `useState` triggers re-renders, `useRef` allows value mutations without component re-evaluation.

Performance Optimization Example

```
function Timer() {
  const intervalRef = useRef(null);
  const [time, setTime] = useState(0);

  const startTimer = () => {
    if (intervalRef.current !== null) return;

    intervalRef.current = setInterval(() => {
      setTime(prevTime => prevTime + 1);
    }, 1000);
  };

  const stopTimer = () => {
    if (intervalRef.current) {
      clearInterval(intervalRef.current);
      intervalRef.current = null;
    }
  };

  return (
    <div>
      <p>Time: {time} seconds</p>
      <button onClick={startTimer}>Start</button>
      <button onClick={stopTimer}>Stop</button>
    </div>
  );
}
```

13.3 useRef vs. useState

Key Differences in State Management

Feature	useRef	useState
Re-renders	No re-render	Triggers re-render
Mutability	Directly mutable	Requires setter function
Use Case	Persistent values, DOM references	Component state changes

Practical Comparison

```
function ComparisonDemo() {
  // State-based counter (causes re-renders)
  const [stateCounter, setStateCounter] = useState(0);

  // Ref-based counter (no re-renders)
  const refCounter = useRef(0);

  const incrementState = () => {
    setStateCounter(stateCounter + 1);
    // Each increment triggers a re-render
  };

  const incrementRef = () => {
    refCounter.current += 1;
    // No re-render occurs
    console.log('Ref counter:', refCounter.current);
  };

  return (
    <div>
      <p>State Counter: {stateCounter}</p>
      <button onClick={incrementState}>Increment State</
button>
      <button onClick={incrementRef}>Increment Ref</
button>
    </div>
  );
}
```

13.4 Forwarding Refs

Understanding Ref Forwarding

Ref forwarding allows passing refs through components, enabling more flexible component composition.

Basic Ref Forwarding

```
const CustomInput = React.forwardRef((props, ref) => {
  return (
    <input
      ref={ref}
      {...props}
      className="custom-input"
    />
  );
});

function ParentComponent() {
  const inputRef = useRef(null);

  const focusInput = () => {
    inputRef.current.focus();
  };

  return (
    <div>
      <CustomInput ref={inputRef} />
      <button onClick={focusInput}>Focus Input</button>
    </div>
  );
}
```

Advanced Ref Forwarding Patterns

- Conditional ref passing
- Higher-order component ref management
- Transparent component interfaces

13.5 Real-World useRef Examples

Complex Use Cases

Video Player Controller

```
function VideoPlayer() {
  const videoRef = useRef(null);
  const [isPlaying, setIsPlaying] = useState(false);

  const togglePlay = () => {
    if (videoRef.current) {
      if (isPlaying) {
        videoRef.current.pause();
      } else {
        videoRef.current.play();
      }
      setIsPlaying(!isPlaying);
    }
  };

  return (
    <div>
      <video
        ref={videoRef}
        src="/path/to/video.mp4"
        width="500"
      />
      <button onClick={togglePlay}>
        {isPlaying ? 'Pause' : 'Play'}
      </button>
    </div>
  );
}
```

Performance Monitoring Technique

```
function PerformanceTracker() {
  const startTimeRef = useRef(null);

  const startTracking = () => {
    startTimeRef.current = performance.now();
  };

  const stopTracking = () => {
    if (startTimeRef.current) {
      const duration = performance.now() -
startTimeRef.current;
      console.log(`Operation took ${duration}
milliseconds`);
    }
  };

  return (
    <div>
      <button onClick={startTracking}>Start</button>
      <button onClick={stopTracking}>Stop</button>
    </div>
  );
}
```

5 Essential Tips for useRef

- Maintain immutability in your application architecture
- Never mutate refs directly in render methods
- Leverage refs for performance-critical operations
- Use ref forwarding for transparent component interfaces
- Implement refs as a last resort after state management techniques

7 Actionable Strategies

- Create wrapper functions for ref manipulations
- Implement precise lifecycle management for refs
- Utilize typescript for enhanced ref type safety
- Minimize direct DOM interactions
- Combine refs with custom hooks for complex logic
- Implement memoization techniques with refs
- Design component interfaces with ref transparency

Chapter 14: Custom Hooks

14.1 What Are Custom Hooks?

Understanding the Concept of Custom Hooks

Custom hooks represent a powerful mechanism in React for extracting component logic into reusable functions. Unlike regular functions, custom hooks leverage React's hook system, allowing developers to share stateful logic across multiple components without changing their component hierarchy.

Key Characteristics of Custom Hooks

- Starts with the prefix "use"
- Can call other React hooks
- Encapsulate complex logic and state management
- Promote code reusability and separation of concerns

Anatomy of a Custom Hook

A custom hook follows these fundamental principles:

- Always begin the function name with "use"
- Can use built-in React hooks like useState, useEffect, useContext
- Return values or functions that can be destructured by components
- Maintain the rules of hooks (only call hooks at the top level)

Basic Structure Example

```
function useCustomLogic() {
  const [state, setState] = useState(initialState);

  useEffect(() => {
    // Perform side effects or additional logic
  }, [/* dependencies */]);

  const customMethod = () => {
    // Custom logic implementation
  };

  return { state, customMethod };
}
```

14.2 Creating a useFetch Hook

Comprehensive Data Fetching Hook

The `useFetch` hook simplifies data retrieval from APIs, managing loading states, error handling, and data storage.

Complete Implementation

```
import { useState, useEffect } from 'react';

function useFetch(url, options = {}) {
  const [data, setData] = useState(null);
  const [loading, setLoading] = useState(true);
  const [error, setError] = useState(null);

  useEffect(() => {
    let isMounted = true;

    const fetchData = async () => {
      try {
        const response = await fetch(url, options);

        if (!response.ok) {
          throw new Error(`HTTP error! status: $
{response.status}`);
        }

        const result = await response.json();

        if (isMounted) {
          setData(result);
          setLoading(false);
        }
      } catch (err) {
        if (isMounted) {
          setError(err);
          setLoading(false);
        }
      }
    };

    fetchData();

    // Cleanup function to prevent state updates on
unmounted component
    return () => {
      isMounted = false;
    };
  }, [url, JSON.stringify(options)]);
```

Advanced Features

- Supports custom fetch options
- Handles loading and error states
- Prevents memory leaks with cleanup
- Flexible for various API interactions

14.3 useLocalStorage Hook

Persistent State Management

The `useLocalStorage` hook provides a seamless way to synchronize component state with browser's local storage.

Comprehensive Implementation

```
import { useState, useEffect } from 'react';

function useLocalStorage(key, initialValue) {
  // Retrieve stored value or use initial value
  const readStoredValue = () => {
    try {
      const item = window.localStorage.getItem(key);
      return item ? JSON.parse(item) : initialValue;
    } catch (error) {
      console.error(error);
      return initialValue;
    }
  };

  // State management with local storage sync
  const [storedValue, setStoredValue] =
useState(readStoredValue);

  // Update local storage when state changes
  useEffect(() => {
    try {
      window.localStorage.setItem(key,
JSON.stringify(storedValue));
    } catch (error) {
      console.error(error);
    }
  }, [key, storedValue]);

  // Custom setter with optional transformation
  const setValue = (value) => {
    const valueToStore =
      value instanceof Function ? value(storedValue) :
value;
    setStoredValue(valueToStore);
  };

  return [storedValue, setValue];
}

// Usage Example
function ThemeSelector() {
  const [theme, setTheme] = useLocalStorage('app-theme',
```

14.4 useToggle Hook

Simple State Toggling Mechanism

The `useToggle` hook provides a straightforward way to manage boolean state transitions.

Implementation and Usage

```
import { useState } from 'react';

function useToggle(initialState = false) {
  const [state, setState] = useState(initialState);

  // Toggle function with optional override
  const toggle = (value) => {
    setState(prevState =>
      value !== undefined ? value : !prevState
    );
  };

  return [state, toggle];
}

// Practical Example
function PasswordVisibility() {
  const [isVisible, toggleVisibility] = useToggle(false);

  return (
    <div>
      <input
        type={isVisible ? 'text' : 'password'}
        placeholder="Password"
      />
      <button onClick={toggleVisibility}>
        {isVisible ? 'Hide' : 'Show'} Password
      </button>
    </div>
  );
}
```

14.5 Rules of Hooks

Critical Guidelines for Hook Usage

Top-Level Hook Calls

- Call hooks only at the top level of React function components
- Never call hooks inside loops, conditions, or nested functions
- Ensures predictable state management and rendering behavior

Consistent Rendering

```
// Correct Usage
function Counter() {
  const [count, setCount] = useState(0);

  useEffect(() => {
    document.title = `Count: ${count}`;
  }, [count]);

  return <div>{count}</div>;
}

// Incorrect Usage
function BadCounter() {
  if (count > 5) {
    // WRONG: Conditional hook call
    const [count, setCount] = useState(0);
  }
}
```

Hook Order Dependency

- React relies on hook call order for maintaining state
- Breaking this order can lead to unexpected behavior
- Always maintain a consistent hook invocation pattern

Performance Considerations

- Minimize unnecessary re-renders
- Use dependency arrays in useEffect and other hooks
- Memoize complex computations with useMemo and useCallback

5 Tips for Mastering Custom Hooks

- Optimize hook logic for maximum reusability
- Create hooks with clear, single-responsibility principles
- Handle edge cases and potential errors gracefully
- Use TypeScript for enhanced type safety with hooks
- Test custom hooks thoroughly with various scenarios

7 Actionable Strategies for Custom Hook Development

- Extract repetitive logic into custom hooks
- Implement comprehensive error handling
- Use custom hooks to abstract complex state management
- Design hooks with flexible configuration options
- Leverage existing hooks for composition
- Document hook usage and expected behaviors
- Continuously refactor and improve hook implementations

Chapter 15: React Router

15.1 Setting Up React Router

Installation and Initial Configuration

Installing React Router

To begin working with React Router, you'll need to install the package using npm or yarn:

```
npm install react-router-dom
```

```
# or
```

```
yarn add react-router-dom
```

Basic Setup in Application

Implementing React Router requires wrapping your application's root component with `BrowserRouter`:

```
import React from 'react';
import { BrowserRouter as Router } from 'react-router-dom';
import App from './App';

function Root() {
  return (
    <Router>
      <App />
    </Router>
  );
}

export default Root;
```

Router Types in React Router

BrowserRouter

- Uses HTML5 history API
- Creates clean URLs without hash (#)
- Recommended for modern web applications

```
import { BrowserRouter } from 'react-router-dom';

function App() {
  return (
    <BrowserRouter>
      {/* Application components */}
    </BrowserRouter>
  );
}
```

HashRouter

- Uses URL hash for routing
- Useful for legacy browser support
- Adds hash (#) to URLs

```
import { HashRouter } from 'react-router-dom';

function App() {
  return (
    <HashRouter>
      {/* Application components */}
    </HashRouter>
  );
}
```

15.2 Route, Routes, and Link

Defining Routes

The `Routes` and `Route` components create the navigation structure of your application:

```
import { Routes, Route } from 'react-router-dom';
import Home from './pages/Home';
import About from './pages/About';
import Contact from './pages/Contact';

function App() {
  return (
    <div>
      <nav>
        {/* Navigation links */}
      </nav>

      <Routes>
        <Route path="/" element={<Home />} />
        <Route path="/about" element={<About />} />
        <Route path="/contact" element={<Contact />} />
      </Routes>
    </div>
  );
}
```

Navigation with Link Component

The `Link` component prevents full page reloads during navigation:

```
import { Link } from 'react-router-dom';

function Navigation() {
  return (
    <nav>
      <Link to="/">Home</Link>
      <Link to="/about">About</Link>
      <Link to="/contact">Contact</Link>
    </nav>
  );
}
```

NavLink for Active State

`NavLink` provides additional styling for active routes:

```
import { NavLink } from 'react-router-dom';

function Navigation() {
  return (
    <nav>
      <NavLink
        to="/"
        className={({ isActive }) =>
          isActive ? 'active-link' : 'nav-link'
        }
      >
        Home
      </NavLink>
    </nav>
  );
}
```

15.3 Dynamic Routing with Params

Implementing Route Parameters

Capture dynamic segments in your routes:

```
import { Routes, Route, useParams } from 'react-router-
dom';

function ProductDetail() {
  // Extract route parameters
  const { productId } = useParams();

  return (
    <div>
      <h1>Product Details for ID: {productId}</h1>
    </div>
  );
}

function App() {
  return (
    <Routes>
      <Route
        path="/product/:productId"
        element={<ProductDetail />}
      />
    </Routes>
  );
}
```

Multiple Parameters

Handle complex routing scenarios:

```
function UserProfile() {
  const { userId, tab } = useParams();

  return (
    <div>
      <h1>User {userId}'s {tab} Section</h1>
    </div>
  );
}

function App() {
  return (
    <Routes>
      <Route
        path="/user/:userId/:tab"
        element={<UserProfile />}
      />
    </Routes>
  );
}
```

15.4 Nested Routes

Creating Hierarchical Routes

Implement nested routing structures:

```
import { Routes, Route, Outlet } from 'react-router-dom';

function Dashboard() {
  return (
    <div>
      <h1>User Dashboard</h1>
      <Outlet /> {/* Renders child routes */}
    </div>
  );
}

function DashboardProfile() {
  return <h2>Profile Information</h2>;
}

function DashboardSettings() {
  return <h2>Account Settings</h2>;
}

function App() {
  return (
    <Routes>
      <Route path="/dashboard" element={<Dashboard />}>
        <Route path="profile"
element={<DashboardProfile />} />
        <Route path="settings"
element={<DashboardSettings />} />
      </Route>
    </Routes>
  );
}
```

Nested Navigation

Create complex navigation hierarchies:

```
function Dashboard() {
  return (
    <div>
      <nav>
        <Link to="profile">Profile</Link>
        <Link to="settings">Settings</Link>
      </nav>
      <Outlet />
    </div>
  );
}
```

15.5 Redirects and 404 Pages

Implementing Redirects

Handle navigation and routing conditions:

```
import {
  Routes,
  Route,
  Navigate,
  useLocation
} from 'react-router-dom';

function ProtectedRoute({ children }) {
  const isAuthenticated = checkUserAuthentication();
  const location = useLocation();

  if (!isAuthenticated) {
    // Redirect to login, preserve original destination
    return <Navigate
      to="/login"
      state={{ from: location }}
      replace
    />;
  }

  return children;
}

function App() {
  return (
    <Routes>
      <Route
        path="/dashboard"
        element={
          <ProtectedRoute>
            <Dashboard />
          </ProtectedRoute>
        }
      />
      <Route
        path="/login"
        element={<LoginPage />}
      />
    </Routes>
  );
}
```

Creating 404 Not Found Page

Handle undefined routes:

```
function NotFoundPage() {
  return (
    <div>
      <h1>404 - Page Not Found</h1>
      <Link to="/">Return to Home</Link>
    </div>
  );
}

function App() {
  return (
    <Routes>
      <Route path="/" element={<Home />} />
      <Route path="/about" element={<About />} />
      {/* Catch-all route for undefined paths */}
      <Route path="*" element={<NotFoundPage />} />
    </Routes>
  );
}
```

Advanced Routing Techniques

Programmatic Navigation

Use `useNavigate` hook for imperative routing:

```
import { useNavigate } from 'react-router-dom';

function LoginButton() {
  const navigate = useNavigate();

  const handleLogin = () => {
    // Perform login logic
    navigate('/dashboard');
  };

  return <button onClick={handleLogin}>Login</button>;
}
```

5 Tips for Effective React Router Usage

- Organize routes modularly and logically
- Implement proper authentication checks
- Use nested routes for complex layouts
- Leverage route parameters for dynamic content
- Handle error states and 404 scenarios

7 Actionable Strategies for React Router Development

- Centralize route configurations Implement role-based route protection
- Create reusable routing components
- Optimize performance with code splitting
- Handle complex navigation flows
- Implement consistent error handling
- Use TypeScript for enhanced type safety

Chapter 16: Styling in React

16.1 Inline Styles

Understanding Inline Styling in React

Inline styles in React represent a fundamental approach to component styling, utilizing JavaScript objects to define styles directly within component render methods. Unlike traditional HTML inline styles, React's inline styling leverages a JavaScript object syntax that transforms CSS properties into camelCased keys.

Key Characteristics of Inline Styles

- Styles are defined as JavaScript objects
- CSS properties use camelCase notation
- Numeric values are automatically appended with 'px'
- Styles are applied using the `style` attribute

Basic Inline Style Example

```
function ButtonComponent() {
    const buttonStyle = {
        backgroundColor: 'blue',
        color: 'white',
        padding: '10px 15px',
        borderRadius: '5px',
        fontSize: '16px',
        border: 'none',
        cursor: 'pointer',
        transition: 'background-color 0.3s ease'
    };

    return (
        <button style={buttonStyle}>
            Click Me
        </button>
    );
}
```

Advanced Inline Styling Techniques

Dynamic Styling

```
function ConditionalStyleComponent({ isActive }) {
    const dynamicStyle = {
        backgroundColor: isActive ? 'green' : 'gray',
        opacity: isActive ? 1 : 0.5,
        transform: isActive ? 'scale(1.05)' : 'scale(1)'
    };

    return (
        <div style={dynamicStyle}>
            Conditional Styled Element
        </div>
    );
}
```

Performance and Limitations

- Inline styles create new style objects on each render
- Less efficient for complex styling scenarios
- Limited CSS feature support
- No pseudo-class or media query support

16.2 CSS Modules

Introduction to CSS Modules

CSS Modules provide a scoped styling approach, solving global CSS namespace conflicts by generating unique class names during build time.

Core Concepts

- Local scoping of CSS classes
- Automatic generation of unique class names
- Direct import of CSS files into React components
- Prevents style leakage between components

CSS Module Implementation

```
/* Button.module.css */
.primaryButton {
    background-color: #007bff;
    color: white;
    padding: 10px 15px;
    border-radius: 5px;
}

.secondaryButton {
    background-color: #6c757d;
    color: white;
    padding: 10px 15px;
    border-radius: 5px;
}
```

```
import styles from './Button.module.css';

function ButtonComponent() {
    return (
        <div>
            <button className={styles.primaryButton}>
                Primary Button
            </button>
            <button className={styles.secondaryButton}>
                Secondary Button
            </button>
        </div>
    );
}
```

Advanced CSS Module Techniques

- Composing classes
- Conditional class applications
- Handling multiple classes

16.3 Styled-Components

Understanding Styled-Components

Styled-Components is a popular CSS-in-JS library that allows writing actual CSS code within JavaScript template literals.

Key Features

- Component-level styling
- Dynamic prop-based styling
- Automatic vendor prefixing
- Server-side rendering support

Basic Styled-Component Example

```
import styled from 'styled-components';

const StyledButton = styled.button`
    background-color: ${props => props.primary ?
'#007bff' : '#6c757d'};
    color: white;
    padding: 10px 15px;
    border-radius: 5px;
    transition: all 0.3s ease;

    &:hover {
        opacity: 0.8;
        transform: scale(1.05);
    }
`;

function ButtonComponent() {
    return (
        <div>
            <StyledButton primary>
                Primary Button
            </StyledButton>
            <StyledButton>
                Secondary Button
            </StyledButton>
        </div>
    );
}
```

Advanced Theming

```
import { ThemeProvider } from 'styled-components';

const theme = {
    colors: {
        primary: '#007bff',
        secondary: '#6c757d'
    }
};

function App() {
    return (
        <ThemeProvider theme={theme}>
            {/* Components with theme access */}
        </ThemeProvider>
    );
}
```

16.4 Tailwind CSS with React

Integrating Tailwind CSS

Tailwind CSS provides utility-first styling approach, enabling rapid UI development through pre-defined classes.

Setup and Configuration

```
npm install -D tailwindcss postcss autoprefixer
npx tailwindcss init -p
```

Tailwind Configuration

```
// tailwind.config.js
module.exports = {
    content: [
        "./src/**/*.{js,jsx,ts,tsx}",
    ],
    theme: {
        extend: {
            colors: {
                'custom-blue': '#007bff'
            }
        }
    }
}
```

Practical Tailwind Usage

```
function UserCard() {
    return (
        <div className="max-w-sm rounded overflow-hidden
shadow-lg p-4 bg-white">
            <img
                className="w-full h-48 object-cover
rounded-t-lg"
                src="/user-image.jpg"
                alt="User Profile"
            />
            <div className="px-6 py-4">
                <div className="font-bold text-xl mb-2
text-gray-800">
                    John Doe
                </div>
                <p className="text-gray-700 text-base">
                    Front-end Developer
                </p>
            </div>
        </div>
    );
}
```

16.5 Best Styling Practices

Performance Optimization

- Minimize dynamic style generations
- Use memoization techniques
- Prefer CSS Modules for complex layouts
- Lazy load styles for large applications

Consistency and Maintainability

- Establish a design system
- Use consistent naming conventions
- Implement theme providers
- Create reusable style components

Cross-Browser Compatibility

- Use autoprefixer
- Test styles across multiple browsers
- Implement fallback styles
- Use normalize or reset CSS

Accessibility Considerations

- Ensure sufficient color contrast
- Support system preferences (dark/light mode)
- Use semantic HTML with appropriate styling
- Maintain keyboard navigation styles

Performance Monitoring

- Analyze style bundle size
- Implement code splitting
- Use performance profiling tools
- Optimize CSS delivery

Actionable Strategies

- Develop a consistent design language across your React application
- Leverage utility-first CSS frameworks for rapid prototyping
- Implement component-level styling for better encapsulation
- Create a centralized theme management system
- Use CSS-in-JS for dynamic, prop-based styling
- Optimize style performance through memoization and lazy loading
- Implement responsive design using utility classes and media queries

Tips

- Always prioritize readability and maintainability in your styling approach
- Avoid over-complicated styling solutions
- Test your styles across different devices and browsers
- Keep your styling consistent with your design system
- Stay updated with the latest styling techniques and tools

Chapter 17: API Calls in React

17.1 Fetch API

Understanding Native Fetch API in React

Core Fetch Mechanism

The Fetch API provides a modern, promise-based approach to making network requests directly within JavaScript and React applications. Unlike older XMLHttpRequest methods, Fetch offers a more streamlined and flexible way to interact with web resources.

Basic Fetch Request Structure

```
import React, { useState, useEffect } from 'react';

function UserList() {
    const [users, setUsers] = useState([]);
    const [isLoading, setIsLoading] = useState(true);
    const [error, setError] = useState(null);

    useEffect(() => {
        const fetchUsers = async () => {
            try {
                const response = await fetch('https://
api.example.com/users');

                if (!response.ok) {
                    throw new Error(`HTTP error! status:
${response.status}`);
                }

                const data = await response.json();
                setUsers(data);
                setIsLoading(false);
            } catch (error) {
                setError(error.message);
                setIsLoading(false);
            }
        };

        fetchUsers();
    }, []);

    if (isLoading) return <div>Loading...</div>;
    if (error) return <div>Error: {error}</div>;

    return (
        <ul>
            {users.map(user => (
                <li key={user.id}>{user.name}</li>
            ))}
        </ul>
    );
}
```

Advanced Fetch Techniques

POST Request Example

```
const createUser = async (userData) => {
    try {
        const response = await fetch('https://
api.example.com/users', {
            method: 'POST',
            headers: {
                'Content-Type': 'application/json',
                'Authorization': `Bearer ${authToken}`
            },
            body: JSON.stringify(userData)
        });

        if (!response.ok) {
            throw new Error('Network response was not
ok');
        }

        const result = await response.json();
        return result;
    } catch (error) {
        console.error('Error creating user:', error);
    }
};
```

Handling Different Response Types

```
// Fetching different types of responses
const fetchData = async () => {
    // JSON Response
    const jsonResponse = await fetch('/api/
data').then(res => res.json());

    // Text Response
    const textResponse = await fetch('/api/
text').then(res => res.text());

    // Blob (for files)
    const blobResponse = await fetch('/api/
file').then(res => res.blob());

    // FormData
    const formDataResponse = await fetch('/api/
form').then(res => res.formData());
};
```

17.2 Axios

Comprehensive Axios Integration

Why Choose Axios?

Axios provides additional features over native Fetch:

- Automatic transforms for JSON data
- Better error handling
- Request and response interceptors
- Client-side protection against XSRF

Basic Axios Setup

```
import axios from 'axios';
import React, { useState, useEffect } from 'react';

// Create an axios instance with base configuration
const api = axios.create({
    baseURL: 'https://api.example.com',
    timeout: 5000,
    headers: {
        'Content-Type': 'application/json'
    }
});

function ProductList() {
    const [products, setProducts] = useState([]);
    const [error, setError] = useState(null);

    useEffect(() => {
        const fetchProducts = async () => {
            try {
                const response = await api.get('/
products');
                setProducts(response.data);
            } catch (error) {
                setError(error.response?.data || 'An
error occurred');
            }
        };

        fetchProducts();
    }, []);

    return (
        <div>
            {error && <div>Error: {error}</div>}
            {products.map(product => (
                <div key={product.id}>{product.name}</
div>
            ))}
        </div>
    );
}
```

Axios Interceptors

```
// Request interceptor
api.interceptors.request.use(
    config => {
        const token = localStorage.getItem('authToken');
        if (token) {
            config.headers['Authorization'] = `Bearer $
{token}`;
        }
        return config;
    },
    error => Promise.reject(error)
);

// Response interceptor
api.interceptors.response.use(
    response => response,
    error => {
        if (error.response?.status === 401) {
            // Handle unauthorized access
            window.location = '/login';
        }
        return Promise.reject(error);
    }
);
```

17.3 Handling Loading & Error States

Comprehensive State Management for API Calls

Creating Robust Loading States

```
function DataFetchComponent() {
    const [data, setData] = useState(null);
    const [isLoading, setIsLoading] = useState(true);
    const [error, setError] = useState(null);

    useEffect(() => {
        const fetchData = async () => {
            try {
                setIsLoading(true);
                const response = await fetch('/api/
data');

                if (!response.ok) {
                    throw new Error(`HTTP error! status:
${response.status}`);
                }

                const result = await response.json();
                setData(result);
            } catch (error) {
                setError({
                    message: error.message,
                    status: error.status || 'Unknown'
                });
            } finally {
                setIsLoading(false);
            }
        };

        fetchData();
    }, []);

    if (isLoading) {
        return (
            <div className="loading-spinner">
                <div className="spinner"></div>
                <p>Loading data...</p>
            </div>
        );
    }

    if (error) {
```

17.4 useEffect for Data Fetching

Advanced Data Fetching Patterns

Cancelling Unnecessary Requests

```
function UserProfile({ userId }) {
    const [user, setUser] = useState(null);
    const [isLoading, setIsLoading] = useState(true);

    useEffect(() => {
        let isMounted = true;
        const controller = new AbortController();

        const fetchUser = async () => {
            try {
                setIsLoading(true);
                const response = await fetch(`/api/users/
${userId}`, {
                    signal: controller.signal
                });

                const userData = await response.json();

                if (isMounted) {
                    setUser(userData);
                    setIsLoading(false);
                }
            } catch (error) {
                if (error.name === 'AbortError') {
                    console.log('Fetch aborted');
                } else {
                    console.error('Fetch error:', error);
                }
            }
        };

        fetchUser();

        // Cleanup function
        return () => {
            isMounted = false;
            controller.abort();
        };
    }, [userId]);

    if (isLoading) return <div>Loading user...</div>;
    if (!user) return <div>No user found</div>;
```

17.5 Caching API Responses

Implementing Response Caching

Simple In-Memory Caching

```
const cache = new Map();

function useCachedFetch(url) {
    const [data, setData] = useState(null);
    const [isLoading, setIsLoading] = useState(true);

    useEffect(() => {
        const fetchData = async () => {
            // Check cache first
            if (cache.has(url)) {
                setData(cache.get(url));
                setIsLoading(false);
                return;
            }

            try {
                const response = await fetch(url);
                const result = await response.json();

                // Store in cache
                cache.set(url, result);
                setData(result);
            } catch (error) {
                console.error('Fetch error:', error);
            } finally {
                setIsLoading(false);
            }
        };

        fetchData();
    }, [url]);

    return { data, isLoading };
}
```

Advanced Caching with Expiration

```
class CacheManager {
    constructor() {
        this.cache = new Map();
    }

    set(key, value, ttl = 5 * 60 * 1000) { // 5 minutes
default
        const record = {
            value,
            expiry: Date.now() + ttl
        };
        this.cache.set(key, record);
    }

    get(key) {
        const record = this.cache.get(key);

        if (!record) return null;

        if (Date.now() > record.expiry) {
            this.cache.delete(key);
            return null;
        }

        return record.value;
    }
}
```

Actionable Strategies

- Master promise-based asynchronous data fetching techniques
- Implement comprehensive error handling for network requests
- Create reusable data fetching hooks
- Optimize API call performance through caching
- Manage loading states effectively
- Utilize interceptors for global request/response management
- Implement retry mechanisms for failed network requests

Tips

- Always handle potential network errors gracefully
- Use AbortController to cancel unnecessary requests
- Implement proper loading and error states
- Optimize API calls with intelligent caching
- Stay consistent with your data fetching approach

Chapter 18: Error Boundaries in React.js

18.1 What Are Error Boundaries?

Understanding the Concept of Error Boundaries

Error boundaries are React components designed to catch JavaScript errors anywhere in their child component tree, log those errors, and display a fallback UI instead of the component tree that crashed. Unlike traditional error handling in JavaScript, error boundaries provide a robust mechanism to gracefully handle runtime errors in React applications.

The Problem Error Boundaries Solve

In standard JavaScript and React applications, a single component error can break the entire application, rendering it unusable. Without error boundaries, an error in a deeply nested component would cause the entire React component tree to unmount, leading to a poor user experience.

Key Characteristics of Error Boundaries

- Catch errors during rendering
- Catch errors in lifecycle methods
- Catch errors in constructors
- Prevent entire application from crashing
- Provide a mechanism to log errors
- Allow partial UI recovery

How Error Boundaries Work

Error boundaries are class components that implement either (or both) of these lifecycle methods:

- `static getDerivedStateFromError()`
- `componentDidCatch()`

```
class ErrorBoundary extends React.Component {
  constructor(props) {
    super(props);
    this.state = { hasError: false };
  }

  static getDerivedStateFromError(error) {
    // Update state so the next render will show the
fallback UI
    return { hasError: true };
  }

  componentDidCatch(error, errorInfo) {
    // You can log the error to an error reporting
service
    logErrorToService(error, errorInfo);
  }

  render() {
    if (this.state.hasError) {
      // You can render any custom fallback UI
      return <h1>Something went wrong.</h1>;
    }

    return this.props.children;
  }
}
```

18.2 Creating an Error Boundary

Implementing Basic Error Boundary Component

To create an error boundary, you must define a class component with specific error-handling lifecycle methods:

```
class ProductDetailErrorBoundary extends React.Component
{
  constructor(props) {
    super(props);
    this.state = {
      hasError: false,
      errorMessage: null
    };
  }

  static getDerivedStateFromError(error) {
    return {
      hasError: true,
      errorMessage: error.toString()
    };
  }

  componentDidCatch(error, errorInfo) {
    // Send error to monitoring service
    errorTrackingService.report({
      error,
      errorInfo,
      componentStack: errorInfo.componentStack
    });
  }

  render() {
    if (this.state.hasError) {
      return (
        <div className="error-container">
          <h2>Product Loading Failed</h2>
          <p>We couldn't load the product details.
{this.state.errorMessage}</p>
          <button onClick={() =>
window.location.reload()}>
            Reload Page
          </button>
        </div>
      );
    }

    return this.props.children;
```

Wrapping Components with Error Boundary

You can wrap individual components or entire sections of your application:

```
function App() {
  return (
    <ErrorBoundary>
      <ProductList>
        <ProductDetailErrorBoundary>
          <ProductDetail productId={123} />
        </ProductDetailErrorBoundary>
      </ProductList>
    </ErrorBoundary>
  );
}
```

18.3 Handling Component Errors

Types of Errors Caught by Error Boundaries

- Rendering errors
- Lifecycle method errors
- Constructor errors
- State update errors

Common Error Scenarios

1. **Network Request Failures**

```
class DataFetcher extends React.Component {
  state = { data: null, error: null }

  async componentDidMount() {
    try {
      const response = await fetchData();
      this.setState({ data: response });
    } catch (error) {
      this.setState({ error });
    }
  }

  render() {
    if (this.state.error) {
      throw this.state.error;
    }
    // Render data
  }
}
```

2 **Prop Type Validation Errors**

```
class UserProfile extends React.Component {
  render() {
    // Validate critical props
    if (!this.props.user || !this.props.user.id) {
      throw new Error('Invalid user data');
    }

    return (
      <div>
        <h1>{this.props.user.name}</h1>
        {/* Render user details */}
      </div>
    );
  }
}
```

18.4 Logging Errors

Error Tracking Strategies

- Implement client-side error logging
- Send error details to monitoring services
- Create comprehensive error reports

```
function logErrorToService(error, errorInfo) {
  const errorLog = {
    message: error.toString(),
    stack: errorInfo.componentStack,
    timestamp: new Date().toISOString(),
    url: window.location.href,
    userAgent: navigator.userAgent
  };

  // Send to error tracking service
  fetch('/api/error-log', {
    method: 'POST',
    headers: {
      'Content-Type': 'application/json'
    },
    body: JSON.stringify(errorLog)
  });
}
```

18.5 Fallback UI

Designing Effective Error Fallback Interfaces

- Provide clear error messages
- Offer user recovery options
- Maintain consistent design
- Include relevant troubleshooting information

```
function GlobalErrorFallback({ error,
resetErrorBoundary }) {
  return (
    <div role="alert" className="error-fallback">
      <h2>Oops! Something went wrong</h2>
      <pre style={{ color: "red" }}>{error.message}</pre>
      <button onClick={resetErrorBoundary}>
        Try again
      </button>
      <div className="error-support-info">
        <p>Need help? Contact support at
support@example.com</p>
        <p>Error Code: {generateErrorCode()}</p>
      </div>
    </div>
  );
}
```

Advanced Error Boundary Techniques

Nested Error Boundaries

```
function App() {
  return (
    <RootErrorBoundary>
      <NavigationErrorBoundary>
        <Navigation />
      </NavigationErrorBoundary>
      <ContentErrorBoundary>
        <MainContent>
          <DetailPageErrorBoundary>
            <DetailPage />
          </DetailPageErrorBoundary>
        </MainContent>
      </ContentErrorBoundary>
    </RootErrorBoundary>
  );
}
```

5 Tips for Effective Error Boundaries

- Create modular and specific error boundaries
- Handle errors at appropriate component levels
- Log errors for debugging and monitoring
- Provide user-friendly fallback interfaces
- Test error scenarios thoroughly

7 Actionable Strategies for Error Management

- Implement comprehensive error tracking mechanisms
- Design granular error boundary components
- Use error boundaries to isolate failure points
- Normalize error handling across application
- Develop clear error communication protocols
- Build resilient fallback user interfaces
- Continuously improve error detection and reporting

Chapter 19: React Fragments

19.1 Why Use Fragments?

The Problem with Multiple Root Elements

In React, components typically return a single root element. Prior to fragments, developers were forced to wrap multiple elements in unnecessary container elements like `<div>` or `<span>`, which created additional DOM nodes and impacted performance and semantic structure.

Challenges of Wrapper Elements

- Unnecessary DOM node creation
- Potential CSS layout complications
- Semantic HTML structure disruption
- Performance overhead

How Fragments Solve the Problem

React Fragments provide a way to group multiple elements without adding extra nodes to the DOM. They allow developers to return multiple elements from a component without introducing additional wrapper elements.

Example of the Problem

```
// Without Fragments
function UserProfile() {
  return (
    <div>
      <h1>User Profile</h1>
      <p>Name: John Doe</p>
      <p>Email: john@example.com</p>
    </div>
  );
}

// With Fragments
function UserProfile() {
  return (
    <>
      <h1>User Profile</h1>
      <p>Name: John Doe</p>
      <p>Email: john@example.com</p>
    </>
  );
}
```

Performance and Rendering Benefits

- Zero additional DOM nodes
- Cleaner rendered HTML
- Improved component readability
- More efficient rendering

19.2 `<></>` vs `<Fragment>`

Short Syntax: <></>

The most common and concise way to use fragments is the short syntax <></>. This syntax is perfect for simple use cases where you don't need additional properties.

```
function Navigation() {
  return (
    <>
      <nav>Home</nav>
      <nav>About</nav>
      <nav>Contact</nav>
    </>
  );
}
```

Explicit `<Fragment>` Syntax

The explicit `React.Fragment` syntax becomes necessary when you need to add keys or other attributes to the fragment.

```
function List({ items }) {
  return (
    <React.Fragment>
      {items.map((item, index) => (
        <React.Fragment key={item.id}>
          <dt>{item.term}</dt>
          <dd>{item.description}</dd>
        </React.Fragment>
      ))}
    </React.Fragment>
  );
}
```

Key Differences

Feature	`<>`	`<React.Fragment>`
Key Support	Not Supported	Supported
Attributes	No Additional Attributes	Supports Additional Attributes
Import Required	No	Yes (import React)
Performance	Slightly Faster	Slightly Overhead

When to Use Each Syntax

- Use <> for simple grouping without special requirements
- Use `<React.Fragment>` when:
    - Adding keys to fragment
    - Adding other attributes
    - Working with dynamic content requiring identification

19.3 Keyed Fragments

Understanding Keyed Fragments

When rendering lists or dynamically generated content, fragments may require keys to help React identify which items have changed, been added, or removed.

```
function TodoList({ todos }) {
  return (
    <dl>
      {todos.map(todo => (
        <React.Fragment key={todo.id}>
          <dt>{todo.title}</dt>
          <dd>{todo.description}</dd>
        </React.Fragment>
      ))}
    </dl>
  );
}
```

Scenarios Requiring Keyed Fragments

- Rendering lists
- Dynamic content generation
- Conditional rendering with multiple elements
- Complex nested structures

Key Generation Strategies

```
function DynamicContent({ data }) {
  return (
    <>
      {data.map((item, index) => (
        // Avoid using index as key if possible
        <React.Fragment key={item.uniqueIdentifier ||
`fragment-${index}`}>
          <h2>{item.title}</h2>
          <p>{item.content}</p>
        </React.Fragment>
      ))}
    </>
  );
}
```

19.4 Avoiding Div Soup

The Problem of Unnecessary Wrappers

Overusing `<div>` elements creates "div soup" - a cluttered, semantically meaningless HTML structure that complicates styling and accessibility.

Negative Impacts of Div Soup

- Reduced HTML semantic clarity
- Increased DOM complexity
- Performance overhead
- CSS styling challenges
- Accessibility impediments

Fragment-Based Solutions

```
// Div Soup
function BadComponent() {
  return (
    <div>
      <div>
        <div>
          <h1>Title</h1>
          <div>
            <p>Content</p>
          </div>
        </div>
      </div>
    </div>
  );
}

// Clean Fragment Approach
function CleanComponent() {
  return (
    <>
      <h1>Title</h1>
      <p>Content</p>
    </>
  );
}
```

Semantic HTML Alternatives

```
function ProductDetails() {
  return (
    <article>
      <header>
        <h2>Product Name</h2>
      </header>
      <>
        <section>Description</section>
        <section>Specifications</section>
      </>
      <footer>Additional Information</footer>
    </article>
  );
}
```

19.5 Fragment Best Practices

Performance Considerations

- Minimize nested fragments
- Use fragments for logical grouping
- Avoid unnecessary wrapping

Compatibility and Support

- Supported in React 16.2 and later
- Works with server-side rendering
- Compatible with most build tools and environments

Advanced Fragment Techniques

```
function ConditionalRendering({ isLoggedIn, user }) {
  return (
    <>
      {isLoggedIn && (
        <>
          <UserProfile user={user} />
          <Dashboard />
        </>
      )}
      {!isLoggedIn && (
        <>
          <LoginForm />
          <RegisterPrompt />
        </>
      )}
    </>
  );
}
```

Error Handling and Debugging

- Use explicit `React.Fragment` for easier debugging
- Add meaningful comments for complex fragment structures

- Utilize React DevTools to inspect fragment usage

5 Tips for Effective Fragment Usage

- Prioritize semantic HTML structure
- Minimize unnecessary DOM nodes
- Use appropriate fragment syntax
- Keep fragment nesting minimal
- Leverage fragments for conditional rendering

7 Actionable Strategies for Fragment Management

- Standardize fragment usage across project
- Create reusable fragment patterns
- Optimize rendering performance
- Maintain clean component structures
- Implement consistent key generation
- Reduce unnecessary wrapper elements
- Improve overall code readability

Chapter 20: React Portals

20.1 What Are Portals?

Understanding the Concept of Portals

React Portals provide a powerful mechanism to render child components into a DOM node that exists outside the DOM hierarchy of the parent component. In standard React rendering, components are typically nested within their parent's DOM structure. Portals break this conventional rendering pattern by allowing developers to render a component's children at a different location in the DOM tree.

The Technical Mechanics of Portals

The `ReactDOM.createPortal()` method is the key to implementing portals. This method takes two primary arguments:

1. The React element to be rendered
2. The DOM element where the component should be mounted

Basic Portal Syntax

```
import ReactDOM from 'react-dom';

function Portal({ children }) {
  return ReactDOM.createPortal(
    children,
    document.getElementById('portal-root')
  );
}
```

Why Portals Matter

Portals solve several critical rendering challenges:

- Breaking out of component containment
- Rendering overlays like modals, tooltips, and dropdowns
- Managing z-index and stacking context complications
- Handling complex UI interactions that require DOM manipulation outside normal component hierarchy

20.2 Creating a Modal with Portals

Modal Component Implementation

```
import React, { useState } from 'react';
import ReactDOM from 'react-dom';

function Modal({ isOpen, onClose, children }) {
  if (!isOpen) return null;

  return ReactDOM.createPortal(
    <div className="modal-overlay">
      <div className="modal-content">
        <button
          className="modal-close-button"
          onClick={onClose}
        >
          &times;
        </button>
        {children}
      </div>
    </div>,
    document.getElementById('modal-root')
  );
}

function App() {
  const [isModalOpen, setIsModalOpen] = useState(false);

  return (
    <div>
      <button onClick={() => setIsModalOpen(true)}>
        Open Modal
      </button>
      <Modal
        isOpen={isModalOpen}
        onClose={() => setIsModalOpen(false)}
      >
        <h2>Portal Modal Content</h2>
        <p>This modal is rendered using React Portals!</
p>
      </Modal>
    </div>
  );
}
```

Portal Modal Best Practices

- Always provide a close mechanism
- Implement keyboard accessibility
- Manage focus trapping
- Add appropriate ARIA attributes for screen readers

Accessibility Considerations

```
function AccessibleModal({ isOpen, onClose, children }) {
  const modalRef = useRef(null);

  useEffect(() => {
    if (isOpen) {
      // Trap focus within modal
      const focusableElements =
modalRef.current.querySelectorAll(
        'button, [href], input, select, textarea,
[tabindex]:not([tabindex="-1"])'
      );

      const firstElement = focusableElements[0];
      const lastElement =
focusableElements[focusableElements.length - 1];

      const trapFocus = (e) => {
        if (e.key === 'Tab') {
          if (e.shiftKey && document.activeElement ===
firstElement) {
            lastElement.focus();
            e.preventDefault();
          } else if (!e.shiftKey &&
document.activeElement === lastElement) {
            firstElement.focus();
            e.preventDefault();
          }
        }
      };

      document.addEventListener('keydown', trapFocus);
      firstElement?.focus();

      return () => {
        document.removeEventListener('keydown',
trapFocus);
      };
    }
  }, [isOpen]);

  if (!isOpen) return null;
```

20.3 Event Bubbling in Portals

Event Propagation Mechanics

Despite being rendered outside the normal DOM hierarchy, events in portals still propagate through React's synthetic event system. This means event handlers work similarly to standard React components.

```
function PortalWithEvents() {
  const handleOverlayClick = (e) => {
    console.log('Overlay clicked');
  };

  const handleModalClick = (e) => {
    console.log('Modal content clicked');
    // Prevents event from bubbling to overlay
    e.stopPropagation();
  };

  return ReactDOM.createPortal(
    <div
      onClick={handleOverlayClick}
      className="overlay"
    >
      <div
        onClick={handleModalClick}
        className="modal"
      >
        Modal Content
      </div>
    </div>,
    document.getElementById('portal-root')
  );
}
```

Event Bubbling Nuances

- Events trigger from the portal's rendered location
- Parent component event handlers still work
- `stopPropagation()` functions identically to standard React events

20.4 Styling Portals

CSS Strategies

```
#modal-root {
  position: fixed;
  top: 0;
  left: 0;
  width: 100%;
  height: 100%;
  z-index: 1000;
  display: flex;
  justify-content: center;
  align-items: center;
}

.modal-overlay {
  background: rgba(0, 0, 0, 0.5);
  position: absolute;
  top: 0;
  left: 0;
  right: 0;
  bottom: 0;
}

.modal-content {
  background: white;
  padding: 20px;
  border-radius: 5px;
  max-width: 500px;
  width: 100%;
}
```

Styling Considerations

- Use fixed positioning for full-screen overlays
- Implement high z-index values
- Create responsive and adaptive designs
- Ensure cross-browser compatibility

20.5 When to Use Portals

Ideal Use Cases

1. **Modal Dialogs**: Render without disrupting parent component layout
2. **Tooltips**: Position precisely regardless of parent's CSS
3. **Dropdown Menus**: Escape overflow and clipping constraints
4. **Notifications**: Create global alert systems
5. **Floating Elements**: Manage complex positioning scenarios

Performance and Architectural Implications

- Minimal performance overhead
- Clean separation of concerns
- Enhanced UI flexibility
- Improved component composition

Strategic Implementation Tips

Break through conventional rendering limitations by understanding portal's unique capabilities and strategically implementing them in complex UI architectures.

Practical Recommendations

- Minimize portal usage to essential scenarios
- Maintain clean, predictable component structures
- Prioritize accessibility and user experience
- Test thoroughly across different browser environments

Advanced Portal Techniques

Dynamic Portal Rendering

```
function DynamicPortal({ children, target }) {
  const [portalRoot, setPortalRoot] = useState(null);

  useEffect(() => {
    const root = document.getElementById(target);
    setPortalRoot(root);
  }, [target]);

  return portalRoot
    ? ReactDOM.createPortal(children, portalRoot)
    : null;
}
```

5 Strategic Tips

- Leverage React Portals as precision tools for complex UI rendering challenges, maintaining clean architectural patterns while solving intricate DOM manipulation requirements.
- Implement portals with meticulous attention to performance, accessibility, and user interaction design principles.
- Create reusable portal components that encapsulate complex rendering logic and provide consistent, maintainable solutions.
- Prioritize semantic HTML and appropriate ARIA attributes when constructing portal-based interfaces to ensure robust accessibility.
- Master the nuanced event propagation mechanisms to create intuitive and responsive portal-based user interfaces.

7 Actionable Strategies

- Develop a comprehensive modal management system using portal-based components.
- Create a global notification mechanism utilizing React Portals for consistent UI messaging.
- Implement advanced tooltip systems that transcend traditional CSS positioning

constraints.

- Design adaptive dropdown menus with precise positioning and interaction models.
- Construct complex overlay interfaces with granular control over rendering and interaction.
- Build screen reader-friendly interfaces that leverage portal's unique rendering capabilities.
- Optimize performance by strategically implementing portal-based rendering for complex UI components.

Chapter 21: Performance Optimization in React

21.1 React.memo

Understanding Memoization in React

Memoization represents a critical optimization technique that prevents unnecessary re-rendering of React components. `React.memo` serves as a higher-order component designed to wrap functional components, implementing a shallow comparison of props to determine whether a component should update.

Core Mechanics of React.memo

```
import React from 'react';

// Basic React.memo Implementation
const ExpensiveComponent = React.memo(function
MyComponent(props) {
  return (
    <div>
      {props.value}
    </div>
  );
});

// Custom Comparison Function
const ComplexComponent = React.memo(function
MyComponent(props) {
  return (
    <div>
      {props.complexObject.name}
    </div>
  );
}, (prevProps, nextProps) => {
  // Custom comparison logic
  return (
    prevProps.complexObject.id ===
nextProps.complexObject.id
  );
});
```

Performance Implications

- Reduces unnecessary re-renders
- Minimizes computational overhead
- Optimizes rendering cycle for complex components

Deep Dive into Prop Comparison

```
function ParentComponent() {
  const [count, setCount] = useState(0);
  const [name, setName] = useState('John');

  // Memoized callback to prevent unnecessary re-creation
  const handleClick = useCallback(() => {
    setCount(c => c + 1);
  }, []);

  return (
    <div>
      <MemoizedChildComponent
        name={name}
        onClick={handleClick}
      />
      <button onClick={() => setName('Jane')}>
        Change Name
      </button>
    </div>
  );
}

// Memoized component with prop comparison
const MemoizedChildComponent = React.memo(function
ChildComponent({ name, onClick }) {
  console.log('Child component rendered');
  return (
    <div>
      <h1>{name}</h1>
      <button onClick={onClick}>Increment</button>
    </div>
  );
});
```

21.2 useCallback Hook

Preventing Unnecessary Function Recreations

`useCallback` acts as a critical optimization hook that memoizes function definitions, preventing unnecessary recreations during component re-renders.

Basic useCallback Implementation

```
import React, { useState, useCallback } from 'react';

function ParentComponent() {
  const [count, setCount] = useState(0);

  // Memoized callback function
  const incrementCount = useCallback(() => {
    setCount(prevCount => prevCount + 1);
  }, []); // Empty dependency array means function never
changes

  return (
    <div>
      <ChildComponent
        onIncrement={incrementCount}
        count={count}
      />
    </div>
  );
}

// Child component with memoization
const ChildComponent = React.memo(({ onIncrement,
count }) => {
  return (
    <div>
      <p>Count: {count}</p>
      <button onClick={onIncrement}>Increment</button>
    </div>
  );
});
```

Dependency Management

```
function ComplexComponent() {
  const [value, setValue] = useState('');
  const [items, setItems] = useState([]);

  // Callback with dependencies
  const processItems = useCallback(() => {
    return items.filter(item => item.includes(value));
  }, [items, value]); // Dependencies trigger function
recreation

  return (
    <div>
      <input
        value={value}
        onChange={(e) => setValue(e.target.value)}
      />
      <ItemList processItems={processItems} />
    </div>
  );
}
```

21.3 useMemo Hook

Memoizing Computational Expensive Operations

`useMemo` optimizes complex calculations by caching results and preventing unnecessary recalculations.

Advanced Memoization Techniques

```
import React, { useMemo, useState } from 'react';

function ExpensiveCalculationComponent() {
  const [numbers, setNumbers] = useState([10, 20, 30, 40,
50]);
  const [increment, setIncrement] = useState(0);

  // Memoized expensive calculation
  const totalSum = useMemo(() => {
    console.log('Calculating sum...');
    return numbers.reduce((acc, number) => acc + number,
0);
  }, [numbers]); // Only recalculates when numbers change

  // Memoized complex object creation
  const user = useMemo(() => ({
    name: 'John Doe',
    age: 30,
    scores: numbers
  }), [numbers]);

  return (
    <div>
      <p>Total Sum: {totalSum}</p>
      <p>User Details: {JSON.stringify(user)}</p>
      <button onClick={() => setIncrement(i => i + 1)}>
        Increment: {increment}
      </button>
    </div>
  );
}
```

Performance Comparison Strategies

```
function PerformanceComparison() {
  const [data, setData] = useState([]);

  // Non-memoized expensive calculation
  const expensiveCalculation = () => {
    return data.map(item => item * 2)
      .filter(value => value > 100)
      .reduce((acc, val) => acc + val, 0);
  };

  // Memoized calculation
  const memoizedCalculation = useMemo(() => {
    return data.map(item => item * 2)
      .filter(value => value > 100)
      .reduce((acc, val) => acc + val, 0);
  }, [data]);

  return <div>{memoizedCalculation}</div>;
}
```

21.4 Code Splitting

Dynamic Import Mechanisms

```
import React, { Suspense, lazy } from 'react';

// Lazy load components
const Dashboard = lazy(() => import('./Dashboard'));
const AdminPanel = lazy(() => import('./AdminPanel'));

function App() {
  return (
    <Suspense fallback={<div>Loading...</div>}>
      <Routes>
        <Route path="/dashboard" element={<Dashboard /
>} />
        <Route path="/admin" element={<AdminPanel />} />
      </Routes>
    </Suspense>
  );
}
```

Route-Based Code Splitting

```
import { BrowserRouter, Routes, Route } from 'react-
router-dom';

function AppRouter() {
  return (
    <BrowserRouter>
      <Suspense fallback={<LoadingSpinner />}>
        <Routes>
          <Route
            path="/users"
            element={lazy(() => import('./
UserManagement'))}
          />
          <Route
            path="/products"
            element={lazy(() => import('./
ProductCatalog'))}
          />
        </Routes>
      </Suspense>
    </BrowserRouter>
  );
}
```

21.5 Lazy Loading Components

Dynamic Component Loading Strategies

```
function DynamicComponentLoader() {
  const [Component, setComponent] = useState(null);

  const loadComponent = async (componentName) => {
    switch(componentName) {
      case 'Chart':
        const { default: ChartComponent } = await
import('./ChartComponent');
        setComponent(() => ChartComponent);
        break;
      case 'Table':
        const { default: TableComponent } = await
import('./TableComponent');
        setComponent(() => TableComponent);
        break;
    }
  };

  return (
    <div>
      <button onClick={() => loadComponent('Chart')}>
        Load Chart
      </button>
      {Component && <Component />}
    </div>
  );
}
```

Conditional Rendering with Lazy Loading

```
function ConditionalLazyLoader() {
  const [activeModule, setActiveModule] = useState(null);

  const ModuleMap = {
    'analytics': lazy(() => import('./AnalyticsModule')),
    'reporting': lazy(() => import('./ReportingModule')),
    'dashboard': lazy(() => import('./DashboardModule'))
  };

  return (
    <Suspense fallback={<LoadingIndicator />}>
      {activeModule &&
React.createElement(ModuleMap[activeModule])}
    </Suspense>
  );
}
```

5 Strategic Tips

- Optimize render cycles by minimizing unnecessary component updates through precise memoization techniques.
- Implement intelligent code splitting strategies to reduce initial load times and improve application performance.
- Create modular, lazy-loadable components that enhance application scalability and responsiveness.
- Develop comprehensive performance monitoring mechanisms to identify and address rendering bottlenecks.
- Master dependency management in memoization hooks to prevent over-optimization and unnecessary computational overhead.

7 Actionable Strategies

- Construct a sophisticated performance profiling system for React applications.
- Implement intelligent lazy loading mechanisms across complex application architectures.

- Design modular component structures that maximize code reusability and performance.
- Create advanced memoization patterns that adapt to dynamic application states.
- Develop comprehensive performance optimization workflows.
- Establish robust error handling and fallback strategies for dynamically loaded components.
- Build scalable application architectures that prioritize runtime efficiency.

Chapter 22: Testing React Apps

22.1 Jest Basics

Understanding Jest as a Testing Framework

Jest stands as the premier testing framework for JavaScript and React applications, providing a comprehensive solution for writing and running tests with minimal configuration.

Setting Up Jest

```
npm install --save-dev jest @types/jest
```

Configuring Package.json

```
{
  "scripts": {
    "test": "jest",
    "test:watch": "jest --watch"
  }
}
```

Core Testing Concepts

Basic Test Structure

```
// mathFunctions.js
export function add(a, b) {
  return a + b;
}
```

```
// mathFunctions.test.js
import { add } from './mathFunctions';

describe('Math Functions', () => {
  test('adds two numbers correctly', () => {
    expect(add(2, 3)).toBe(5);
  });

  test('handles negative numbers', () => {
    expect(add(-1, -1)).toBe(-2);
  });
});
```

Advanced Jest Matchers

```
describe('Advanced Matchers', () => {
  test('object matching', () => {
    const data = { name: 'John', age: 30 };

    // Exact match
    expect(data).toEqual({ name: 'John', age: 30 });

    // Partial match
    expect(data).toMatchObject({ name: 'John' });

    // Specific property checks
    expect(data).toHaveProperty('name');
    expect(data).toHaveProperty('age', 30);
  });

  test('array operations', () => {
    const fruits = ['apple', 'banana', 'orange'];

    expect(fruits).toContain('banana');
    expect(fruits).toHaveLength(3);
  });
});
```

22.2 React Testing Library

Core Principles of React Testing Library

React Testing Library focuses on testing components from the user's perspective, prioritizing accessibility and realistic interaction scenarios.

Installation

```
npm install --save-dev @testing-library/react @testing-
library/jest-dom
```

Rendering and Querying Components

```
import React from 'react';
import { render, screen } from '@testing-library/react';
import UserProfile from './UserProfile';

describe('UserProfile Component', () => {
  test('renders user name', () => {
    const user = { name: 'John Doe', email:
'john@example.com' };

    render(<UserProfile user={user} />);

    // Different query methods
    const nameElement = screen.getByText('John Doe');
    const emailElement = screen.getByTestId('user-
email');

    expect(nameElement).toBeInTheDocument();

expect(emailElement).toHaveTextContent('john@example.com'
);
  });
});
```

User Interactions

```
import { render, screen, fireEvent } from '@testing-
library/react';
import Button from './Button';

describe('Button Component', () => {
  test('handles click events', () => {
    const mockClickHandler = jest.fn();

    render(<Button onClick={mockClickHandler}>Click Me</
Button>);

    const button = screen.getByText('Click Me');
    fireEvent.click(button);

    expect(mockClickHandler).toHaveBeenCalledTimes(1);
  });
});
```

22.3 Testing Components

Component Rendering Strategies

```
import React from 'react';
import { render, screen } from '@testing-library/react';
import ComplexComponent from './ComplexComponent';

describe('Complex Component Testing', () => {
  test('renders with different props', () => {
    const { rerender } = render(
      <ComplexComponent mode="view" />
    );

    // Initial render check
    expect(screen.getByTestId('view-
mode')).toBeInTheDocument();

    // Re-render with different props
    rerender(<ComplexComponent mode="edit" />);

    expect(screen.getByTestId('edit-
mode')).toBeInTheDocument();
  });

  test('handles conditional rendering', () => {
    render(<ComplexComponent isLoggedIn={true} />);

    expect(screen.getByTestId('logged-in-
content')).toBeInTheDocument();
    expect(screen.queryByTestId('login-
prompt')).not.toBeInTheDocument();
  });
});
```

Context and Provider Testing

```
import { render, screen } from '@testing-library/react';
import { ThemeProvider } from './ThemeContext';
import ThemedComponent from './ThemedComponent';

describe('Context-Based Testing', () => {
  test('renders with correct theme', () => {
    render(
      <ThemeProvider initialTheme="dark">
        <ThemedComponent />
      </ThemeProvider>
    );

    const componentElement = screen.getByTestId('themed-
component');
    expect(componentElement).toHaveClass('dark-theme');
  });
});
```

22.4 Mocking API Calls

Axios Mocking Techniques

```
import axios from 'axios';
import { render, screen, waitFor } from '@testing-
library/react';
import UserList from './UserList';

// Mock entire axios module
jest.mock('axios');

describe('API Call Testing', () => {
  test('fetches and displays users', async () => {
    const mockUsers = [
      { id: 1, name: 'John Doe' },
      { id: 2, name: 'Jane Smith' }
    ];

    // Setup mock implementation
    axios.get.mockResolvedValue({ data: mockUsers });

    render(<UserList />);

    // Wait for async operations
    await waitFor(() => {
      expect(screen.getByText('John
Doe')).toBeInTheDocument();
      expect(screen.getByText('Jane
Smith')).toBeInTheDocument();
    });
  });

  test('handles error scenarios', async () => {
    // Mock error response
    axios.get.mockRejectedValue(new Error('Network
Error'));

    render(<UserList />);

    await waitFor(() => {
      expect(screen.getByTestId('error-
message')).toBeInTheDocument();
    });
  });
});
```

Mock Service Worker for API Mocking

```
import { rest } from 'msw';
import { setupServer } from 'msw/node';
import { render, screen, waitFor } from '@testing-
library/react';
import ProductComponent from './ProductComponent';

const server = setupServer(
  rest.get('/api/products', (req, res, ctx) => {
    return res(ctx.json([
      { id: 1, name: 'Product 1' },
      { id: 2, name: 'Product 2' }
    ]));
  })
);

beforeAll(() => server.listen());
afterEach(() => server.resetHandlers());
afterAll(() => server.close());

describe('Product API Testing', () => {
  test('renders products from API', async () => {
    render(<ProductComponent />);

    await waitFor(() => {
      expect(screen.getByText('Product
1')).toBeInTheDocument();
      expect(screen.getByText('Product
2')).toBeInTheDocument();
    });
  });
});
```

22.5 Snapshot Testing

Implementing Snapshot Tests

```
import React from 'react';
import renderer from 'react-test-renderer';
import Button from './Button';

describe('Snapshot Testing', () => {
  test('Button renders correctly', () => {
    const tree = renderer
      .create(<Button primary>Click Me</Button>)
      .toJSON();

    expect(tree).toMatchSnapshot();
  });

  test('Button appearance changes', () => {
    const primaryButton = renderer
      .create(<Button primary>Primary</Button>)
      .toJSON();

    const secondaryButton = renderer
      .create(<Button>Secondary</Button>)
      .toJSON();

    expect(primaryButton).not.toEqual(secondaryButton);
  });
});
```

Dynamic Snapshot Testing

```
import React from 'react';
import renderer from 'react-test-renderer';
import UserCard from './UserCard';

describe('Dynamic Snapshot Testing', () => {
  const testCases = [
    {
      name: 'John Doe',
      role: 'Developer',
      active: true
    },
    {
      name: 'Jane Smith',
      role: 'Designer',
      active: false
    }
  ];

  testCases.forEach(user => {
    test(`renders ${user.name} correctly`, () => {
      const tree = renderer
        .create(<UserCard user={user} />)
        .toJSON();

      expect(tree).toMatchSnapshot();
    });
  });
});
```

5 Strategic Tips

- Construct comprehensive test suites that cover multiple scenarios and edge cases.
- Implement rigorous mocking strategies to isolate component behavior.
- Develop test-driven development practices that prioritize code quality.
- Create modular and reusable testing utilities across the application.
- Maintain high test coverage while focusing on meaningful and impactful tests.

7 Actionable Strategies

- Establish a robust testing infrastructure for React applications.
- Develop advanced mocking techniques for complex dependency scenarios.
- Create comprehensive test suites that validate critical application flows.
- Implement continuous integration testing workflows.
- Design performance-optimized testing strategies.
- Build adaptive testing frameworks that scale with application complexity.
- Construct intelligent test coverage measurement systems.

Chapter 23: Deploying React Apps

23.1 Building for Production

Understanding Production Builds

Creating a production build is the critical first step in deploying any React application. Production builds optimize your application for performance, reducing file sizes and improving load times. The process involves several key optimization techniques:

Minification and Compression

When you run the production build command, your React application undergoes a comprehensive optimization process:

```
npm run build
```

```
# or
```

```
yarn build
```

This command triggers several crucial transformations:

- JavaScript and CSS files get minified
- Unnecessary comments and whitespace are removed
- Code is compressed to reduce overall bundle size
- Static assets are optimized

Code Splitting and Lazy Loading

Production builds leverage advanced bundling techniques:

```
// Example of code splitting
import React, { lazy, Suspense } from 'react';

const DashboardComponent = lazy(() => import('./
DashboardComponent'));

function App() {
  return (
    <Suspense fallback={<div>Loading...</div>}>
      <DashboardComponent />
    </Suspense>
  );
}
```

This approach ensures that:

- Only necessary code is loaded initially
- Large components load on-demand
- Initial page load becomes significantly faster

Build Optimization Configurations

Typical `build` script in `package.json`:

```
{
  "scripts": {
    "build": "react-scripts build",
    "production": "NODE_ENV=production webpack --config
webpack.prod.js"
  }
}
```

Performance Auditing

Before deployment, run performance checks:

```
# Using Lighthouse CLI
npx lighthouse http://localhost:3000 --view
```

23.2 Deploying to Netlify

Netlify Deployment Workflow

Direct GitHub Integration

1. Connect your GitHub repository
2. Configure build settings:

```
# netlify.toml configuration
[build]
  command = "npm run build"
  publish = "build/"

[build.environment]
  NODE_VERSION = "16"
```

CLI Deployment Method

```
# Install Netlify CLI
npm install netlify-cli -g

# Login to Netlify
netlify login

# Deploy your project
netlify deploy
```

Continuous Deployment Setup

- Automatic builds on repository push
- Preview deployments for pull requests
- Custom domain configuration
- HTTPS SSL certificates

Netlify Build Configurations

Create a `netlify.toml` file in your project root:

```
[build]
  command = "npm run build"
  publish = "build"

[[redirects]]
  from = "/*"
  to = "/index.html"
  status = 200
```

23.3 Deploying to Vercel

Vercel Deployment Process

One-Click GitHub Deployment

- Connect GitHub/GitLab repository
- Automatic project detection
- Instant deployments

Vercel CLI Deployment

```
# Install Vercel CLI
npm i -g vercel

# Login to Vercel
vercel login

# Deploy project
vercel
```

Configuration File

Create `vercel.json`:

```json
{
  "version": 2,
  "builds": [
    {
      "src": "package.json",
      "use": "@vercel/static-build",
      "config": { "distDir": "build" }
    }
  ],
  "routes": [
    {
      "src": "/static/(.*)",
      "headers": {
        "cache-control": "v-max-age=31536000,immutable"
      }
    },
    {
      "src": "/(.*)",
      "dest": "/index.html"
    }
  ]
}
```

23.4 GitHub Pages Deployment

Setting Up GitHub Pages

Repository Configuration

1. Create GitHub repository
2. Configure GitHub Pages settings

```
# Install gh-pages package
npm install gh-pages --save-dev

# Update package.json
```

```
{
  "homepage": "https://yourusername.github.io/repository-name",
  "scripts": {
    "predeploy": "npm run build",
    "deploy": "gh-pages -d build"
  }
}
```

Deployment Command

```
npm run deploy
```

Custom Domain Configuration

- Add CNAME file in `public/` directory
- Configure DNS settings

23.5 Environment Variables

Managing Sensitive Configuration

Local Environment Setup

Create `.env` files:

```
# .env.development
REACT_APP_API_URL=http://localhost:3000/api


# .env.production
REACT_APP_API_URL=https://production-api.com/api
```

Secure Variable Injection

```
// Accessing environment variables
const apiUrl = process.env.REACT_APP_API_URL;

function fetchData() {
  return axios.get(apiUrl);
}
```

Netlify/Vercel Environment Variables

- Web interface configuration
- Secure secret management
- Different environments support

Security Best Practices

- Never commit `.env` files
- Use `.gitignore`
- Use environment-specific configurations
- Rotate access tokens regularly

Top 5 Deployment Tips

- Automate deployment workflows
- Implement comprehensive error tracking
- Optimize asset delivery
- Use CDN for static assets
- Monitor application performance post-deployment

7 Actionable Deployment Strategies

- Implement progressive deployment
- Use feature flags for controlled rollouts
- Set up comprehensive monitoring
- Create deployment pipelines
- Integrate automated testing
- Manage version control rigorously
- Develop rollback mechanisms

Chapter 24: React Hooks Deep Dive

24.1 useReducer

Understanding State Management with useReducer

Core Concepts of useReducer

The `useReducer` hook provides a powerful alternative to `useState` for managing complex state logic. It follows the Redux-like reducer pattern, offering more structured state management for intricate component states.

Basic Reducer Structure

```
function counterReducer(state, action) {
  switch (action.type) {
    case 'INCREMENT':
      return { count: state.count + 1 };
    case 'DECREMENT':
      return { count: state.count - 1 };
    case 'RESET':
      return { count: 0 };
    default:
      return state;
  }
}

function CounterComponent() {
  const [state, dispatch] = useReducer(counterReducer,
{ count: 0 });

  return (
    <div>
      <p>Count: {state.count}</p>
      <button onClick={() => dispatch({ type:
'INCREMENT' })}>
        Increment
      </button>
      <button onClick={() => dispatch({ type:
'DECREMENT' })}>
        Decrement
      </button>
      <button onClick={() => dispatch({ type: 'RESET' })}
>
        Reset
      </button>
    </div>
  );
}
```

Advanced useReducer Patterns

Complex State Management

```
// Todo List Reducer Example
function todoReducer(state, action) {
  switch (action.type) {
    case 'ADD_TODO':
      return {
        ...state,
        todos: [
          ...state.todos,
          {
            id: Date.now(),
            text: action.payload,
            completed: false
          }
        ]
      };
    case 'TOGGLE_TODO':
      return {
        ...state,
        todos: state.todos.map(todo =>
          todo.id === action.payload
            ? { ...todo, completed: !todo.completed }
            : todo
        )
      };
    case 'REMOVE_TODO':
      return {
        ...state,
        todos: state.todos.filter(todo => todo.id !==
action.payload)
      };
    default:
      return state;
  }
}

function TodoListComponent() {
  const [state, dispatch] = useReducer(todoReducer, {
    todos: [],
    filter: 'all'
  });

  const addTodo = (text) => {
```

24.2 useLayoutEffect

Synchronous Effect Rendering

Comparison with useEffect

`useLayoutEffect` operates synchronously after all DOM mutations, before the browser repaints the screen. This makes it crucial for scenarios requiring precise DOM measurements or synchronous updates.

Practical Implementation

```
function MeasureComponent() {
  const [height, setHeight] = useState(0);
  const ref = useRef(null);

  useLayoutEffect(() => {
    const measuredHeight = ref.current.clientHeight;
    setHeight(measuredHeight);
  }, []);

  return (
    <div ref={ref}>
      <p>Component Height: {height}px</p>
    </div>
  );
}
```

Performance Considerations

- Use sparingly, as it blocks visual updates
- Prefer `useEffect` for most scenarios
- Critical for precise DOM manipulations

Advanced Synchronization

```
function AnimatedComponent() {
  const [position, setPosition] = useState({ x: 0, y:
0 });
  const elementRef = useRef(null);

  useLayoutEffect(() => {
    const handleResize = () => {
      const element = elementRef.current;
      const rect = element.getBoundingClientRect();
      setPosition({
        x: rect.left,
        y: rect.top
      });
    };

    handleResize();
    window.addEventListener('resize', handleResize);
    return () => window.removeEventListener('resize',
handleResize);
  }, []);

  return (
    <div
      ref={elementRef}
      style={{
        position: 'absolute',
        left: `${position.x}px`,
        top: `${position.y}px`
      }}
    >
      Positioned Element
    </div>
  );
}
```

24.3 useImperativeHandle

Customizing Imperative Methods

Component Reference Customization

`useImperativeHandle` allows fine-grained control over the methods exposed to parent components through refs.

Implementation Example

```
function CustomInput(props, ref) {
  const inputRef = useRef(null);

  useImperativeHandle(ref, () => ({
    focus: () => {
      inputRef.current.focus();
      inputRef.current.select();
    },
    clear: () => {
      inputRef.current.value = '';
    },
    getValue: () => inputRef.current.value
  }));

  return <input ref={inputRef} {...props} />;
}

const ForwardedInput = forwardRef(CustomInput);

function ParentComponent() {
  const inputRef = useRef(null);

  const handleAction = () => {
    inputRef.current.focus();
    console.log(inputRef.current.getValue());
  };

  return (
    <div>
      <ForwardedInput ref={inputRef} />
      <button onClick={handleAction}>
        Focus and Log Input
      </button>
    </div>
  );
}
```

Advanced Reference Techniques

- Limit exposed methods
- Maintain component encapsulation
- Provide clear, specific interfaces

24.4 useDebugValue

Custom Hook Debugging

Development Tools Integration

`useDebugValue` enhances React DevTools by providing custom labels for custom hooks.

Practical Implementation

```
function useCustomTimer(initialTime = 0) {
  const [time, setTime] = useState(initialTime);

  useDebugValue(time, time => `Timer: ${time} seconds`);

  useEffect(() => {
    const timer = setInterval(() => {
      setTime(prevTime => prevTime + 1);
    }, 1000);

    return () => clearInterval(timer);
  }, []);

  return time;
}

function TimerComponent() {
  const elapsedTime = useCustomTimer();
  return <div>Elapsed: {elapsedTime} seconds</div>;
}
```

Debugging Best Practices

- Use for complex custom hooks
- Provide meaningful debug information
- Optimize for development environments

24.5 Rules of Hooks Recap

Fundamental Hook Guidelines

Hook Usage Rules

1. **Call Hooks at Top Level**
    - Never call hooks inside loops
    - Avoid conditional hook calls
    - Place hooks directly in function component body

```
// Correct Hook Usage
function UserProfile() {
  // Hooks called at top level
  const [user, setUser] = useState(null);
  const [loading, setLoading] = useState(true);

  useEffect(() => {
    // Effect logic
  }, []);

  // Render logic
}

// Incorrect Usage
function BadComponent() {
  if (someCondition) {
    // DO NOT do this
    const [state] = useState();
  }
}
```

2. **Only Call Hooks from React Functions**
    - Use hooks in functional components
    - Use hooks in custom hooks
    - Never use hooks in regular JavaScript functions

Hook Composition Patterns

Custom Hook Creation

```
// Composing Multiple Hooks
function useUserData() {
  const [user, setUser] = useState(null);
  const [loading, setLoading] = useState(true);

  useEffect(() => {
    fetchUserData()
      .then(data => {
        setUser(data);
        setLoading(false);
      });
  }, []);

  return { user, loading };
}
```

Top 5 Hooks Optimization Tips

- Minimize re-renders with memoization
- Use custom hooks for reusable logic
- Understand hook dependency arrays
- Avoid unnecessary effect dependencies
- Profile and optimize complex hook interactions

7 Actionable Hooks Strategies

- Implement precise memoization techniques
- Create modular, reusable custom hooks
- Leverage useReducer for complex states
- Optimize performance with useMemo and useCallback
- Design clean, predictable state management
- Minimize side effects in hooks
- Implement comprehensive error handling

Chapter 25: State Management with Redux

25.1 What is Redux?

Understanding State Management Challenges

The Problem of Complex State

Modern web applications often struggle with state management as applications grow in complexity. Tracking state across multiple components becomes increasingly difficult, leading to:

- Prop drilling
- Inconsistent state updates
- Difficult-to-trace data flows

Redux: Centralized State Solution

Core Principles of Redux

Redux introduces a predictable state container for JavaScript applications, solving complex state management problems through:

- Single source of truth
- Read-only state
- Changes made through pure functions

Redux Architecture Breakdown

```
// Visualization of Redux Flow
const reduxArchitecture = {
  components: "React UI",
  actions: "Describe State Changes",
  reducers: "Update State",
  store: "Centralized State Container"
};
```

Historical Context

Redux emerged from Facebook's Flux architecture, providing a more streamlined approach to managing application state.

25.2 Redux Store, Actions, Reducers

Creating a Redux Store

Store Configuration

```
import { createStore } from 'redux';

// Initial State Structure
const initialState = {
  users: [],
  loading: false,
  error: null
};

// Reducer Function
function rootReducer(state = initialState, action) {
  switch (action.type) {
    case 'FETCH_USERS_START':
      return {
        ...state,
        loading: true
      };
    case 'FETCH_USERS_SUCCESS':
      return {
        ...state,
        loading: false,
        users: action.payload
      };
    case 'FETCH_USERS_FAILURE':
      return {
        ...state,
        loading: false,
        error: action.payload
      };
    default:
      return state;
  }
}

// Create Redux Store
const store = createStore(rootReducer);
```

Actions in Depth

Action Creators

```
// Action Creators
function fetchUsersStart() {
  return {
    type: 'FETCH_USERS_START'
  };
}

function fetchUsersSuccess(users) {
  return {
    type: 'FETCH_USERS_SUCCESS',
    payload: users
  };
}

function fetchUsersFailure(error) {
  return {
    type: 'FETCH_USERS_FAILURE',
    payload: error
  };
}

// Async Action with Thunk
function fetchUsers() {
  return async (dispatch) => {
    dispatch(fetchUsersStart());
    try {
      const response = await fetch('/api/users');
      const users = await response.json();
      dispatch(fetchUsersSuccess(users));
    } catch (error) {
      dispatch(fetchUsersFailure(error.message));
    }
  };
}
```

Reducer Principles

- Pure functions
- No side effects
- Immutable state updates

25.3 useSelector & useDispatch

React-Redux Hooks

Connecting Components

```
import { useSelector, useDispatch } from 'react-redux';

function UserList() {
  // Select state from store
  const users = useSelector(state => state.users);
  const loading = useSelector(state => state.loading);
  const error = useSelector(state => state.error);

  // Dispatch actions
  const dispatch = useDispatch();

  useEffect(() => {
    dispatch(fetchUsers());
  }, [dispatch]);

  if (loading) return <div>Loading...</div>;
  if (error) return <div>Error: {error}</div>;

  return (
    <ul>
      {users.map(user => (
        <li key={user.id}>{user.name}</li>
      ))}
    </ul>
  );
}
```

Advanced Selector Techniques

```
// Memoized Selectors with Reselect
import { createSelector } from 'reselect';

const getUserState = state => state.users;

const getActiveUsers = createSelector(
  [getUserState],
  (users) => users.filter(user => user.isActive)
);
```

25.4 Redux Toolkit

Simplifying Redux Setup

Toolkit Configuration

```
import { configureStore, createSlice } from '@reduxjs/
toolkit';

// User Slice
const userSlice = createSlice({
  name: 'users',
  initialState: {
    list: [],
    loading: false,
    error: null
  },
  reducers: {
    fetchUsersStart: (state) => {
      state.loading = true;
    },
    fetchUsersSuccess: (state, action) => {
      state.loading = false;
      state.list = action.payload;
    },
    fetchUsersFailure: (state, action) => {
      state.loading = false;
      state.error = action.payload;
    }
  }
});

// Create Store
const store = configureStore({
  reducer: {
    users: userSlice.reducer
  }
});

// Export Actions
export const {
  fetchUsersStart,
  fetchUsersSuccess,
  fetchUsersFailure
} = userSlice.actions;
```

Async Thunks

```
import { createAsyncThunk } from '@reduxjs/toolkit';

const fetchUsers = createAsyncThunk(
  'users/fetchUsers',
  async (_, { rejectWithValue }) => {
    try {
      const response = await fetch('/api/users');
      const data = await response.json();
      return data;
    } catch (error) {
      return rejectWithValue(error.response.data);
    }
  }
);
```

25.5 When to Use Redux

State Management Decision Matrix

Complexity Indicators

Scenarios ideal for Redux:

- Global state shared across multiple components
- Complex state logic
- Frequent state updates
- Need for time-travel debugging
- Large-scale applications

1. Global State Shared Across Multiple Components

When your application has state that needs to be accessed by many components across different parts of your component tree, Redux provides a centralized store that eliminates prop drilling.

Example: E-commerce Shopping Cart

```
// store/cartSlice.js
```

```
import { createSlice } from '@reduxjs/toolkit';

export const cartSlice = createSlice({
  name: 'cart',
  initialState: {
    items: [],
    totalQuantity: 0,
    totalAmount: 0
  },
  reducers: {
    addItemToCart(state, action) {
      const newItem = action.payload;
      const existingItem = state.items.find(item =>
item.id === newItem.id);

      if (!existingItem) {
        state.items.push({
          id: newItem.id,
          price: newItem.price,
          quantity: 1,
          totalPrice: newItem.price,
          name: newItem.title
        });
      } else {
        existingItem.quantity++;
        existingItem.totalPrice = existingItem.totalPrice
+ newItem.price;
      }
      state.totalQuantity++;
      state.totalAmount = state.totalAmount +
newItem.price;
    },
    removeItemFromCart(state, action) {
      const id = action.payload;
      const existingItem = state.items.find(item =>
item.id === id);

      if (existingItem.quantity === 1) {
        state.items = state.items.filter(item => item.id !
== id);
      } else {
        existingItem.quantity--;
```

```
        existingItem.totalPrice = existingItem.totalPrice
- existingItem.price;
      }
      state.totalQuantity--;
      state.totalAmount = state.totalAmount -
existingItem.price;
    }
  }
});

export const { addItemToCart, removeItemFromCart } =
cartSlice.actions;
export default cartSlice.reducer;

// store/index.js
import { configureStore } from '@reduxjs/toolkit';
import cartReducer from './cartSlice';

const store = configureStore({
  reducer: {
    cart: cartReducer
  }
});

export default store;

// ProductItem.js - Can add items to cart
import React from 'react';
import { useDispatch } from 'react-redux';
import { addItemToCart } from '../store/cartSlice';

const ProductItem = ({ id, title, price, description }) =>
{
  const dispatch = useDispatch();

  const addToCartHandler = () => {
    dispatch(addItemToCart({
      id,
      title,
      price
    }));
  };
```

```
  return (
    <div className="product-item">
      <h3>{title}</h3>
      <p>${price.toFixed(2)}</p>
      <p>{description}</p>
      <button onClick={addToCartHandler}>Add to Cart</
button>
    </div>
  );
};

export default ProductItem;

// CartIcon.js - Shows cart quantity in header
import React from 'react';
import { useSelector } from 'react-redux';

const CartIcon = () => {
  const cartQuantity = useSelector(state =>
state.cart.totalQuantity);

  return (
    <div className="cart-icon">
      <span>🛒</span>
      <span className="badge">{cartQuantity}</span>
    </div>
  );
};

export default CartIcon;

// CartPage.js - Full cart details on a separate page
import React from 'react';
import { useSelector, useDispatch } from 'react-redux';
import { addItemToCart, removeItemFromCart } from '../
store/cartSlice';

const CartPage = () => {
  const dispatch = useDispatch();
  const cartItems = useSelector(state =>
```

```
state.cart.items);
  const totalAmount = useSelector(state =>
state.cart.totalAmount);

  const incrementItemHandler = (item) => {
    dispatch(addItemToCart(item));
  };

  const decrementItemHandler = (id) => {
    dispatch(removeItemFromCart(id));
  };

  return (
    <div className="cart">
      <h2>Your Shopping Cart</h2>
      <ul>
        {cartItems.map(item => (
          <li key={item.id}>
            <div>
              <h3>{item.name}</h3>
              <div>
                <span>${item.price.toFixed(2)} x
{item.quantity}</span>
              </div>
            </div>
            <div>
              <button onClick={() =>
decrementItemHandler(item.id)}>-</button>
              <span>{item.quantity}</span>
              <button onClick={() =>
incrementItemHandler({
                id: item.id,
                title: item.name,
                price: item.price
              })}>+</button>
            </div>
          </li>
        ))}
      </ul>
      <div>
        <span>Total Amount: ${totalAmount.toFixed(2)}</
span>
```

```
      </div>
    </div>
  );
};

export default CartPage;

// App.js
import React from 'react';
import { Provider } from 'react-redux';
import store from './store';
import Header from './components/Header';
import ProductsList from './components/ProductsList';
import CartPage from './components/CartPage';

const App = () => {
  return (
    <Provider store={store}>
      <Header />
      <main>
        <ProductsList />
        <CartPage />
      </main>
    </Provider>
  );
};

export default App;
```

In this example, the shopping cart state is accessed and modified from multiple components:

- ProductItem components can add items to the cart
- CartIcon shows the total quantity in the header
- CartPage displays and modifies the full cart contents

Without Redux, you would need to lift state up to a common ancestor and pass it down through props, which becomes unwieldy in larger applications.

2. Complex State Logic

When your application has complex state transitions, business logic, or validation requirements, Redux helps to centralize and organize this logic.

Example: Multi-step Form with Validation and Dependencies

```
// store/formSlice.js
import { createSlice } from '@reduxjs/toolkit';

export const formSlice = createSlice({
  name: 'form',
  initialState: {
    currentStep: 1,
    totalSteps: 3,
    formData: {
      personalInfo: {
        firstName: '',
        lastName: '',
        email: '',
        isValid: false,
      },
      addressInfo: {
        street: '',
        city: '',
        state: '',
        zipCode: '',
        isValid: false,
      },
      paymentInfo: {
        cardType: '',
        cardNumber: '',
        cvv: '',
        expiryDate: '',
        isValid: false,
      }
    },
    formCompleted: false,
    submitting: false,
    submitError: null
  },
  reducers: {
    updatePersonalInfo(state, action) {
      state.formData.personalInfo = {
        ...state.formData.personalInfo,
        ...action.payload
      };
```

```
      // Validate personal info
      const { firstName, lastName, email } =
state.formData.personalInfo;
      const emailRegex = /^[^\s@]+@[^\s@]+\.[^\s@]+$/;
      state.formData.personalInfo.isValid =
        firstName.trim().length > 0 &&
        lastName.trim().length > 0 &&
        emailRegex.test(email);
    },
    updateAddressInfo(state, action) {
      state.formData.addressInfo = {
        ...state.formData.addressInfo,
        ...action.payload
      };

      // Validate address info
      const { street, city, state, zipCode } =
state.formData.addressInfo;
      const zipRegex = /^\d{5}(-\d{4})?$/;
      state.formData.addressInfo.isValid =
        street.trim().length > 0 &&
        city.trim().length > 0 &&
        state.trim().length > 0 &&
        zipRegex.test(zipCode);
    },
    updatePaymentInfo(state, action) {
      state.formData.paymentInfo = {
        ...state.formData.paymentInfo,
        ...action.payload
      };

      // Validate payment info based on card type
      const { cardType, cardNumber, cvv, expiryDate } =
state.formData.paymentInfo;
      let cardNumberRegex;

      switch(cardType) {
        case 'visa':
          cardNumberRegex = /^4[0-9]{12}(?:[0-9]{3})?$/;
          break;
        case 'mastercard':
```

```
          cardNumberRegex = /^5[1-5][0-9]{14}$/;
          break;
        case 'amex':
          cardNumberRegex = /^3[47][0-9]{13}$/;
          break;
        default:
          cardNumberRegex = /^[0-9]{13,19}$/;
      }

      const cvvRegex = cardType === 'amex' ? /^[0-9]
{4}$/ : /^[0-9]{3}$/;
      const expiryRegex = /^(0[1-9]|1[0-2])\/[0-9]{2}$/;

      state.formData.paymentInfo.isValid =
        cardType.trim().length > 0 &&
        cardNumberRegex.test(cardNumber) &&
        cvvRegex.test(cvv) &&
        expiryRegex.test(expiryDate);
    },
    goToNextStep(state) {
      if (state.currentStep < state.totalSteps) {
        state.currentStep += 1;
      }
    },
    goToPreviousStep(state) {
      if (state.currentStep > 1) {
        state.currentStep -= 1;
      }
    },
    submitForm(state) {
      state.submitting = true;
      state.submitError = null;
    },
    submitFormSuccess(state) {
      state.formCompleted = true;
      state.submitting = false;
    },
    submitFormFailure(state, action) {
      state.submitting = false;
      state.submitError = action.payload;
    }
  }
```

```
});

export const {
  updatePersonalInfo,
  updateAddressInfo,
  updatePaymentInfo,
  goToNextStep,
  goToPreviousStep,
  submitForm,
  submitFormSuccess,
  submitFormFailure
} = formSlice.actions;

export default formSlice.reducer;

// store/formThunks.js
import {
  submitForm,
  submitFormSuccess,
  submitFormFailure
} from './formSlice';

export const submitFormData = (formData) => async
(dispatch) => {
  dispatch(submitForm());

  try {
    // Simulate API call
    await new Promise(resolve => setTimeout(resolve,
1500));

    // Check if all sections are valid before submission
    if (!formData.personalInfo.isValid ||
        !formData.addressInfo.isValid ||
        !formData.paymentInfo.isValid) {
      throw new Error("Please complete all required fields
correctly.");
    }

    // Simulate successful submission
    dispatch(submitFormSuccess());
    return { success: true };
```

```
  } catch (error) {
    dispatch(submitFormFailure(error.message));
    return { success: false, error: error.message };
  }
};

// Components using the complex state logic
// PersonalInfoStep.js
import React from 'react';
import { useSelector, useDispatch } from 'react-redux';
import { updatePersonalInfo, goToNextStep } from '../
store/formSlice';

const PersonalInfoStep = () => {
  const dispatch = useDispatch();
  const { firstName, lastName, email, isValid } =
useSelector(
    state => state.form.formData.personalInfo
  );

  const handleInputChange = (e) => {
    const { name, value } = e.target;
    dispatch(updatePersonalInfo({ [name]: value }));
  };

  const handleNext = () => {
    if (isValid) {
      dispatch(goToNextStep());
    }
  };

  return (
    <div className="form-step">
      <h2>Personal Information</h2>
      <div className="form-group">
        <label htmlFor="firstName">First Name:</label>
        <input
          type="text"
          id="firstName"
          name="firstName"
          value={firstName}
          onChange={handleInputChange}
```

```
        />
      </div>
      <div className="form-group">
        <label htmlFor="lastName">Last Name:</label>
        <input
          type="text"
          id="lastName"
          name="lastName"
          value={lastName}
          onChange={handleInputChange}
        />
      </div>
      <div className="form-group">
        <label htmlFor="email">Email:</label>
        <input
          type="email"
          id="email"
          name="email"
          value={email}
          onChange={handleInputChange}
        />
      </div>
      <button
        onClick={handleNext}
        disabled={!isValid}
      >
        Next
      </button>
    </div>
  );
};

// FormContainer.js
import React from 'react';
import { useSelector, useDispatch } from 'react-redux';
import { submitFormData } from '../store/formThunks';
import PersonalInfoStep from './PersonalInfoStep';
import AddressInfoStep from './AddressInfoStep';
import PaymentInfoStep from './PaymentInfoStep';
import FormSuccess from './FormSuccess';

const FormContainer = () => {
```

```
  const dispatch = useDispatch();
  const {
    currentStep,
    formData,
    formCompleted,
    submitting,
    submitError
  } = useSelector(state => state.form);

  const handleSubmit = () => {
    dispatch(submitFormData(formData));
  };

  if (formCompleted) {
    return <FormSuccess />;
  }

  const renderCurrentStep = () => {
    switch (currentStep) {
      case 1:
        return <PersonalInfoStep />;
      case 2:
        return <AddressInfoStep />;
      case 3:
        return <PaymentInfoStep onSubmit={handleSubmit} /
>;
      default:
        return <PersonalInfoStep />;
    }
  };

  return (
    <div className="form-container">
      <div className="progress-bar">
        <div className="steps">
          <div className={`step ${currentStep >= 1 ?
'active' : ''}`}>
            Personal Info
          </div>
          <div className={`step ${currentStep >= 2 ?
'active' : ''}`}>
            Address
```

```
          </div>
          <div className={`step ${currentStep >= 3 ?
'active' : ''}`}>
            Payment
          </div>
        </div>
      </div>

      {renderCurrentStep()}

      {submitting && <div
className="loader">Processing...</div>}
      {submitError && <div className="error">{submitError}
</div>}
    </div>
  );
};

export default FormContainer;
```

This example demonstrates complex state logic handling:

- Multi-step form with validation for each step
- Dependencies between form sections
- Complex validation rules
- Form submission with error handling
- State-based UI rendering

Redux helps manage this complexity by providing a centralized location for state and business logic.

3. Frequent State Updates

When your application requires frequent state updates, especially at different rates or from different sources, Redux provides an optimized way to handle these changes.

Example: Real-time Dashboard with Multiple Data Sources

```
// store/dashboardSlice.js
import { createSlice } from '@reduxjs/toolkit';

export const dashboardSlice = createSlice({
  name: 'dashboard',
  initialState: {
```

```
    userMetrics: {
      activeUsers: 0,
      newSignups: 0,
      conversionRate: 0,
      lastUpdated: null,
      loading: false,
      error: null
    },
    systemMetrics: {
      cpuUsage: 0,
      memoryUsage: 0,
      networkTraffic: 0,
      lastUpdated: null,
      loading: false,
      error: null
    },
    salesMetrics: {
      dailySales: 0,
      totalRevenue: 0,
      averageOrderValue: 0,
      lastUpdated: null,
      loading: false,
      error: null
    },
    refreshIntervals: {
      userMetrics: 30000, // 30 seconds
      systemMetrics: 5000, // 5 seconds
      salesMetrics: 60000  // 1 minute
    }
  },
  reducers: {
    fetchUserMetricsStart(state) {
      state.userMetrics.loading = true;
      state.userMetrics.error = null;
    },
    fetchUserMetricsSuccess(state, action) {
      state.userMetrics = {
        ...state.userMetrics,
        ...action.payload,
        lastUpdated: new Date().toISOString(),
        loading: false,
        error: null
```

```
    };
  },
  fetchUserMetricsFailure(state, action) {
    state.userMetrics.loading = false;
    state.userMetrics.error = action.payload;
  },
  fetchSystemMetricsStart(state) {
    state.systemMetrics.loading = true;
    state.systemMetrics.error = null;
  },
  fetchSystemMetricsSuccess(state, action) {
    state.systemMetrics = {
      ...state.systemMetrics,
      ...action.payload,
      lastUpdated: new Date().toISOString(),
      loading: false,
      error: null
    };
  },
  fetchSystemMetricsFailure(state, action) {
    state.systemMetrics.loading = false;
    state.systemMetrics.error = action.payload;
  },
  fetchSalesMetricsStart(state) {
    state.salesMetrics.loading = true;
    state.salesMetrics.error = null;
  },
  fetchSalesMetricsSuccess(state, action) {
    state.salesMetrics = {
      ...state.salesMetrics,
      ...action.payload,
      lastUpdated: new Date().toISOString(),
      loading: false,
      error: null
    };
  },
  fetchSalesMetricsFailure(state, action) {
    state.salesMetrics.loading = false;
    state.salesMetrics.error = action.payload;
  },
  updateRefreshInterval(state, action) {
    const { metricType, interval } = action.payload;
```

```
      state.refreshIntervals[metricType] = interval;
    }
  }
});

export const {
  fetchUserMetricsStart,
  fetchUserMetricsSuccess,
  fetchUserMetricsFailure,
  fetchSystemMetricsStart,
  fetchSystemMetricsSuccess,
  fetchSystemMetricsFailure,
  fetchSalesMetricsStart,
  fetchSalesMetricsSuccess,
  fetchSalesMetricsFailure,
  updateRefreshInterval
} = dashboardSlice.actions;

export default dashboardSlice.reducer;

// store/dashboardThunks.js
import {
  fetchUserMetricsStart,
  fetchUserMetricsSuccess,
  fetchUserMetricsFailure,
  fetchSystemMetricsStart,
  fetchSystemMetricsSuccess,
  fetchSystemMetricsFailure,
  fetchSalesMetricsStart,
  fetchSalesMetricsSuccess,
  fetchSalesMetricsFailure
} from './dashboardSlice';

// User metrics thunk
export const fetchUserMetrics = () => async (dispatch) =>
{
  dispatch(fetchUserMetricsStart());

  try {
    // Simulate API call
    const response = await fetch('/api/metrics/users');
    const data = await response.json();
```

```
    dispatch(fetchUserMetricsSuccess({
      activeUsers: data.activeUsers,
      newSignups: data.newSignups,
      conversionRate: data.conversionRate
    }));
  } catch (error) {
    dispatch(fetchUserMetricsFailure(error.message));
  }
};

// System metrics thunk
export const fetchSystemMetrics = () => async (dispatch)
=> {
  dispatch(fetchSystemMetricsStart());

  try {
    // Simulate API call
    const response = await fetch('/api/metrics/system');
    const data = await response.json();

    dispatch(fetchSystemMetricsSuccess({
      cpuUsage: data.cpuUsage,
      memoryUsage: data.memoryUsage,
      networkTraffic: data.networkTraffic
    }));
  } catch (error) {
    dispatch(fetchSystemMetricsFailure(error.message));
  }
};

// Sales metrics thunk
export const fetchSalesMetrics = () => async (dispatch) =>
{
  dispatch(fetchSalesMetricsStart());

  try {
    // Simulate API call
    const response = await fetch('/api/metrics/sales');
    const data = await response.json();

    dispatch(fetchSalesMetricsSuccess({
```

```
      dailySales: data.dailySales,
      totalRevenue: data.totalRevenue,
      averageOrderValue: data.averageOrderValue
    }));
  } catch (error) {
    dispatch(fetchSalesMetricsFailure(error.message));
  }
};

// Dashboard.js - Main component
import React, { useEffect, useRef } from 'react';
import { useSelector, useDispatch } from 'react-redux';
import {
  fetchUserMetrics,
  fetchSystemMetrics,
  fetchSalesMetrics
} from '../store/dashboardThunks';
import { updateRefreshInterval } from '../store/
dashboardSlice';
import UserMetricsPanel from './UserMetricsPanel';
import SystemMetricsPanel from './SystemMetricsPanel';
import SalesMetricsPanel from './SalesMetricsPanel';

const Dashboard = () => {
  const dispatch = useDispatch();
  const refreshIntervals = useSelector(state =>
state.dashboard.refreshIntervals);

  // References to store interval IDs
  const userMetricsIntervalRef = useRef(null);
  const systemMetricsIntervalRef = useRef(null);
  const salesMetricsIntervalRef = useRef(null);

  // Setup refresh intervals
  useEffect(() => {
    // Initial fetch
    dispatch(fetchUserMetrics());
    dispatch(fetchSystemMetrics());
    dispatch(fetchSalesMetrics());

    // Setup intervals
    userMetricsIntervalRef.current = setInterval(() => {
```

```
      dispatch(fetchUserMetrics());
    }, refreshIntervals.userMetrics);

    systemMetricsIntervalRef.current = setInterval(() => {
      dispatch(fetchSystemMetrics());
    }, refreshIntervals.systemMetrics);

    salesMetricsIntervalRef.current = setInterval(() => {
      dispatch(fetchSalesMetrics());
    }, refreshIntervals.salesMetrics);

    // Cleanup
    return () => {
      clearInterval(userMetricsIntervalRef.current);
      clearInterval(systemMetricsIntervalRef.current);
      clearInterval(salesMetricsIntervalRef.current);
    };
  }, [dispatch, refreshIntervals]);

  const handleIntervalChange = (metricType, newInterval)
=> {
    dispatch(updateRefreshInterval({ metricType, interval:
newInterval }));

    // Reset the corresponding interval
    if (metricType === 'userMetrics') {
      clearInterval(userMetricsIntervalRef.current);
      userMetricsIntervalRef.current = setInterval(() => {
        dispatch(fetchUserMetrics());
      }, newInterval);
    } else if (metricType === 'systemMetrics') {
      clearInterval(systemMetricsIntervalRef.current);
      systemMetricsIntervalRef.current = setInterval(() =>
{
        dispatch(fetchSystemMetrics());
      }, newInterval);
    } else if (metricType === 'salesMetrics') {
      clearInterval(salesMetricsIntervalRef.current);
      salesMetricsIntervalRef.current = setInterval(() =>
{
        dispatch(fetchSalesMetrics());
      }, newInterval);
```

```
    }
  };

  return (
    <div className="dashboard">
      <h1>Real-time Dashboard</h1>

      <div className="dashboard-grid">
        <UserMetricsPanel
          refreshInterval={refreshIntervals.userMetrics}
          onIntervalChange={(newInterval) =>
handleIntervalChange('userMetrics', newInterval)}
        />

        <SystemMetricsPanel
          refreshInterval={refreshIntervals.systemMetrics}
          onIntervalChange={(newInterval) =>
handleIntervalChange('systemMetrics', newInterval)}
        />

        <SalesMetricsPanel
          refreshInterval={refreshIntervals.salesMetrics}
          onIntervalChange={(newInterval) =>
handleIntervalChange('salesMetrics', newInterval)}
        />
      </div>
    </div>
  );
};

export default Dashboard;

// UserMetricsPanel.js - Component for displaying user
metrics
import React from 'react';
import { useSelector } from 'react-redux';

const UserMetricsPanel = ({ refreshInterval,
onIntervalChange }) => {
  const { activeUsers, newSignups, conversionRate,
lastUpdated, loading, error } =
    useSelector(state => state.dashboard.userMetrics);
```

```
  return (
    <div className="dashboard-panel">
      <div className="panel-header">
        <h2>User Metrics</h2>
        <div className="refresh-controls">
          <select
            value={refreshInterval}
            onChange={(e) =>
onIntervalChange(parseInt(e.target.value))}
          >
            <option value={5000}>5 seconds</option>
            <option value={10000}>10 seconds</option>
            <option value={30000}>30 seconds</option>
            <option value={60000}>1 minute</option>
          </select>
          {lastUpdated && (
            <div className="last-updated">
              Last updated: {new
Date(lastUpdated).toLocaleTimeString()}
            </div>
          )}
        </div>
      </div>

      {loading ? (
        <div className="loading">Loading...</div>
      ) : error ? (
        <div className="error">{error}</div>
      ) : (
        <div className="metrics-content">
          <div className="metric">
            <h3>Active Users</h3>
            <div className="metric-value">{activeUsers}</
div>
          </div>
          <div className="metric">
            <h3>New Signups</h3>
            <div className="metric-value">{newSignups}</
div>
          </div>
          <div className="metric">
```

```
            <h3>Conversion Rate</h3>
            <div className="metric-value">{conversionRate}
%</div>
          </div>
        </div>
      )}
    </div>
  );
};

export default UserMetricsPanel;
```

This example demonstrates handling frequent state updates:

- Multiple data sources updating at different intervals
- Configurable refresh rates for each data source
- Loading and error states for each data source
- Timestamp tracking for last updates
- Clean interval management with useEffect

Redux helps manage these concurrent data flows by providing a centralized store and predictable state transitions.

4. Need for Time-Travel Debugging

One of Redux's most powerful features is the ability to track state changes over time, which enables time-travel debugging.

Example: To-Do Application with Undo/Redo Functionality

```
// store/todoSlice.js
import { createSlice } from '@reduxjs/toolkit';

const todoSlice = createSlice({
  name: 'todos',
  initialState: {
    items: [],
    history: {
      past: [],
      future: []
    },
    filter: 'all' // 'all', 'active', 'completed'
  },
  reducers: {
```

```
    addTodo: (state, action) => {
      // Save current state to history
      state.history.past.push({
        items: [...state.items],
        filter: state.filter
      });
      state.history.future = []; // Clear future when new
action occurs

      // Add new todo
      state.items.push({
        id: Date.now(),
        text: action.payload,
        completed: false
      });
    },
    toggleTodo: (state, action) => {
      // Save current state to history
      state.history.past.push({
        items: [...state.items],
        filter: state.filter
      });
      state.history.future = []; // Clear future when new
action occurs

      // Toggle todo completion status
      const todo = state.items.find(todo => todo.id ===
action.payload);
      if (todo) {
        todo.completed = !todo.completed;
      }
    },
    deleteTodo: (state, action) => {
      // Save current state to history
      state.history.past.push({
        items: [...state.items],
        filter: state.filter
      });
      state.history.future = []; // Clear future when new
action occurs

      // Delete todo
```

```
      state.items = state.items.filter(todo => todo.id !==
action.payload);
    },
    setFilter: (state, action) => {
      state.filter = action.payload;
    },
    undo: (state) => {
      if (state.history.past.length > 0) {
        // Get the last state from history
        const lastState =
state.history.past[state.history.past.length - 1];

        // Save current state to future
        state.history.future.unshift({
          items: [...state.items],
          filter: state.filter
        });

        // Restore items and filter from past state
        state.items = lastState.items;
        state.filter = lastState.filter;

        // Remove the used state from past
        state.history.past.pop();
      }
    },
    redo: (state) => {
      if (state.history.future.length > 0) {
        // Get the next state from future
        const nextState = state.history.future[0];

        // Save current state to past
        state.history.past.push({
          items: [...state.items],
          filter: state.filter
        });

        // Restore items and filter from future state
        state.items = nextState.items;
        state.filter = nextState.filter;

        // Remove the used state from future
```

```
        state.history.future.shift();
      }
    }
  }
});

export const {
  addTodo,
  toggleTodo,
  deleteTodo,
  setFilter,
  undo,
  redo
} = todoSlice.actions;

export default todoSlice.reducer;

// TodoApp.js
import React, { useState } from 'react';
import { useSelector, useDispatch } from 'react-redux';
import {
  addTodo,
  toggleTodo,
  deleteTodo,
  setFilter,
  undo,
  redo
} from '../store/todoSlice';

const TodoApp = () => {
  const [newTodoText, setNewTodoText] = useState('');
  const dispatch = useDispatch();

  const todos = useSelector(state => state.todos.items);
  const filter = useSelector(state => state.todos.filter);
  const hasPast = useSelector(state =>
state.todos.history.past.length > 0);
  const hasFuture = useSelector(state =>
state.todos.history.future.length > 0);

  const handleAddTodo = (e) => {
    e.preventDefault();
```

```
    if (newTodoText.trim()) {
      dispatch(addTodo(newTodoText));
      setNewTodoText('');
    }
  };

  const handleToggleTodo = (id) => {
    dispatch(toggleTodo(id));
  };

  const handleDeleteTodo = (id) => {
    dispatch(deleteTodo(id));
  };

  const handleFilterChange = (newFilter) => {
    dispatch(setFilter(newFilter));
  };

  const handleUndo = () => {
    dispatch(undo());
  };

  const handleRedo = () => {
    dispatch(redo());
  };

  // Filter todos based on current filter
  const filteredTodos = todos.filter(todo => {
    if (filter === 'active') return !todo.completed;
    if (filter === 'completed') return todo.completed;
    return true; // 'all' filter
  });

  return (
    <div className="todo-app">
      <h1>Todo List with Time Travel</h1>

      <div className="time-travel-controls">
        <button onClick={handleUndo} disabled={!hasPast}>
          ↩ Undo
        </button>
        <button onClick={handleRedo} disabled={!hasFuture}
```

```
>
          Redo ↪
        </button>
      </div>

      <form onSubmit={handleAddTodo}>
        <input
          type="text"
          value={newTodoText}
          onChange={(e) => setNewTodoText(e.target.value)}
          placeholder="Add a new todo"
        />
        <button type="submit">Add</button>
      </form>

      <div className="filters">
        <button
          className={filter === 'all' ? 'active' : ''}
          onClick={() => handleFilterChange('all')}
        >
          All
        </button>
        <button
          className={filter === 'active' ? 'active' : ''}
          onClick={() => handleFilterChange('active')}
        >
          Active
        </button>
        <button
          className={filter === 'completed' ? 'active' :
''}
          onClick={() => handleFilterChange('completed')}
        >
          Completed
        </button>
      </div>

      <ul className="todo-list">
        {filteredTodos.map(todo => (
          <li key={todo.id} className={todo.completed ?
'completed' : ''}>
            <span
```

```
            onClick={() => handleToggleTodo(todo.id)}
            className="todo-text"
          >
            {todo.text}
          </span>
          <button
            onClick={() => handleDeleteTodo(todo.id)}
            className="delete-btn"
          >
            ×
          </button>
        </li>
      ))}
    </ul>

    <div className="todo-count">
      {todos.filter(todo => !todo.completed).length}
items left
    </div>
  </div>
 );
};

export default TodoApp;
```

This example demonstrates time-travel debugging with Redux:

- Every state-changing action (add, toggle, delete) preserves the previous state in history
- Undo functionality restores the previous state
- Redo functionality allows moving forward through undone actions
- History is tracked within the Redux store
- The UI reflects the ability to undo/redo based on history availability

While this example implements a simple version, Redux DevTools provides professional time-travel debugging capabilities that allow developers to:

- Inspect every action that has occurred
- View the complete state at any point in time
- Jump to any previous state during development
- Export and import state for debugging purposes
- Trace the impact of specific actions on the application state

5. Large-scale Applications

Redux shines in large applications with many components, complex data flows, and multiple teams working together.

Example: E-commerce Platform with Modular Architecture

```
// File structure example
/*
/src
  /store
    /slices
      cartSlice.js
      productSlice.js
      userSlice.js
      orderSlice.js
      wishlistSlice.js
      reviewSlice.js
      searchSlice.js
    /middleware
      loggingMiddleware.js
      analyticsMiddleware.js
      apiMiddleware.js
    /selectors
      cartSelectors.js
      productSelectors.js
      userSelectors.js
    rootReducer.js
    store.js
  /features
    /products
      /components
        ProductList.js
        ProductDetail.js
        ProductFilters.js
      /hooks
        useProductFilters.js
      productsAPI.js
    /cart
      /components
        CartSummary.js
        CartItem.js
        Checkout.js
      cartAPI.js
```

```
    /user
      /components
        Profile.js
        LoginForm.js
        AddressBook.js
      userAPI.js
    /orders
      /components
        OrderHistory.js
        OrderDetail.js
      ordersAPI.js
  /common
    /components
      Button.js
      Modal.js
      Loader.js
    /hooks
      useDebounce.js
      useLocalStorage.js
    /utils
      formatCurrency.js
      validation.js
*/

// store/rootReducer.js
import { combineReducers } from '@reduxjs/toolkit';
import cartReducer from './slices/cartSlice';
import productReducer from './slices/productSlice';
import userReducer from './slices/userSlice';
import orderReducer from './slices/orderSlice';
import wishlistReducer from './slices/wishlistSlice';
import reviewReducer from './slices/reviewSlice';
import searchReducer from './slices/searchSlice';

const rootReducer = combineReducers({
  cart: cartReducer,
  products: productReducer,
  user: userReducer,
  orders: orderReducer,
  wishlist: wishlistReducer,
  reviews: reviewReducer,
  search: searchReducer
```

```
});

export default rootReducer;

// store/store.js
import { configureStore } from '@reduxjs/toolkit';
import rootReducer from './rootReducer';
import loggingMiddleware from './middleware/
loggingMiddleware';
import analyticsMiddleware from './middleware/
analyticsMiddleware';
import apiMiddleware from './middleware/apiMiddleware';

const store = configureStore({
  reducer: rootReducer,
  middleware: (getDefaultMiddleware) =>
    getDefaultMiddleware()
      .concat(loggingMiddleware)
      .concat(analyticsMiddleware)
      .concat(apiMiddleware)
});

export default store;

// store/slices/productSlice.js
import { createSlice, createAsyncThunk } from '@reduxjs/
toolkit';
import { fetchProducts, fetchProductById,
fetchProductsByCategory } from '../../features/products/
productsAPI';

export const fetchAllProducts = createAsyncThunk(
  'products/fetchAll',
  async (_, { rejectWithValue }) => {
    try {
      const response = await fetchProducts();
      return response.data;
    } catch (error) {
      return rejectWithValue(error.response.data);
    }
  }
);
```

```
export const fetchProduct = createAsyncThunk(
  'products/fetchById',
  async (productId, { rejectWithValue }) => {
    try {
      const response = await fetchProductById(productId);
      return response.data;
    } catch (error) {
      return rejectWithValue(error.response.data);
    }
  }
);

export const fetchProductsInCategory = createAsyncThunk(
  'products/fetchByCategory',
  async (category, { rejectWithValue }) => {
    try {
      const response = await
fetchProductsByCategory(category);
      return response.data;
    } catch (error) {
      return rejectWithValue(error.response.data);
    }
  }
);

const productSlice = createSlice({
  name: 'products',
  initialState: {
    items: [],
    selectedProduct: null,
    categories: [],
    filters: {
      category: null,
      priceRange: { min: 0, max: 1000 },
      sortBy: 'popularity',
      inStock: true
    },
    loading: {
      items: false,
      selectedProduct: false,
      categories: false
```

```
    },
    error: {
      items: null,
      selectedProduct: null,
      categories: null
    }
  },
  reducers: {
    setFilter(state, action) {
      const { filterName, value } = action.payload;
      state.filters[filterName] = value;
    },
    resetFilters(state) {
      state.filters = {
        category: null,
        priceRange: { min: 0, max: 1000 },
        sortBy: 'popularity',
        inStock: true
      };
    },
    sortProducts(state, action) {
      state.filters.sortBy = action.payload;
    }
  },
  extraReducers: (builder) => {
    // Handle fetchAllProducts
    builder.addCase(fetchAllProducts.pending, (state) => {
      state.loading.items = true;
      state.error.items = null;
    });
    builder.addCase(fetchAllProducts.fulfilled, (state,
action) => {
      state.loading.items = false;
      state.items = action.payload;
      // Extract unique categories
      const uniqueCategories = [...new
Set(action.payload.map(product => product.category))];
      state.categories = uniqueCategories;
    });
    builder.addCase(fetchAllProducts.rejected, (state,
action) => {
      state.loading.items = false;
```

```
      state.error.items = action.payload;
    });

    // Handle fetchProduct
    builder.addCase(fetchProduct.pending, (state) => {
      state.loading.selectedProduct = true;
      state.error.selectedProduct = null;
    });
    builder.addCase(fetchProduct.fulfilled, (state,
action) => {
      state.loading.selectedProduct = false;
      state.selectedProduct = action.payload;
    });
    builder.addCase(fetchProduct.rejected, (state, action)
=> {
      state.loading.selectedProduct = false;
      state.error.selectedProduct = action.payload;
    });

    // Handle fetchProductsInCategory
    builder.addCase(fetchProductsInCategory.pending,
(state) => {
      state.loading.items = true;
      state.error.items = null;
    });
    builder.addCase(fetchProductsInCategory.fulfilled,
(state, action) => {
      state.loading.items = false;
      state.items = action.payload;
    });
    builder.addCase(fetchProductsInCategory.rejected,
(state, action) => {
      state.loading.items = false;
      state.error.items = action.payload;
    });
  }
});

export const { setFilter, resetFilters, sortProducts } =
productSlice.actions;
export default productSlice.reducer;
```

```
// store/selectors/productSelectors.js
import { createSelector } from '@reduxjs/toolkit';

// Basic selectors
export const selectAllProducts = state =>
state.products.items;
export const selectSelectedProduct = state =>
state.products.selectedProduct;
export const selectProductFilters = state =>
state.products.filters;
export const selectProductCategories = state =>
state.products.categories;
export const selectProductsLoading = state =>
state.products.loading;
export const selectProductsErrors = state =>
state.products.error;

// Complex selectors
export const selectFilteredProducts = createSelector(
  [selectAllProducts, selectProductFilters],
  (products, filters) => {
    return products.filter(product => {
      // Apply category filter
      if (filters.category && product.category !==
filters.category) {
        return false;
      }

      // Apply price range filter
      if (product.price < filters.priceRange.min ||
          product.price > filters.priceRange.max) {
        return false;
      }

      // Apply in-stock filter
      if (filters.inStock && !product.inStock) {
        return false;
      }

      return true;
    }).sort((a, b) => {
      // Apply sorting
```

```
      switch (filters.sortBy) {
        case 'price-low-to-high':
          return a.price - b.price;
        case 'price-high-to-low':
          return b.price - a.price;
        case 'newest':
          return new Date(b.createdAt) - new
Date(a.createdAt);
        case 'rating':
          return b.rating - a.rating;
        case 'popularity':
        default:
          return b.popularity - a.popularity;
      }
    });
  }
);

export const selectProductsOnSale = createSelector(
  [selectAllProducts],
  (products) => products.filter(product => product.onSale)
);

export const selectProductsByCategory = (category) =>
  createSelector(
    [selectAllProducts],
    (products) => products.filter(product =>
product.category === category)
  );

// features/products/components/ProductList.js
import React, { useEffect } from 'react';
import { useSelector, useDispatch } from 'react-redux';
import { fetchAllProducts } from '../../../store/slices/
productSlice';
import {
  selectFilteredProducts,
  selectProductFilters,
  selectProductsLoading
} from '../../../store/selectors/productSelectors';
import ProductFilters from './ProductFilters';
import ProductCard from './ProductCard';
```

```
import Loader from '../../../common/components/Loader';

const ProductList = () => {
  const dispatch = useDispatch();
  const filteredProducts =
useSelector(selectFilteredProducts);
  const filters = useSelector(selectProductFilters);
  const loading = useSelector(selectProductsLoading);

  useEffect(() => {
    dispatch(fetchAllProducts());
  }, [dispatch]);

  if (loading.items) {
    return <Loader />;
  }

  return (
    <div className="product-page">
      <h1>Products</h1>

      <div className="product-container">
        <aside className="filters-sidebar">
          <ProductFilters />
        </aside>

        <main className="product-list">
          <div className="product-list-header">
            <span className="results-count">
              {filteredProducts.length} products found
            </span>
            <div className="sort-options">
              <label htmlFor="sort">Sort by:</label>
              <select
                id="sort"
                value={filters.sortBy}
                onChange={(e) =>
dispatch(sortProducts(e.target.value))}
              >
                <option value="popularity">Popularity</
option>
                <option value="price-low-to-high">Price:
```

```
Low to High</option>
                <option value="price-high-to-low">Price:
High to Low</option>
                <option value="newest">Newest</option>
                <option value="rating">Rating</option>
              </select>
            </div>
          </div>

          <div className="products-grid">
            {filteredProducts.map(product => (
              <ProductCard key={product.id}
product={product} />
            ))}
          </div>
        </main>
      </div>
    </div>
  );
};

export default ProductList;

// middleware/analyticsMiddleware.js
const analyticsMiddleware = store => next => action => {
  // Track user actions
  if (action.type === 'cart/addItemToCart') {
    // Send product added to cart event
    trackEvent('add_to_cart', {
      product_id: action.payload.id,
      product_name: action.payload.title,
      product_price: action.payload.price
    });
  }

  if (action.type === 'products/fetchById/fulfilled') {
    // Send product view event
    trackEvent('view_item', {
      product_id: action.payload.id,
      product_name: action.payload.title,
      product_category: action.payload.category
    });
```

```
  }

  if (action.type === 'cart/checkout/fulfilled') {
    // Send purchase event
    trackEvent('purchase', {
      transaction_id: action.payload.orderId,
      value: action.payload.totalAmount,
      items: action.payload.items
    });
  }

  return next(action);
};

// Helper function to track events (would connect to
analytics service)
const trackEvent = (eventName, eventData) => {
  // In a real app, this would send data to Google
Analytics, Mixpanel, etc.
  console.log('ANALYTICS EVENT:', eventName, eventData);
};

export default analyticsMiddleware;
```
This example demonstrates how Redux works in large-scale applications:

1. **Modular Structure**:
    - Store is divided into separate slices for different domains
    - Features are organized by business domain rather than technical concern
    - Reusable components and utilities are separated from feature-specific code
2. **Code Organization**:
    - Selectors provide reusable, memoized data access patterns
    - Middleware handles cross-cutting concerns like logging, analytics, and API calls
    - API logic is separated from component and state management code
3. **Performance Optimization**:
    - Memoized selectors prevent unnecessary re-renders
    - Components only subscribe to the specific parts of state they need
    - Normalized state structure optimizes lookups and updates

4 **Team Collaboration**:

- Clear boundaries between features allow teams to work independently
- Standardized patterns make it easier for developers to understand the codebase
- Consistent action patterns create a shared vocabulary

5 **Scalability**:

- New features can be added without modifying existing code
- State is organized in a way that can grow with the application
- Common patterns reduce cognitive load when adding new functionality

Redux provides structure and predictability that becomes increasingly valuable as an application grows in size and complexity.

redo } = todoSlice.actions;

export default todoSlice.reducer;

// TodoApp.js import React, { useState } from 'react'; import { useSelector, useDispatch } from 'react-redux'; import { addTodo, toggleTodo, deleteTodo, setFilter, undo,

Alternative Considerations

- Small applications: React Context
- Medium complexity: React Context with useReducer
- Complex global state: Redux or Redux Toolkit

Performance Considerations

```
// Performance Optimization Patterns
function OptimizedComponent() {
  // Memoize selectors
  const memoizedUsers = useSelector(getActiveUsers,
shallowEqual);

  // Prevent unnecessary re-renders
  return React.memo(function UserDisplay() {
    // Render logic
  });
}
```

State Management Patterns

- Normalize complex nested states
- Use selectors for derived data
- Implement middleware for side effects
- Separate concerns in state management

Top 5 Redux Implementation Tips

- Minimize global state surface
- Use Redux Toolkit for simplification
- Implement memoized selectors
- Normalize complex state structures
- Separate concerns in state management

7 Actionable Redux Strategies

- Implement modular slice architecture
- Optimize state selection mechanisms
- Utilize middleware for complex logic
- Create reusable action creators
- Design predictable state transitions
- Implement comprehensive error handling
- Leverage toolkit for simplified configuration

Chapter 26: Next.js Introduction

26.1 What is Next.js?

Understanding the Next.js Framework

Next.js stands as a powerful React framework that revolutionizes web application development by providing a comprehensive solution for building high-performance, production-ready web applications. Created by Vercel, Next.js extends React's capabilities with built-in optimizations, server-side rendering, and a robust ecosystem of features that address common web development challenges.

Core Characteristics of Next.js

Next.js distinguishes itself through several key architectural advantages:

Performance Optimization

- Automatic code splitting reduces initial load times
- Intelligent prefetching of JavaScript
- Optimized production builds
- Automatic static optimization

Developer Experience

- Zero configuration setup
- Hot module replacement
- Intuitive routing system
- Built-in CSS and Sass support
- TypeScript integration out of the box

Rendering Strategies

Next.js supports multiple rendering approaches:

- Static Site Generation (SSG)
- Server-Side Rendering (SSR)

- Incremental Static Regeneration (ISR)
- Client-Side Rendering (CSR)

Installation and Setup

```
# Create a new Next.js project
npx create-next-app@latest my-nextjs-app

# Navigate to project directory
cd my-nextjs-app

# Start development server
npm run dev
```

26.2 SSR vs. CSR

Server-Side Rendering (SSR)

Server-Side Rendering represents a method where page content is generated on the server for each request. Next.js provides robust SSR capabilities through its `getServerSideProps` function.

SSR Implementation Example

```
export async function getServerSideProps(context) {
  // Fetch data from external API
  const res = await fetch('https://api.example.com/data')
  const data = await res.json()

  // Pass data to the page via props
  return {
    props: { data }, // Will be passed to the page
component as props
  }
}

function ProductPage({ data }) {
  return (
    <div>
      <h1>{data.name}</h1>
      <p>{data.description}</p>
    </div>
  )
}

export default ProductPage
```

Client-Side Rendering (CSR)

Client-Side Rendering generates content directly in the browser using JavaScript, typically through React's standard rendering mechanism.

CSR Implementation

```
import { useState, useEffect } from 'react'

function DataFetchComponent() {
  const [data, setData] = useState(null)

  useEffect(() => {
    async function fetchData() {
      const response = await fetch('/api/data')
      const result = await response.json()
      setData(result)
    }

    fetchData()
  }, [])

  if (!data) return <div>Loading...</div>

  return (
    <div>
      {data.map(item => (
        <div key={item.id}>{item.name}</div>
      ))}
    </div>
  )
}
```

Comparative Analysis

Feature	Server-Side Rendering	Client-Side Rendering
Initial Load	Faster, content immediately visible	Slower, requires JavaScript execution
SEO Performance	Excellent	Limited without additional techniques
First Contentful Paint	Rapid	Delayed
Complex Interactions	More server computation	Lighter server load

26.3 File-Based Routing

Routing Mechanism

Next.js introduces an intuitive file-system based routing approach where file structure directly translates to application routes.

Basic Routing Structure

```
pages/
├── index.js              # Home page (/)
├── about.js              # About page (/about)
├── contact.js            # Contact page (/contact)
└── users/
    ├── index.js          # Users listing page (/users)
    └── [id].js           # Dynamic user profile page (/
users/123)
```

Dynamic Routing

```
// pages/users/[id].js
function UserProfile({ user }) {
  return (
    <div>
      <h1>{user.name}</h1>
      <p>Email: {user.email}</p>
    </div>
  )
}

export async function getServerSideProps({ params }) {
  const res = await fetch(`https://api.example.com/users/
${params.id}`)
  const user = await res.json()

  return { props: { user } }
}

export default UserProfile
```

Nested Routes

Next.js supports complex routing scenarios with nested dynamic routes and catch-all routes.

26.4 API Routes

Creating API Endpoints

Next.js allows creating serverless API routes within the same project structure.

API Route Example

```
// pages/api/users.js
export default function handler(req, res) {
  if (req.method === 'GET') {
    // Handle GET request
    res.status(200).json({ users: [
      { id: 1, name: 'John Doe' },
      { id: 2, name: 'Jane Smith' }
    ]})
  } else if (req.method === 'POST') {
    // Handle POST request
    const newUser = req.body
    res.status(201).json({ message: 'User created', user:
newUser })
  }
}
```

Middleware and Authentication

```
// pages/api/protected-route.js
export default function handler(req, res) {
  // Simple authentication middleware
  const { authorization } = req.headers

  if (!authorization) {
    return res.status(401).json({ error:
'Unauthorized' })
  }

  // Validate token, process request
  res.status(200).json({ message: 'Access granted' })
}
```

26.5 Deploying Next.js Apps

Deployment Platforms

- Vercel (Recommended)
- Netlify
- Heroku
- DigitalOcean
- AWS

Deployment Process

```
# Build production application
npm run build

# Start production server
npm start
```

Optimization Techniques

- Enable compression
- Implement caching strategies
- Minimize external dependencies
- Use static generation where possible

Environment Configuration

```
# .env.local file
DATABASE_URL=your_database_connection_string
API_KEY=your_secret_api_key
```

5 Strategic Tips for Next.js Development

- Configure static optimization for maximum performance
- Leverage incremental static regeneration for dynamic content
- Implement robust error handling in API routes

- Utilize TypeScript for enhanced type safety
- Optimize images and assets using
- Next.js built-in components

7 Actionable Strategies for Next.js Mastery

- Modularize complex components for better maintainability
- Implement progressive loading techniques
- Use server-side props for critical data fetching
- Create reusable API utility functions
- Standardize error management across application
- Integrate comprehensive logging mechanisms
- Design responsive layouts with built-in Next.js utilities

Chapter 27: React Best Practices

27.1 Folder Structure

Scalable Project Architecture

Designing an effective folder structure is critical for maintaining clean, organized, and scalable React applications. A well-thought-out directory layout enhances code readability, maintainability, and developer productivity.

Recommended Folder Structure

```
src/
│
├── components/
│   ├── common/
│   │   ├── Button.js
│   │   ├── Input.js
│   │   └── Modal.js
│   │
│   ├── layout/
│   │   ├── Header.js
│   │   ├── Footer.js
│   │   └── Sidebar.js
│   │
│   └── features/
│       ├── user/
│       │   ├── UserProfile.js
│       │   └── UserSettings.js
│       └── products/
│           ├── ProductList.js
│           └── ProductDetail.js
│
├── pages/
│   ├── Home.js
│   ├── About.js
│   └── Dashboard.js
│
├── hooks/
│   ├── useAuth.js
│   ├── useForm.js
│   └── useApi.js
│
├── context/
│   ├── AuthContext.js
│   └── ThemeContext.js
│
├── utils/
│   ├── validation.js
│   ├── formatters.js
│   └── helpers.js
│
├── services/
│   ├── api.js
```

Principles of Folder Organization

1. **Separation of Concerns**: Divide code into logical, manageable sections
2. **Consistency**: Maintain a uniform structure across the project
3. **Scalability**: Allow easy addition of new features and components
4. **Modularity**: Create self-contained, reusable modules

27.2 Component Organization

Component Classification

React components can be categorized into distinct types based on their responsibilities and behavior:

Presentational Components

```
function UserCard({ name, email, avatar }) {
  return (
    <div className="user-card">
      <img src={avatar} alt={`${name}'s avatar`} />
      <h3>{name}</h3>
      <p>{email}</p>
    </div>
  )
}
```

Container Components

```
function UserProfileContainer() {
  const [user, setUser] = useState(null);
  const [loading, setLoading] = useState(true);

  useEffect(() => {
    async function fetchUserData() {
      try {
        const response = await fetch('/api/user');
        const userData = await response.json();
        setUser(userData);
        setLoading(false);
      } catch (error) {
        console.error('Failed to fetch user data',
error);
        setLoading(false);
      }
    }

    fetchUserData();
  }, []);

  if (loading) return <LoadingSpinner />;

  return <UserCard
    name={user.name}
    email={user.email}
    avatar={user.avatar}
  />;
}
```

Component Composition Strategies

1. **Single Responsibility Principle**
2. **Prop Drilling Minimization**
3. **Composition over Inheritance**

27.3 Naming Conventions

React Component Naming

1. **PascalCase for Components**

```
// Correct
function UserProfile() { ... }
function ProductCard() { ... }

// Incorrect
function userProfile() { ... }
function product_card() { ... }
```

2 Descriptive and Meaningful Names

```
// Good
function ActiveUserList() { ... }
function PremiumProductFilter() { ... }

// Avoid
function List() { ... }
function Filter() { ... }
```

Hook Naming Conventions

```
// Prefix hooks with 'use'
function useAuthentication() {
  const [isLoggedIn, setIsLoggedIn] = useState(false);

  const login = useCallback(() => {
    // Login logic
    setIsLoggedIn(true);
  }, []);

  const logout = useCallback(() => {
    // Logout logic
    setIsLoggedIn(false);
  }, []);

  return { isLoggedIn, login, logout };
}
```

File Naming

- React Component Files: `PascalCase.js`

- Hooks: `use[Functionality].js`
- Utility Files: `camelCase.js`

27.4 Code Reusability

Custom Hooks

```
// Reusable data fetching hook
function useFetch(url) {
  const [data, setData] = useState(null);
  const [loading, setLoading] = useState(true);
  const [error, setError] = useState(null);

  useEffect(() => {
    async function fetchData() {
      try {
        const response = await fetch(url);
        const result = await response.json();
        setData(result);
        setLoading(false);
      } catch (err) {
        setError(err);
        setLoading(false);
      }
    }

    fetchData();
  }, [url]);

  return { data, loading, error };
}

// Usage in component
function ProductList() {
  const { data, loading, error } = useFetch('/api/
products');

  if (loading) return <Spinner />;
  if (error) return <ErrorMessage />;

  return (
    <ul>
      {data.map(product => (
        <li key={product.id}>{product.name}</li>
      ))}
    </ul>
  );
}
```

Higher-Order Components (HOCs)

```
function withLoading(WrappedComponent) {
  return function({ isLoading, ...props }) {
    if (isLoading) {
      return <Spinner />;
    }

    return <WrappedComponent {...props} />;
  };
}

const UserProfileWithLoading = withLoading(UserProfile);
```

27.5 Accessibility (a11y)

Semantic HTML

```
function AccessibleForm() {
  return (
    <form>
      <label htmlFor="username">Username</label>
      <input
        id="username"
        type="text"
        aria-describedby="username-help"
      />
      <p id="username-help">
        Enter your unique username (3-16 characters)
      </p>

      <button type="submit" aria-label="Submit form">
        Submit
      </button>
    </form>
  );
}
```

ARIA Attributes

```
function AdvancedModal({ isOpen, onClose, children }) {
  return (
    <div
      role="dialog"
      aria-modal="true"
      aria-labelledby="modal-title"
      className={isOpen ? 'modal open' : 'modal'}
    >
      <h2 id="modal-title">Modal Title</h2>
      {children}
      <button
        onClick={onClose}
        aria-label="Close modal"
      >
        Close
      </button>
    </div>
  );
}
```

Keyboard Navigation

```
function AccessibleMenu() {
  const [activeIndex, setActiveIndex] = useState(0);
  const menuItems = ['Home', 'Profile', 'Settings'];

  const handleKeyDown = (event) => {
    switch(event.key) {
      case 'ArrowDown':
        setActiveIndex((prev) =>
          (prev + 1) % menuItems.length
        );
        break;
      case 'ArrowUp':
        setActiveIndex((prev) =>
          (prev - 1 + menuItems.length) %
menuItems.length
        );
        break;
    }
  };

  return (
    <ul
      role="menu"
      onKeyDown={handleKeyDown}
      tabIndex={0}
    >
      {menuItems.map((item, index) => (
        <li
          key={item}
          role="menuitem"
          tabIndex={-1}
          aria-selected={index === activeIndex}
        >
          {item}
        </li>
      ))}
    </ul>
  );
}
```

5 Strategic Tips for React Development

- Optimize render performance with memoization techniques
- Implement consistent error boundary mechanisms
- Standardize state management approach
- Prioritize functional component patterns
- Create modular, reusable component libraries

7 Actionable Strategies for React Mastery

- Develop comprehensive testing strategies
- Implement advanced prop type validations
- Create flexible, composable component architectures
- Utilize advanced React hook patterns
- Establish robust code review processes
- Design scalable state management solutions
- Integrate performance monitoring tools

Chapter 28: Common React Mistakes

28.1 Missing Keys in Lists

The Importance of Keys in React Rendering

Performance and Reconciliation

React uses keys to efficiently update the DOM by identifying which items have changed, been added, or removed in a list. Omitting keys leads to critical performance and rendering issues.

Incorrect Implementation

```
function UserList({ users }) {
  // INCORRECT: No keys provided
  return (
    <ul>
      {users.map(user => (
        <li>{user.name}</li> // Missing key prop
      ))}
    </ul>
  )
}
```

Correct Key Implementation

```
function UserList({ users }) {
  return (
    <ul>
      {users.map(user => (
        <li key={user.id}>{user.name}</li> // Unique
identifier key
      ))}
    </ul>
  )
}
```

Key Selection Strategies

1 **Prefer Unique Identifiers**

- Use database IDs
- Avoid using array index as keys
- Generate unique keys for dynamic lists

Problematic Index-Based Keys

```
function BadKeyExample({ items }) {
  // ANTIPATTERN: Using index as key
  return (
    <ul>
      {items.map((item, index) => (
        <li key={index}>
          {item.name}
          <button onClick={() => removeItem(index)}
>Remove</button>
        </li>
      ))}
    </ul>
  )
}
```

Improved Unique Key Implementation

```
function ImprovedList({ items }) {
  return (
    <ul>
      {items.map(item => (
        <li key={item.uniqueId}>
          {item.name}
          <button onClick={() =>
removeItem(item.uniqueId)}>Remove</button>
        </li>
      ))}
    </ul>
  )
}
```

28.2 Direct State Mutations

Immutability in React State Management

Incorrect State Mutation

```
function BadStateManagement() {
  const [users, setUsers] = useState([
    { id: 1, name: 'John' },
    { id: 2, name: 'Jane' }
  ]);

  const addUser = () => {
    // INCORRECT: Directly mutating state
    users.push({ id: 3, name: 'Bob' });
    setUsers(users);
  }

  return (
    <div>
      {users.map(user => (
        <div key={user.id}>{user.name}</div>
      ))}
      <button onClick={addUser}>Add User</button>
    </div>
  )
}
```

Correct State Update Patterns

```
function GoodStateManagement() {
  const [users, setUsers] = useState([
    { id: 1, name: 'John' },
    { id: 2, name: 'Jane' }
  ]);

  const addUser = () => {
    // CORRECT: Creating a new array
    setUsers([...users, { id: 3, name: 'Bob' }]);
  }

  const updateUser = (id, newName) => {
    // CORRECT: Mapping to create a new array
    setUsers(users.map(user =>
      user.id === id ? { ...user, name: newName } : user
    ));
  }

  const removeUser = (id) => {
    // CORRECT: Filtering to create a new array
    setUsers(users.filter(user => user.id !== id));
  }

  return (
    <div>
      {users.map(user => (
        <div key={user.id}>{user.name}</div>
      ))}
      <button onClick={addUser}>Add User</button>
    </div>
  )
}
```

State Mutation Consequences

- React cannot detect changes
- Prevents efficient re-rendering
- Breaks component optimization
- Leads to unpredictable UI states

28.3 Overusing useEffect

Effect Hook Best Practices

Common Misuse Patterns

```
function ProblematicComponent() {
  const [data, setData] = useState(null);
  const [loading, setLoading] = useState(true);

  // ANTIPATTERN: Unnecessary multiple effects
  useEffect(() => {
    fetch('/api/users')
      .then(response => response.json())
      .then(users => {
        setData(users);
        setLoading(false);
      });
  }, []); // Empty dependency array

  useEffect(() => {
    if (data) {
      // Unnecessary secondary effect
      console.log('Data updated:', data);
    }
  }, [data]);

  return (
    <div>
      {loading ? 'Loading...' : JSON.stringify(data)}
    </div>
  )
}
```

Optimized Effect Implementation

```
function OptimizedComponent() {
  const [data, setData] = useState(null);
  const [loading, setLoading] = useState(true);

  // IMPROVED: Single consolidated effect
  useEffect(() => {
    let isMounted = true;

    async function fetchData() {
      try {
        const response = await fetch('/api/users');
        const users = await response.json();

        if (isMounted) {
          setData(users);
          setLoading(false);
        }
      } catch (error) {
        if (isMounted) {
          setLoading(false);
        }
      }
    }

    fetchData();

    // Cleanup function
    return () => {
      isMounted = false;
    };
  }, []); // Single effect with cleanup

  return (
    <div>
      {loading ? 'Loading...' : JSON.stringify(data)}
    </div>
  )
}
```

Effect Hook Guidelines

1 Minimize effect dependencies

2 Use cleanup functions
3 Separate concerns
4 Prefer custom hooks for complex logic

28.4 Prop Drilling Issues

Solving Prop Passing Challenges

Prop Drilling Problem

```
function GrandParentComponent() {
  const [theme, setTheme] = useState('light');

  return (
    <ParentComponent theme={theme} setTheme={setTheme}>
      <ChildComponent theme={theme} setTheme={setTheme} /
>
    </ParentComponent>
  )
}

function ParentComponent({ children, theme, setTheme }) {
  return (
    <div>
      {/* Passing props through intermediate component
*/}
      {React.cloneElement(children, { theme, setTheme })}
    </div>
  )
}

function ChildComponent({ theme, setTheme }) {
  return (
    <button onClick={() => setTheme(theme === 'light' ?
'dark' : 'light')}>
      Toggle Theme
    </button>
  )
}
```

Context API Solution

```
// Create context
const ThemeContext = React.createContext(null);

function ThemeProvider({ children }) {
  const [theme, setTheme] = useState('light');

  return (
    <ThemeContext.Provider value={{ theme, setTheme }}>
      {children}
    </ThemeContext.Provider>
  )
}

function ChildComponent() {
  const { theme, setTheme } = useContext(ThemeContext);

  return (
    <button onClick={() => setTheme(theme === 'light' ?
'dark' : 'light')}>
      Toggle Theme
    </button>
  )
}

function App() {
  return (
    <ThemeProvider>
      <ChildComponent />
    </ThemeProvider>
  )
}
```

Prop Passing Alternatives

```
```

- Context API
- State Management Libraries

- Custom Hooks
- Composition Patterns

28.5 Ignoring Error Boundaries

Error Handling in React Applications

Basic Error Boundary Implementation

```
class ErrorBoundary extends React.Component {
  constructor(props) {
    super(props);
    this.state = { hasError: false };
  }

  static getDerivedStateFromError(error) {
    return { hasError: true };
  }

  componentDidCatch(error, errorInfo) {
    // Log error to monitoring service
    logErrorToService(error, errorInfo);
  }

  render() {
    if (this.state.hasError) {
      return (
        <div>
          <h1>Something went wrong.</h1>
          <button onClick={() =>
this.setState({ hasError: false })}>
            Try again
          </button>
        </div>
      );
    }

    return this.props.children;
  }
}

function App() {
  return (
    <ErrorBoundary>
      <RiskyComponent />
    </ErrorBoundary>
  )
}
```

Error Handling Strategies

1. Implement error boundaries
2. Provide fallback UI
3. Log errors for debugging
4. Graceful error recovery

5 Strategic Tips for Error Prevention

- Implement comprehensive error boundary strategies
- Utilize TypeScript for compile-time type checking
- Create robust input validation mechanisms
- Standardize error logging approaches
- Design predictable state management patterns

7 Actionable Strategies for Robust React Development

- Develop comprehensive unit and integration tests
- Implement strict prop type validations
- Create modular, decoupled component architectures
- Establish consistent code review processes
- Integrate advanced debugging techniques
- Design fault-tolerant application structures
- Implement proactive error monitoring solutions

Chapter 29: React Interview Questions

29.1 Virtual DOM Explained

Understanding the Concept of Virtual DOM

The Virtual DOM represents a lightweight, in-memory representation of the actual Document Object Model (DOM) in React applications. It's a fundamental concept that significantly enhances React's performance and rendering efficiency.

Core Mechanics of Virtual DOM

React creates a virtual representation of the UI in memory, which is a JavaScript object that mirrors the structure of the actual DOM. When state or props change, React first updates this virtual representation, then compares it with the previous version through a process called "diffing".

```
// Simple representation of Virtual DOM structure
const virtualElement = {
  type: 'div',
  props: {
    className: 'container',
    children: [
      {
        type: 'h1',
        props: {
          children: 'Hello, React!'
        }
      }
    ]
  }
};
```

Rendering Process

1. **Initial Render**: React creates a virtual DOM tree
2. **State Change**: A new virtual DOM tree is generated
3. **Diffing Algorithm**: React compares the new and old virtual DOM
4. **Minimal Updates**: Only necessary changes are applied to the actual DOM

Performance Advantages

- Minimizes direct manipulation of the DOM
- Reduces computational overhead
- Enables efficient updates and re-rendering
- Provides a consistent abstraction layer across different platforms

Practical Example of Virtual DOM Optimization

```
function VirtualDOMExample() {
  const [count, setCount] = useState(0);

  // React will optimize renders using Virtual DOM
  return (
    <div>
      <p>Count: {count}</p>
      <button onClick={() => setCount(count + 1)}>
        Increment
      </button>
    </div>
  );
}
```

29.2 Hooks vs. Class Components

Functional Components with Hooks: Modern Approach

Hooks introduced in React 16.8 revolutionized how developers write components, providing a more direct way to use state and lifecycle features in functional components.

Key Differences

Class Components	Functional Components with Hooks
Require `extends React.Component`	Simple JavaScript functions
Use `this` keyword	No `this` context needed
Lifecycle methods like `componentDidMount`	Hooks like `useEffect`
More verbose	Concise and readable

Core Hooks Breakdown

1 **useState**: Manages state in functional components

```
function Counter() {
  const [count, setCount] = useState(0);
  return (
    <div>
      <p>Count: {count}</p>
      <button onClick={() => setCount(count + 1)}>
        Increment
      </button>
    </div>
  );
}
```

2 **useEffect**: Handles side effects and lifecycle events

```
function DataFetcher() {
  const [data, setData] = useState(null);

  useEffect(() => {
    async function fetchData() {
      const response = await fetch('/api/data');
      const result = await response.json();
      setData(result);
    }
    fetchData();
  }, []); // Empty dependency array means run once

  return data ? <DataDisplay data={data} /> :
<LoadingSpinner />;
}
```

3 **useContext**: Simplifies context consumption

```
const ThemeContext = createContext('light');

function ThemedComponent() {
  const theme = useContext(ThemeContext);
  return <div className={theme}>Themed Content</div>;
}
```

Migration Strategies

- Gradually convert class components to functional components
- Leverage hooks for more readable and maintainable code
- Use custom hooks to extract and reuse stateful logic

29.3 Reconciliation in React

Understanding the Reconciliation Process

Reconciliation is React's algorithm for efficiently updating the UI by comparing the new and previous component trees.

Diffing Algorithm Principles

1. **Element Type Comparison**
    - Different types result in complete tree reconstruction
    - Same type allows minimal updates
2. **Key Prop Significance**
    - Helps React identify which child elements have changed
    - Critical for optimizing list rendering

```
function UserList({ users }) {
  return (
    <ul>
      {users.map(user => (
        <li key={user.id}>  // Unique key is crucial
          {user.name}
        </li>
      ))}
    </ul>
  );
}
```

Performance Optimization Techniques

- Use stable, unique keys for list items
- Minimize unnecessary re-renders
- Implement `React.memo` for complex components

Complex Reconciliation Scenario

```
function OptimizedComponent({ data }) {
  // Memoize expensive computations
  const processedData = useMemo(() => {
    return data.map(item =>
expensiveTransformation(item));
  }, [data]);

  // Prevent unnecessary re-renders
  return React.memo(() => (
    <div>{processedData.map(renderItem)}</div>
  ));
}
```

29.4 Controlled vs. Uncontrolled Components

Controlled Components

Components where React manages form data through state.

```
function ControlledForm() {
  const [username, setUsername] = useState('');

  const handleSubmit = (event) => {
    event.preventDefault();
    // Form data is fully controlled by React state
    console.log(username);
  };

  return (
    <form onSubmit={handleSubmit}>
      <input
        type="text"
        value={username}
        onChange={(e) => setUsername(e.target.value)}
      />
      <button type="submit">Submit</button>
    </form>
  );
}
```

Uncontrolled Components

Form data managed by the DOM itself, using refs.

```
function UncontrolledForm() {
  const usernameRef = useRef(null);

  const handleSubmit = (event) => {
    event.preventDefault();
    // Access value directly through DOM
    console.log(usernameRef.current.value);
  };

  return (
    <form onSubmit={handleSubmit}>
      <input
        type="text"
        ref={usernameRef}
      />
      <button type="submit">Submit</button>
    </form>
  );
}
```

Comparison Matrix

Aspect	Controlled Components	Uncontrolled Components
State Management	React State	DOM Ref
Validation	Easier	More Complex
Performance	Slight Overhead	Minimal Overhead
Use Case	Complex Forms	Simple Inputs

29.5 React Fiber Architecture

Understanding React Fiber

React Fiber is a complete rewrite of React's reconciliation and rendering process, introduced to enable more flexible and efficient rendering.

Core Architecture Characteristics

- Incremental rendering
- Ability to pause, abort, or reuse work
- Priority-based update mechanism

Rendering Phases

1. **Reconciliation Phase**
   - Determines what changes need to be made
   - Creates a fiber tree representing component hierarchy
2. **Commit Phase**
   - Applies actual changes to the DOM
   - Handles side effects and lifecycle methods

Fiber Node Structure

```
// Simplified Fiber Node representation
const fiber = {
  tag: WorkTag,                // Component type
  key: null,                   // Unique identifier
  type: ReactComponentType,// Component or DOM type
  stateNode: any,              // Reference to instance
  return: Fiber,               // Parent fiber
  child: Fiber,                // Child fiber
  sibling: Fiber,              // Next sibling fiber
  pendingProps: any,           // Incoming props
  memoizedProps: any,          // Previous props
  updateQueue: UpdateQueue,// Pending state updates
  pendingWorkPriority: PriorityLevel
};
```

Advanced Rendering Techniques

```
function PrioritizedRendering() {
  const [urgentState, setUrgentState] = useState(null);
  const [backgroundState, setBackgroundState] =
useState(null);

  useEffect(() => {
    // Simulate different priority updates
    ReactDOM.unstable_scheduleWork(
      () => setUrgentState('Urgent Update'),
      { priority: ReactDOM.unstable_priorityLevels.high }
    );

    ReactDOM.unstable_scheduleWork(
      () => setBackgroundState('Background Update'),
      { priority: ReactDOM.unstable_priorityLevels.low }
    );
  }, []);

  return (
    <div>
      <UrgentComponent data={urgentState} />
      <BackgroundComponent data={backgroundState} />
    </div>
  );
}
```

5 Strategic Tips for React Development

- Continuously refactor and simplify your component logic
- Prioritize performance optimization techniques
- Master the nuances of hooks and component lifecycle
- Implement robust error boundaries Stay updated with latest
- React ecosystem developments

7 Actionable Strategies for React Mastery

- Create reusable custom hooks
- Leverage code splitting and lazy loading
- Implement proper memoization techniques
- Use TypeScript for enhanced type safety
- Master state management patterns
- Develop comprehensive testing strategies
- Optimize rendering with React.memo and useMemo

Chapter 30: Building a Mini Project

30.1 Planning the App (Todo List)

Project Requirements Analysis

A robust Todo List application requires careful planning to ensure functionality, usability, and scalability. The core features will include:

Key Functional Requirements

- Add new todo items
- Mark items as complete
- Delete todo items
- Filter todos (All, Active, Completed)
- Persist todos in local storage
- Responsive design

Architecture Design

Component Hierarchy

```
App
│
├── TodoHeader
│   └── AddTodoForm
│
├── TodoList
│   └── TodoItem
│
└── TodoFilters
```

Technical Stack Selection

- **Frontend**: React.js
- **State Management**: React Hooks (useState, useEffect)
- **Styling**: CSS Modules or Tailwind CSS
- **Storage**: Local Storage API

Initial Project Setup

```
npx create-react-app todo-list-app
```

```
cd todo-list-app
```

```
# For generating unique IDs
npm install uuid
```

Data Model Definition

```
const todoSchema = {
  id: String,              // Unique identifier
  text: String,            // Todo item text
  completed: Boolean,      // Completion status
  createdAt: Date,         // Creation timestamp
  updatedAt: Date          // Last update timestamp
};
```

30.2 Setting Up Components

Component Structure Implementation

TodoHeader Component

```
import React, { useState } from 'react';

function TodoHeader({ addTodo }) {
  const [input, setInput] = useState('');

  const handleSubmit = (e) => {
    e.preventDefault();
    if (!input.trim()) return;

    addTodo({
      id: crypto.randomUUID(), // Modern UUID generation
      text: input,
      completed: false,
      createdAt: new Date(),
      updatedAt: new Date()
    });

    setInput(''); // Reset input after submission
  };

  return (
    <header>
      <h1>Todo List</h1>
      <form onSubmit={handleSubmit}>
        <input
          type="text"
          value={input}
          onChange={(e) => setInput(e.target.value)}
          placeholder="Add a new todo"
        />
        <button type="submit">Add Todo</button>
      </form>
    </header>
  );
}
```

TodoList Component

```
function TodoList({ todos, toggleTodo, deleteTodo }) {
  return (
    <ul>
      {todos.map(todo => (
        <TodoItem
          key={todo.id}
          todo={todo}
          onToggle={() => toggleTodo(todo.id)}
          onDelete={() => deleteTodo(todo.id)}
        />
      ))}
    </ul>
  );
}
```

TodoItem Component

```
function TodoItem({ todo, onToggle, onDelete }) {
  return (
    <li>
      <input
        type="checkbox"
        checked={todo.completed}
        onChange={onToggle}
      />
      <span
        style={{
          textDecoration: todo.completed ? 'line-
through' : 'none'
        }}
      >
        {todo.text}
      </span>
      <button onClick={onDelete}>Delete</button>
    </li>
  );
}
```

Component Communication Patterns

- Prop Drilling for Simple Applications
- Context API for Complex State Management

- Potential Future Expansion to Redux

30.3 Adding State & Logic

State Management Strategy

```
function App() {
  const [todos, setTodos] = useState(() => {
    // Initialize from local storage
    const savedTodos = localStorage.getItem('todos');
    return savedTodos ? JSON.parse(savedTodos) : [];
  });

  const [filter, setFilter] = useState('all');

  // Persist todos to local storage
  useEffect(() => {
    localStorage.setItem('todos', JSON.stringify(todos));
  }, [todos]);

  // Add Todo Handler
  const addTodo = (newTodo) => {
    setTodos(prevTodos => [...prevTodos, newTodo]);
  };

  // Toggle Todo Completion
  const toggleTodo = (id) => {
    setTodos(prevTodos =>
      prevTodos.map(todo =>
        todo.id === id
          ? { ...todo, completed: !todo.completed,
updatedAt: new Date() }
          : todo
      )
    );
  };

  // Delete Todo
  const deleteTodo = (id) => {
    setTodos(prevTodos =>
      prevTodos.filter(todo => todo.id !== id)
    );
  };

  // Filter Todos
  const filteredTodos = todos.filter(todo => {
    switch(filter) {
      case 'active':
```

Advanced State Management Techniques

- Implement useReducer for complex state logic
- Create custom hooks for reusable logic
- Implement error boundaries

30.4 Styling the App

CSS Modules Approach

```
/* TodoItem.module.css */
.todoItem {
  display: flex;
  align-items: center;
  padding: 10px;
  margin: 5px 0;
  background-color: #f4f4f4;
  border-radius: 5px;
}

.completed {
  text-decoration: line-through;
  color: #888;
}

.deleteButton {
  margin-left: auto;
  background-color: #ff4d4d;
  color: white;
  border: none;
  padding: 5px 10px;
  border-radius: 3px;
}
```

Responsive Design Considerations

```
@media (max-width: 600px) {
  .todoContainer {
    width: 95%;
    margin: 0 auto;
  }
}
```

Tailwind CSS Alternative

```
function TodoItem({ todo, onToggle, onDelete }) {
  return (
    <li className="flex items-center p-2 bg-gray-100
rounded mb-2">
      <input
        type="checkbox"
        checked={todo.completed}
        onChange={onToggle}
        className="mr-2"
      />
      <span
        className={`flex-grow ${todo.completed ? 'line-
through text-gray-500' : ''}`}
      >
        {todo.text}
      </span>
      <button
        onClick={onDelete}
        className="bg-red-500 text-white px-2 py-1
rounded"
      >
        Delete
      </button>
    </li>
  );
}
```

30.5 Deploying the Project

Deployment Preparation

```
# Build production version
npm run build
```

Install deployment tool

```
npm install -g netlify-cli
```

Deploy to Netlify

```
netlify deploy
```

Continuous Integration Setup

.github/workflows/deploy.yml

```
name: Deploy to Netlify

on:
  push:
    branches: [ main ]
  pull_request:
    branches: [ main ]

jobs:
  build:
    runs-on: ubuntu-latest
    steps:
      - uses: actions/checkout@v2
      - name: Use Node.js
        uses: actions/setup-node@v2
        with:
          node-version: '14'
      - run: npm ci
      - run: npm run build
      - name: Deploy to Netlify
        uses: nwtgck/actions-netlify@v1.2
        with:
          publish-dir: './build'
```

Performance Optimization

- Code splitting
- Lazy loading components
- Memoization techniques

5 Strategic Tips for Project Development

- Write clean, modular, and reusable component code
- Implement comprehensive error handling
- Prioritize user experience and intuitive design
- Optimize performance through efficient state management
- Maintain consistent coding standards

7 Actionable Strategies for React Projects

- Create a robust project structure
- Implement comprehensive testing
- Utilize TypeScript for type safety
- Develop responsive and accessible designs
- Integrate state management solutions
- Optimize rendering performance
- Implement continuous integration and deployment

www.ingramcontent.com/pod-product-compliance
Lightning Source LLC
LaVergne TN
LVHW071159210926
848482LV00014B/691